ANTIRACISM IN BALLET TEACHING

This new collection of essays and interviews assembles research on teaching methods, choreographic processes, and archival material that challenges systemic exclusions and provides practitioners with accessible steps to creating more equitable teaching environments, curricula, classes, and artistic settings.

Antiracism in Ballet Teaching gives readers a wealth of options for addressing and dismantling racialized biases in ballet teaching, as well as in approaches to leadership and choreography. Chapters are organized into three sections—Identities, Pedagogies, and Futurities—that illuminate evolving approaches to choreographing and teaching ballet, shine light on artists, teachers, and dancers who are lesser known/less visibile in a racialized canon, and amplify the importance of holistic practices that integrate ballet history with technique and choreography. Chapter authors include award-winning studio owners, as well as acclaimed choreographers, educators, and scholars. The collection ends with interviews featuring ballet company directors (Robert Garland and Alonzo King), world-renowned scholars (Clare Croft, Thomas F. DeFrantz, Brenda Dixon Gottschild), sought-after choreographers (Jennifer Archibald and Claudia Schreier), and teachers (Keesha Beckford, Tai Jimenez, Alicia Graf Mack, and Endalyn Taylor).

This is an essential resource for anyone teaching or learning to teach ballet in the twenty-first century.

Kate Mattingly is an assistant professor in the Department of Communication and Theatre Arts at Old Dominion University, USA.

Iyun Ashani Harrison is an associate professor of the practice of dance and head of ballet at Duke University, USA.

ANTIRACISM IN BALLET TEACHING

Edited by Kate Mattingly and Iyun Ashani Harrison

Routledge
Taylor & Francis Group
LONDON AND NEW YORK

Designed cover image: Dancer Marja' Miller. © Raheem Tutein & Jehbreal Muhammad Jackson

First published 2024
by Routledge
4 Park Square, Milton Park, Abingdon, Oxon OX14 4RN

and by Routledge
605 Third Avenue, New York, NY 10158

Routledge is an imprint of the Taylor & Francis Group, an informa business

© 2024 selection and editorial matter, Kate Mattingly and Iyun Ashani Harrison; individual chapters, the contributors

The right of Kate Mattingly and Iyun Ashani Harrison to be identified as the authors of the editorial material, and of the authors for their individual chapters, has been asserted in accordance with sections 77 and 78 of the Copyright, Designs and Patents Act 1988.

All rights reserved. No part of this book may be reprinted or reproduced or utilised in any form or by any electronic, mechanical, or other means, now known or hereafter invented, including photocopying and recording, or in any information storage or retrieval system, without permission in writing from the publishers.

Trademark notice: Product or corporate names may be trademarks or registered trademarks, and are used only for identification and explanation without intent to infringe.

British Library Cataloguing in Publication Data
A catalogue record for this book is available from the British Library

Library of Congress Cataloging-in-Publication Data
A catalog record has been requested for this book

ISBN: 978-1-032-25420-3 (hbk)
ISBN: 978-1-032-25419-7 (pbk)
ISBN: 978-1-003-28306-5 (ebk)

DOI: 10.4324/9781003283065

Typeset in Galliard
by Taylor & Francis Books

CONTENTS

List of figures	*viii*
Contributors	*x*
Acknowledgements	*xii*
Acknowledgements	*xiv*

Introduction *Kate Mattingly and Iyun Ashani Harrison*	1

PART I
Identities   **21**

1 Teaching for Tomorrow: Antiracism in Ballet *Gabrielle Salvatto*	23
2 Perspective: Artistic Director of Ballet Tech *Dionne Figgins*	32
3 Perspective: Lourdes Lopez, Artistic Director of Miami City Ballet *Lourdes Lopez*	39

4 Native American Dancing beyond Settler Colonial Confines 49
   Kate Mattingly

5 Reflections on Quare Dance: Ballet and Black, Queer, Fem(me)inist Aesthetics 64
   Alyah Baker

PART 2
Pedagogies **73**

6 Classical Perspectives: Performance, Pedagogy, and (Changing) Cultures 75
   Anjali Austin

7 Dear Ballet Teachers, Let's Talk About Race 82
   Ilana Goldman and Paige Cunningham

8 Making Space: Inclusive and Equitable Teaching Practices for Ballet in Higher Education 92
   Alana Isiguen

9 Dismantling Anti-Blackness in Ballet: Pedagogies of Freedom 100
   Maurya Kerr

10 ReCentering the Studio: Ballet Leadership and Learning Through Intersectional and Antiracist Approaches 112
   Renée K. Nicholson and Lisa DeFrank-Cole

11 Credibility and Expertise: Black Women Teaching Classical Ballet 119
   Monica Stephenson

12 Adjusting Pedagogies for Developing Artists: Age-appropriate Classes for Classical Ballet 129
   Misa Oga

13 Ballet as Artistic, Scientific, and Existential Inquiry: Incorporating Ballet's Broader History in a Syllabus and in the Studio 137
Jehbreal Muhammad Jackson

14 Dive In 153
Keesha Beckford

PART 3
Futurities 161

15 A willingness to shed | crafting alternate realms & possibilities in movement: FUTUREFORMS 163
Sidra Bell

16 Honoring the Legacy of Antiracist Ballet Teaching & Leadership as Modeled by Black and Brown-owned, Black and Brown-led, and Black and Brown-serving Dance Organizations 171
Iyun Ashani Harrison

17 Ballet's Ever-Present Presence 184
Thomas F. DeFrantz

18 Twelve Steps to Ballet's Cultural Recovery: A Guide to Creating an Antiracist Organizational Culture 195
Theresa Ruth Howard

19 Creating New Spaces in Ballet Repertoire: Today's Generation of Black Choreographers 206
Brandye Lee

20 Ballet's Futurities: Insights from Choreographers, Educators, and Scholars 214
Iyun Ashani Harrison

Index 243

FIGURES

4.1 "Gaea" photograph by Cara Romero of dancer Crickett Tiger (Muscogee Creek/Cochiti) on the California Coast wearing Leah Mata-Fragua's all-Indigenous dancewear. 50
13.1 The *N'kisi Sarabanda* is a spiritual signature ("firma") of the *mpungo* (spiritual ancestor or natural force) *Sarabanda*. It likely influenced the *en croix* pattern of ballet technique. 138
13.2 The Shabaka/o Stone created in 710 BCE conglomerate stela. The star-like pattern is attributed to it later being used as a nether millstone. 139
13.3a Close-up reduction of eight-point star that anchors the *Murqanas* (stalactite) dome in the "Hall of Two Sisters" in the Alhambra palace built between 1238 and 1370 during the Nasrid Dynasty (the last dynasty of Islamic rule in Spain). It reflects the Kalām philosophy of an atomically interconnected universe. The "created world" is represented by the botanical vines, plant, and flower shapes (#'s 5 & 12) that weave throughout *shabaka* (grid) patterns, and the permanence, order, and exactitude of the creator are shown in the precision of the geometric patterning of points, lines, planes, and right angles (#'s 1–4, 6, 7 & 9). Design: Raheem Tutein 140

13.3b Full view of three-dimensional *Murqanas* design in the "Hall of Two Sisters" in the Alhambra palace. (Wikimedia Commons)   141

13.4   Photo Credit: © RMN-Grand Palais / Art Resource, NY. Artist: Rabel, Daniel (1578–1637) Description: Dancers performing a sarabande, four figures. Album Rabel Daniel - Folio 46. A collection of drawings related to the *Ballet de la Douairière de Billebahaut* danced by Louis XIII in February 1626 in the hall of the Louvre. Ink and watercolor, 28.5 x 44 cm   142

13.5   Upper left corner: Ballet's foundational "zambo" geometric leg rotation within the personal square of eight-point cardinal (*en croix*) and ordinal directions reflecting the eight-pointed Islamic atomic star of creation, a staple of Islamic art. Drawn by Raheem Tutein. Adapted from Jeffrey Scott Longstaff, "Organizations of Chaos in an Infinitely Deflecting Body Space." Below: Ballet dancer, Marja' Miller, in profile with geometrically degreed leg heights and botanical upper half. At the center of the floor is a diagram of the floor patterns (also seen in upper left corner). The three-dimensional ballet vocabulary, like the *Murqanas* dome, is extrapolated from the two dimensional eight-point star and enacts the same geometric, scientific, and cosmological principles as those in the *N'kisi Sarabanda* and the *Alhambra*. Design: Raheem Tutein, derived from Jeffrey Scott Longstaff. "Organizations of Chaos in an Infinitely Deflecting Body Space". *A Conference on Liminality and Performance*. Brunel University Twickenham; 27–30 April 2000.   148

15.1   Image by Sidra Bell   165

15.2   Image by Sidra Bell   170

CONTRIBUTORS

Anjali Austin is a professor in the School of Dance at Florida State University, USA.

Alyah Baker is a dance artist, scholar, entrepreneur, and founder of Ballet for Black and Brown Bodies.

Keesha Beckford is the Youth Division Liaison at the Joffrey Academy.

Sidra Bell is the director of Sidra Bell Dance New York.

Paige Cunningham is an associate professor in the Department of Dance at the University of Illinois Urbana-Champaign, USA.

Lisa DeFrank-Cole is a professor and director of Leadership Studies at West Virginia University, USA.

Thomas F. DeFrantz is a professor in the departments of Performance Studies and Theatre at Northwestern University, USA.

Dionne Figgins is the artistic director of Ballet Tech: New York City's Public School for Dance.

List of contributors xi

Ilana Goldman is an associate professor in the School of Dance at Florida State University, USA.

Iyun Ashani Harrison is an associate professor of the practice of dance and head of ballet at Duke University, USA.

Theresa Ruth Howard is the founder and curator of Memoirs of Blacks in Ballet.

Alana Isiguen is the artist in residence with the Department of Dance at the University of Washington, USA.

Jehbreal Muhammad Jackson is an artist and doctoral candidate at Columbia University, USA.

Maurya Kerr is a poet, educator, and the artistic director of tinypistol.

Brandye Lee is a ballet instructor at Jones-Haywood Dance School and dance lecturer at Howard University, USA.

Lourdes Lopez is the artistic director of Miami City Ballet.

Kate Mattingly is an assistant professor in the Department of Communication and Theatre Arts at Old Dominion University, USA.

Renée K. Nicholson is an associate professor and director of the Humanities Center and of the Programs for Multi- and Interdisciplinary Studies at West Virginia University, USA.

Misa Oga is the director of MOGA Conservatory of Dance in Utah.

Gabrielle Salvatto is a professional dancer, amateur activist, and writer, and is currently dancing with Saarland State Ballet in Germany.

Monica Stephenson is the Director of Preparatory Dance at the University of North Carolina School of the Arts and a doctoral candidate at Texas Woman's University.

ACKNOWLEDGEMENTS

First and foremost, I thank Routledge for proposing the topic of this book and asking if I would be interested in creating an anthology. I am indebted to chapter authors I had the pleasure of being in dialogue with—Keesha Beckford, Paige Cunningham and Ilana Goldman, Theresa Ruth Howard, Alana Isiguen, Jehbreal Muhammad Jackson, Maurya Kerr, Misa Oga, Gabrielle Salvatto, and Monica Stephenson—and leaders I interviewed who generously shared their wisdom and insights, Lourdes Lopez and Dionne Figgins. I am especially grateful for my teachers, including the faculty at The Washington School of Ballet where I trained while I was in high school, and left high school early each day to attend pre-professional classes. I also learned a great deal about ballet as a graduate student at NYU in classes taught by Cherylyn Lavagnino, James Martin, Cassandra Phifer, and James Sutton, and while performing choreography by William Forsythe and Amanda Miller. I had the great joy of teaching dance history at Ballet Tech: New York's Public School for Dance, led by Eliot Feld and Maggie Christ. Since completing my doctorate I have been fortunate to find a home in the Dance Program at Old Dominion University (ODU) where colleagues and students are invested in equitable and transformative learning environments. I am especially grateful for ODU's Dance Program Director Megan Thompson who supported and helped to organize the Antiracism in the Arts symposium that took place in October of 2022, and which featured guest speakers from this anthology. Working on this anthology has led me reflect on teaching as a form of collaboration, and how often ballet is taught in highly competitive and individualistic ways. I believe this approach not only contributes to othering and hierarchies that undergird racialized, gendered, and ableist exclusions, but also makes it difficult for ballet teachers to honor dialogue and collaboration. Compiling this anthology has been an illuminating experience and I am indebted to friends who listened patiently and shared their own perspectives on teaching and living, most notably, James Ady, Cheryl Sladkin Altschuler, Elizabeth Craft, Garit Lawson, Catherine Long, Elisabeth Motley, Serena Orloff, Caitlin Sims, Elizabeth Weldon, Helanius J. Wilkins, and Kristina Windom.

Kate Mattingly

ACKNOWLEDGEMENTS

I acknowledge Dr. Kate Mattingly for including me in this crucial work and opening up an intriguing area of research for me. I am indebted to Duke University's Trinity College and former Trinity Dean, Dr. Valerie S. Ashby, for providing the necessary resources for me to pursue this work. To my intellectual and artistic community, I would not be able to do this work without your continued support and feedback. Thank you, Dr. Thomas F. DeFrantz, Dr. Esther Hernández-Medina, Dr. Adanna J. Johnson, Dr. Jarvis C. McInnis, and my Juilliard School, Dance Theatre of Harlem, and Ailey School families. I am also sending a heartfelt shoutout to my family and friends and Ballet Ashani and Duke Dance Program colleagues for listening to my random epiphanies and rants and receiving them with kindness and love.

Iyun Ashani Harrison

INTRODUCTION

Kate Mattingly and Iyun Ashani Harrison

During the summer of 2021, when we discussed this anthology on Zoom, we noticed a gap in books about teaching ballet. Most writing by white authors does not mention racism or white supremacy in teaching practices. Books on dance that address racialized exclusions often do not include ballet, or do not address ballet pedagogy. In addition, there seems to be very little writing about teaching that centers dancers of color in ballet, especially in pre-professional training. We hope that this anthology fills this gap by providing teachers, students, and leaders with tangible practices and sustainable policies that dismantle inequities in ballet settings and amplify the joy in learning.

Our focus on pedagogy stems from the belief that teachers play a pivotal role in upholding—as well as dismantling—aesthetic hierarchies that present barriers. While the title of the book addresses antiracism, we view this anthology as invested in eradicating obstacles that take many forms. Racism is one of several pervasive and damaging systemic exclusions in ballet settings, alongside sexism, genderism, classism, ageism, and ableism. In agreement with Kimberlé Crenshaw's theories of intersectionality, we consider these exclusions inextricably linked to one another, and each chapter foregrounds authors' approaches to challenging barriers, assumptions, and biases.[1] Following the work of Patricia Hill Collins, we view systemic forms of inequality in ballet as a "matrix of domination," which exists at institutional, group, and individual levels.[2]

With over 40 years of combined experience as students, performers, teachers, researchers, and practitioners invested in ballet, we are well-aware of how our identities and our backgrounds have both opened and foreclosed certain paths. Kate is a white cisgender female, who trained at the Washington School of Ballet and was a scholarship student in summer programs with San Francisco Ballet School and Ballet West. She chose to attend Princeton University at age 18 instead of pursuing a dance career. She graduated with a degree in Architecture, and received her Master of Fine Arts (MFA) degree in Dance from New York University's Tisch School of the Arts, where she was taught by Cassandra Phifer, and performed choreography by William Forsythe and Cherylyn Lavagnino.

Iyun identifies as a Black, gay, male Jamaican who began his ballet training studying the Royal Academy of Dancing children's syllabus in the Caribbean. He received his BFA from The Juilliard School, danced professionally with the Dance Theatre of Harlem, Ballet Hispanico of New York, Ailey II, and appeared in television specials. After completing his MFA at Hollins University, Iyun taught at Cornish College of the Arts, Goucher College, Webster University, Pomona College, Duke University, Pacific Northwest Ballet, Peabody Conservatory, and The Ailey School. He is a commissioned choreographer and the founder and director of Ballet Ashani, a contemporary ballet company.

During conversations about this anthology, our different backgrounds produced moments of intense debates, and we invited friends and colleagues into these discussions by asking them to author chapters. We seek to interrogate notions of "ideal" teaching methods, to question "authenticity" as a metric, and to expand perspectives on ballet pedagogy. We hope that readers notice there are multiple and, at times, conflicting notions of "inclusion" in the chapters that follow and, as editors, we have differing definitions of what "very diverse" students look and feel like in a ballet class.

While there are some people today who view conversations about identities as divisive and exclusionary, we seek to differentiate between naming identities as a path to dismantling barriers, and using identities to uphold exclusions. As editors and educators, we have a shared belief in the generative aspects of diversity and belonging, and seek to amplify Blackness, queerness, and feminist knowledges. Until we exist in a world where identities are not treated as barriers to entry, we will continue to work toward this future. We do not subscribe to essentialist notions of identities as indicators of preferences or character traits, and agree with educators, choreographers, and students who do not want to be pigeon-holed into identity-driven selections. We are working towards a world where teachers are aware of biases and barriers, and dancers are appreciated for skills and artistry.

We focus on what is called the United States, currently home to 574 federally-recognized Nations. In the chapter "Native American Dancing beyond Settler Colonial Confines," Kate describes how ballet's imbrications with whiteness undergird its presumed superiority, and how deeper awareness and appreciation of Indigenous epistemologies would benefit both dance education and university curricula. We decided to bracket our focus to the United States as a necessary delimitation, and hope that each community will work to eradicate systemic exclusions in ballet, and extend and modify authors' recommendations.

We distinguish our focus from recent publications by questioning if it is possible to repair the damages—or "heal" our communities—without addressing the sources of harm and trauma. We notice a tendency among white authors and teachers to avoid discussions of any topic that produces embarrassment or exposes wrongdoing. We consider this a tactic of white supremacy, theorized as "right to comfort," that responds to conflict by blaming the person who raises the issue rather than examining the problem. Herein we find one of the double-binds of addressing racism in ballet: as an art form and technique, ballet has, historically and currently, privileged obedience and docile dancers. This can be traced to the courts of France in the 1600s, where ballet was used as a "Weapon of State" to quell uprisings and maintain order, control, and hierarchies.[3] Authoritarian teaching methods in ballet continue to exist in many settings, including universities, conservatories, and private studios. When these teaching approaches are mixed with white supremacy characteristics, we see why students, especially students of color, have been met with resistance and dismissal.

This anthology seeks to eradicate exclusions as well as address the pain that they create. But the intended readers for this anthology are not only teachers and students of ballet. White supremacy in ballet is held in place by the predominantly white and male directors, administrators, and leaders who continually make decisions that benefit other white men and harm women, especially women of color.

To offer one seemingly benign example of how these exclusions are reproduced by administrators and leaders, Kate shares an incident from the University of Utah where she was an assistant professor: "A graduate student in the Ballet MFA program, a woman of color, asked if I could serve as a liaison between her and the School of Dance Director, a white man. When I asked if everything was okay, she responded that she had met with him in his office a day earlier about a mistake he had made in her funding application for conference travel, and he had yelled at her with such force and aggression she no longer felt safe meeting with him alone. As I thought about this lack of safety and respect in a university setting, I asked if it would be okay to tell the director's supervisor, the Associate Dean for Faculty & Academic Affairs, about the incident, and the student said yes. I relayed the information to the Associate Dean, a white woman, who implied that sharing the incident with the Dean, another white man and the Director's supervisor, might jeopardize her good relationship with him, so she could not. I served as a liaison for the student for a year, until she graduated with her MFA, and I left the university soon after. The MFA student who was mistreated is currently an acclaimed ballet teacher and studio owner, and contributed a chapter to this anthology. The incident magnified barriers held in place by leaders who ignore racialized bias, who know they will not be held accountable, and administrators who value their reputations more than students' health and well-being."[4]

Kwame Ture and Charles V. Hamilton write, "Institutional racism has been maintained deliberately by the power structure and through indifference, inertia, and lack of courage on the part of white masses as well as petty officials… The line between purposeful suppression and indifference blurs."[5]

We hope our anthology brings attention to both suppression and indifference, and to notice when leaders prioritize "kindness" over uncomfortable conversations, or demand "resilience" of students of color, rather than dismantle barriers and biases. We seek to show how the rhetoric of "kindness" and "resilience" stifle much-needed action, while deflecting responsibility for inhumane policies and behaviors by teachers and leaders.

While we are committed to making ballet classes accessible, we also wish to dismantle notions of ballet's entitlement, which reveals itself when ballet is perceived as more valuable than other techniques, or a necessary part of dance education. As co-editors we are aware of the privileged status that ballet occupies in this country: a Dance Data Project report found U.S. ballet companies' aggregate expenses were about $664 million, and contemporary/modern dance companies operated with about $150 million in fiscal year 2019.[6] This disproportionate attention and funding can be traced to ballet's cultural capital, analyzed by Thomas F. DeFrantz in this anthology, and its associations with sophistication. When this country sought to establish itself as a refined nation-state, ballet became a path to validation: in 1840 when Fanny Elssler performed in the United States, President Martin van Buren and his cabinet received her in an official audience. Congress adjourned each evening that she danced in Washington. At a formal banquet in the Capitol, the Congressmen drank to her health from a dance slipper.[7]

Ballet is just one of many significant approaches to dancing, and teachers and directors are responsible for challenging the myth of ballet's supremacy. We invest in writing because we hope these insightful chapters will be accessible and widely circulated, and that future anthologies amplify other dance techniques and teachers' knowledge.

Nevertheless, we are well-aware of the scarcity of Asian/Asian American and Indigenous perspectives in the following pages, and acknowledge that this anthology, curated with the hopes of dismantling barriers, is also complicit with the exclusions of academic publishing, which is inaccessible to many brilliant writers and teachers.[8] When the *Oxford Handbook of Contemporary Ballet* published its 53 chapters in 2021, there were no mentions of prominent Asian and Asian-American contemporary ballet choreographers in the United States, such as Edwaard Liang or Choo San Goh. When we invited an acclaimed author to write a chapter for this anthology, the stipend of $70 per contributor that we negotiated with Routledge was too low a fee for his time and insights. Many anthologies published by academic presses do not provide any stipend for authors: their contributions are "rewarded" in university tenure and promotion reviews. Several Native scholars affiliated with universities were asked to contribute chapters, but the topic of ballet pedagogy, the relatively short length of chapters, or the schedule for submitting chapters made the invitation unappealing or undoable.

We look forward to learning from readers' feedback and questions and invite people to begin with any of the three sections that follow: Part 1, "Identities," begins with an essay by Gabrielle Salvatto that illuminates her experiences as a student and professional. An interview with Dionne

Figgins, now director of one of the schools described by Salvatto, follows. We hope readers notice the frequently mentioned organizations throughout the chapters and consider their significance in antiracist work. Chapters 3 to 5 include an interview with Lourdes Lopez, a chapter by Mattingly, and one by Alyah Baker.

Part 2, "Pedagogies," explores teaching methods of Anjali Austin, Misa Oga, Jehbreal Muhammad Jackson, Maurya Kerr, Alana Isiguen, Ilana Goldman and Paige Cunningham, and Monica Stephenson, who writes about the influential Jones Haywood School of Ballet. The anthology closes with Part 3, "Futurities," a rich mosaic of insights from choreographers, educators, and scholars, with the anthology's final chapter amplifying the voices of people invested in the future of ballet. We extend a special thank you to these interviewees: Jennifer Archibald, Keesha Beckford, Clare Croft, Thomas F. DeFrantz, Brenda Dixon Gottschild, Robert Garland, Alicia Graf Mack, Tai Jimenez, Alonzo King, Endalyn Taylor Outlaw, and Claudia Schreier.

A History of Racism in Ballet: Comments, Casting, and Caricatures

Kate Mattingly

When I teach courses in dance history, I use the metaphor of an algorithm to explain how leaders in schools and dance companies make decisions that uphold white supremacy: when I search "ballet" in Google, an algorithm produces images of mostly white dancers of a certain body type. This algorithm is not only responding to a query but also determining the boundaries of "ballet dancer," and algorithms are mathematical formulations made by human beings.[9] A more analog example could be, prior to 2018, Freed of London, a major pointe shoe manufacturer, did not make shoes that matched dancers with beige or brown skin. Dancers of color were excluded from Freed's definition of "ballet dancers."

These examples support the research of Dr. Ruha Benjamin, who writes, "Robots are not sentient beings, sure, but racism flourishes well beyond hate-filled hearts."[10] In other words, systemic exclusions do not need intentional choices by humans to exclude other people: they thrive through lack of awareness. For instance, how often do history courses include one of the earliest dance companies in this country: the American Negro Ballet, which formed in 1934 and debuted in 1937?

Indigenous dancers and dancers of color[11] have been performing leading roles with American Ballet Theatre (ABT) and New York City Ballet (NYCB) since the 1940s: Rosella Hightower (Choctow) and Sono Osato (Japanese-Irish) were principal dancers with Ballet Theatre, precursor to ABT.[12] In 1948, when NYCB was established, performances by Maria Tallchief (Osage) expanded definitions of ballet. In 1952, Louis Johnson (African American) performed as a guest artist with NYCB, and in 1955, Arthur Mitchell (African American) joined the company; in 1971, Debra Austin (African American) was handpicked by George Balanchine to join NYCB, and she became a principal dancer with Pennsylvania Ballet in 1982. Latina Lourdes Lopez joined NYCB in 1974 and was promoted to principal in 1984. Lauren Anderson (African American) joined Houston Ballet in 1983 and was promoted to principal in 1990. Edwaard Liang (Taiwanese American) joined NYCB in 1993 and was promoted to soloist in 1998. Aesha Ash joined NYCB as a corps de ballet dancer in 1996 and became the first African American female faculty member at the School of American Ballet. Karen Brown (African American) spent 22 years performing and teaching with Dance Theatre of Harlem, and then directed Oakland Ballet from 2000 to 2006.[13]

These artists illustrate that Indigenous dancers and dancers of color in ballet are a constant. Barriers to their promotion and acclaim have been perpetuated by predominately white leadership. One of the intentions of this anthology is to reframe conversations about equity by insisting on long-term action and accountability from white leaders and teachers. As education scholar Brian Gibbs writes, "Racism is a White problem, a problem of White supremacy and a lack of White understanding and acknowledgment that there is a problem..." Gibbs continues with the recommendation, "Rather than avoiding or causing additional harm, teachers seek to help students better understand the harm, where it came from, how it manifested, and ultimately, how it can be prevented. The possibilities of healing come from knowledge, understanding, and the possibility of something different."[14]

Theresa Ruth Howard describes the pervasive resistance to change in ballet as "the desire to change without changing." Howard notes the disconnect of

> doing the small incremental things to give the illusion of change, like hiring more brown people to say 'oh look at us we're so

brown,' but then what you're hearing is that those spaces don't feel inclusive, people don't feel heard, there's not a feeling of belonging or ownership, or even access to that inner circle.[15]

Incremental, stand-alone "fixes" do not erase ongoing decision-making that reproduces exclusions. Persistent behaviors, assumptions, and policies reinforce racialized biases in ballet, and are made visible through comments, casting, and caricatures.

Comments

Students of color describe many barriers faced in ballet, from policies about hair styles to the tendency of white teachers to ignore their effort and accomplishments. Comments like "Beautiful" or "Well done" are given to white students, while students of color are told, "That's better" or "Keep up the good work." Students interpret these differences as white dancers tending to match what a teacher "expects" a ballet dancer to do, while students of color are perpetually in process, never achieving "beauty" or "elegance."

Word choice is powerful because language can solidify movement that is transient and ephemeral. When a teacher acknowledges a student's dancing as "beautiful" the entire class hears this affirmation: words adhere. Writing about dancers of color by critics both informs and influences these comments. Descriptors like "fierce" and "powerful" emphasize a dancer's athleticism, often overshadowing a dancer's subtlety and ingenuity. Since dance is an art form that communicates through our bodies it is very difficult to separate our identity markers—gender, race, ethnicity, ability-status—from our movement. When critics connect certain words to identities, racialized assumptions are presented and perpetuated.

White dance critic John Martin published books on dance and wrote for the *New York Times* from 1927 to 1962, perpetuating barriers for Black ballet dancers. Martin defined "Negro dance" as "not designed to delve into philosophy or psychology but to externalize the impulses of a high-spirited, rhythmic, and gracious race."[16] Martin further restricted this category by scolding Talley Beatty in this 1940 article for his ballet technique, noting "a distressing tendency to introduce the technique of the academic ballet."[17] In another 1940 article, entitled "De Mille Ballet Seen as Novelty," Martin described a ballet choreographed by Agnes de

Mille for the "Negro Unit" of American Ballet Theatre as succeeding "remarkably well with limited material." Martin could not accept the possibility of sixteen Black women performing a ballet, and criticized the cast of "Negro girls" for being "manifestly inexperienced." Martin's use of the infantilizing term "girls" is noteworthy because several dancers—Maudelle Bass, Leonore Cox, and Ann Jones—were in their mid-30s. Although the cast was composed of professional dancers, Martin castigates the performers for a lack of "experience," ironic given tremendous obstacles Black ballet dancers navigated to gain training and performance opportunities.

By giving more attention to critics of color and the Black press in the 20th century, historians can trace a different narrative of ballet in the United States. As early as 1908, the *New York Age* documented a performance by Aida Overton Walker, "Surrounding her are several nimble chorus girls, who, by their work, prove to the public that a colored show can put on a ballet possessing as much dash and artistic finesse as a white ballet."[18] These words suggest "white ballet" was synonymous with refinement, and dancers of color were considered lesser than.

Since critics have doubled as authors of dance history books, their racialized biases often extend to students of dance history. When history students become the next generation of teachers, these assumptions are continued. There are direct correlations between the prejudices of ballet teachers and the biases presented by critics and historians. For instance, white critic Sarah Kaufman often wrote about artists of color with a sense of condescension, extending John Martin's values. Kaufman frequently denigrated choreographic choices by Dance Theatre of Harlem, writing in 1998: "Louis Johnson's 'Soul on Pointe' was like a poke in the eye. Dredge up memories of your high school talent show and you'll be pretty close to the sophomoric flash and not-quite-rock music that closed the program."[19]

When critics do not account for biases that uphold white supremacy and its characteristics, entire communities and practices are dismissed.

Casting

Dancer Debra Austin recalls a particularly revealing moment as a principal with Pennsylvania Ballet. White director Robert Weiss advocated for her to dance the sylph in *La Sylphide*, but the white repetiteur rebuffed the recommendation, saying, "I've never seen a Black sylph before." Weiss responded, "Have you ever seen a sylph?"[20]

Such interactions signal how casting reveals implicit biases: the repetiteur's statement exposes the assumption—the algorithm—that historical roles belong to white dancers, extending the conflation of "classical" ballet with "white" ballet. The repetiteur, having never seen a dancer of color perform the role, assumed Austin was incapable of the part. Just as John Martin segregated genres of dance, like "Modern Dance" and "Negro Dance," racialized assumptions contribute to the scarcity of dancers of color in predominantly white companies. To address this problem, the International Association of Blacks in Dance (IABD) started holding annual auditions for dancers of color in 2018, attended by more than 20 representatives from professional ballet companies. IABD mitigates the expense of auditioning for multiple companies—dancers typically pay travel expenses plus an audition fee of $30 to $50 per company—while reducing the tendency of dancers of color to be seen as outliers in classes of predominantly white dancers. This event is especially important because dancers of color often face numerous obstacles in their pursuit of preprofessional training, as detailed by authors in this anthology.

A university student recently described the longterm damage of tokenizing dancers of color: a studio where she trained decided to present a piece about Rosa Parks in a dance competition. As the only dancer of color in the advanced level that was competing, she was cast as Parks. She had never been offered a lead role prior to this moment, and questioned, "Was it my dance ability or my skin tone?" The corrosive effects of self-doubt are well-documented in psychology research and, as this anthology reveals, are frequently experienced by dancers of color in predominantly white settings.[21]

Caricature

La Bayadère, choreographed by Marius Petipa in 1877, and revised in 1941 by Vakhtang Chabukiani and Vladimir Ponomarev, continues to present caricatures of Indian people, with young dancers in blackface.[22] In *Petrocuhka*, choreographed by Mikhail Fokine in 1911 and performed to this day, the role of the Blackamoor presents primitive gestures in blackface. When Lar Lubovitch choreographed *Othello* for American Ballet Theatre in 1997, the company hired Desmond

Richardson because there were no Black principal men for the title role. Another cast featured Keith Roberts, and Lubovitch told me in 1997 that he would perform in blackface, since "it's something that has been done in opera for decades."[23] Critic Anna Kisselgoff noted Roberts's "dark makeup."[24]

In 2017, Phil Chan and Georgina Pazcoguin brought heightened attention to the representation of Asian characters in ballet through their website and pledge, "Final Bow for Yellowface." Many ballet companies have signed the pledge and taken action to eradicate harmful caricatures. Scholar Josephine Lee notes,

> [Y]ellowface performance unfortunately has a long history in all branches of the performing arts. But that doesn't mean it has to have a long future... Working artists, producers, choreographers, writers, directors must make the choice to break away from these tired clichés—and spend their generative energies on something wonderful and new.[25]

This anthology takes this call to action to heart. We hope that contributors' insights and tangible practices amplify the work being done to foster inclusive, welcoming, and generative classes for ballet dancers.

Learning Environments Matter: Effects of Racial Bias in Ballet Teaching

Iyun Ashani Harrison

Racial bias in teaching can be detrimental to ballet dancers of color. Teaching and institutional practices that exhibit racialized attitudes, behaviors, and policies can cause internalized trauma, feelings of inadequacy, and otherness, leading to adverse physical, emotional, behavioral, and psychological outcomes for students of color. Psychologist Adanna J. Johnson has constructed a guide for developing racial competencies and effective communication strategies for treating patients of color, and they can also provide a critical model for ballet teachers.[26] Dr. Johnson analyzes racialized biases' impact on students, which results in stress and behavioral responses, including frustration, anger, resentment, fear, headaches, pounding heart, high blood pressure, sleep disturbances, impatience, and poor performance. She reveals that racialized comments, and anticipating such comments, can trigger these responses. Johnson's research clarifies why attending to perceptions and language shared with students of color is essential.

In 2003 Brenda Dixon Gottschild, published *The Black Dancing Body: A Geography from Coon to Cool*, which analyzed racial biases projected onto movement practitioners of color. Through interviews, professional dancers reflected on prejudice encountered in the dance industry. Twenty years later, her analysis of the disputed geographies of the bodies of dancers of color still rings true. Take, for instance, ballet dancer Zane Booker's reflection:

> I have a huge running joke with a white guy who was a good friend of mine in Ballets de Monte-Carlo. He'd always talk about my feet. And I would tell him, 'My feet point. Your feet don't point.' And I really wonder if he saw my feet… I wonder if he saw what was there.[27]

Gottschild identifies the underpinning values in Booker's reflection when she explains:

> Booker points up the issue of the stereotype… Indeed, we can be blinded by our presupposition, particularly when they are racial; and that is the juncture at which assumptions become prejudices. Like its counterpart in the larger society, the black dancing body has been demonized by blind-sighted observers.[28]

Regrettably, prejudice against minoritized dancers is still prevalent. Though diversity initiatives in ballet are now commonplace in the United States, ballet dancers of color still face tremendous challenges. A 2021 report detailed discriminatory incidents experienced by Staatsballett's ballerina Chloé Lopes Gomes, who was mocked for her skin color and, at times, pressured to wear white skin makeup, leaving her feeling unsupported and humiliated.[29] Furthermore, Lopes Gomes was told her mistakes stood out because she is Black.[30] Similarly, in a 2023 *New York Times* Op-Ed, Gabe Stone Shayer, an American Ballet Theatre soloist of African descent, shared his frustrations with feeling unseen by artistic leadership, the company's practices of racial stereotypes in casting, and divisive use of Black dancers' images to disingenuously promote its diversity, rather and their artistic excellence."[31]

Fortunately, teachers can play an essential role in challenging regressive racial beliefs about dancers of color. Teachers nurture young people inside and outside of the studio. We inscribe our values on our students physically, emotionally, and psychologically. Since values are personal and deep-seated, they require constant evaluation. Teachers must confront biases that exclude minoritized dancers to become more effective educators.

For The Love of Ballet

Some teachers resist change due to their love of the art form. Many spent decades studying and performing, and romanticizing these experiences, even when they were abusive. Some educators view teaching careers as a calling, often making financial and personal sacrifices to work in the field. Together, their love of ballet, sense of service, and traditionalism—privileging outdated knowledge over current information—can make it difficult for educators to make meaningful changes to their teaching.

However, suspending this love may lead teachers away from antiquated methods and create opportunities to strategize and develop antiracist teaching praxes. It is crucial not to privilege the love of ballet over the responsibility to be fair and just educators who are invested in developing healthy young people.

Half a Lifetime in Ballet Teaching

I have taught on the faculties of recreational, preprofessional, professional, and collegiate ballet programs for over sixteen years and have worked with politically and racially progressive white colleagues who exhibited racial and cultural competency. However, despite their awareness and good intentions, I observed that, in high-stakes situations, my white counterparts sometimes retreated into silence, deflected, or defended racial biases. They took a gatekeeping stance, arguing against inclusion to maintain aesthetic "standards."

Five critical factors hinder the development of progressive ballet pedagogies; 1) Ignorance – not knowing what attitudes, behaviors, and policies contribute to racism; 2) Fear and resentment when faced with the crucial antiracist work of reflecting on personal bias; 3) Denial of past actions which implicate them in larger racist structures; 4)

Avoidance of /delaying complex diversity, equity, and inclusion (DEI) work, and 5) Imagining that racism is only represented in "gross and obvious" acts and not the "subtle, cumulative mini-assault[s]" which represent racism in much of contemporary life.[32]

These factors create toxic organizational cultures that affect minoritized staff, faculty, and students. Microaggressions—also known as mini-assaults—detrimentally impact people. Whether conscious of bias or not, many ballet teachers perpetuate the marginalization of dancers of color and model for white students that their racial biases are permissible and should be emulated.

Ballet Students of Color: A Unique Positioning

Students of color in ballet settings in the United States negotiate more significant challenges than learning the intricacies of the art form. Before entering the studio, they navigate complex, collective traumas, including police violence against people of color, environmental injustices (Flint, MI water crisis), neglect (Hurricane Katrina), inhumane immigration and deportation policies, and demeaning societal messages.[33] These factors impact students of color and affect their ability to learn effectively, feel safe, and experience a sense of belonging.

Racialized Bias in The Studio, on Stage, and in Social Settings

Some ballet teachers need help identifying attitudes, behaviors, and policies that constitute racialized bias in education. The following sections provide examples of experiences of racial discrimination typically encountered by ballet students of color in the studio, on stage, and in social settings.

Studio

Most ballet teachers in the United States have learned it is dangerous to make explicit comments to students of color that might be perceived as racist and, as a result, have developed coded language to express racialized attitudes—microaggressions. Some teachers express bias by making insensitive and inappropriate comments that undermine the race and culture of students. Derogatory remarks about pop culture, expressions of xenophobia, and discussing politically and culturally

charged topics, such as the Black Lives Matter movement, can be stress-inducing and create hostile learning environments.

Microaggressions toward students appear as comments about "standards" of physical appearance regarding students' hair, makeup, and complexion. They can be framed positively, emphasizing students' differences. For example, a white ballet teacher complimenting Black students' skin, clothing, or body parts can trigger discomfort and feelings of Otherness. Backhanded compliments about students' abilities to dance well in classes outside of ballet, such as contemporary or hip-hop, or unsolicited encouragement to attend non-ballet-focused summer training can deter students from investing in their ballet education. Other microaggressions might include making public and disparaging remarks about the abilities and physical attributes of professional dancers of color or being overly critical of institutions dedicated to increasing diversity in ballet. Similarly, as large ballet companies diversify their leadership, creative teams, and dancers, some teachers may openly express correlations between diversifying hiring practices and lowered institutional and artistic standards. As Dr. Johnson explains, these interactions can lead to stress, chip away at the self-worth and racial and cultural pride of students of color, and reduce their investment in ballet.

Furthermore, many expressions of racial bias in ballet are invisible to students since they occur in faculty meetings or informal conversations between teachers. Too often, ballet teachers act as gatekeepers, positioning themselves between students and opportunities that affirm their talents. Teachers' biases influence student recruitment and admission auditions, class-level placement and promotion, grading and evaluation, casting, image selection for marketing, and retention efforts. Unfortunately, when faced with complaints about their actions, some teachers downplay or dismiss concerns, citing generational and cultural differences or arguing that students are too sensitive and need to become tougher or more resilient to succeed.

Stage

Class demonstrations and stage productions are public-facing facets of ballet training, where some of the most adverse instances of racially biased interactions occur between teachers and students of color. From auditions to casting, rehearsals to costuming (including makeup and hair styling), to staging and lighting, productions are rife with decisions that keep whiteness at the center and push students of color to the periphery. Many of these issues can be attributed to a failure of imagination: the inability of educators to view ballet as current and their clinging to racialized attitudes and whiteness in the name of tradition.

As an example, let us explore a hypothetical scenario: a ballet school plans to stage a production of *Swan Lake*. The teachers hold significant responsibilities and power, selecting choreography and casts and rehearsing students. Teachers usually understand which students can portray the lead role, Odette/Odile, based on their technique, stamina, strength, body line, qualitative range, musicality, and acting skills. After narrowing down the group of students with these attributes, some teachers may consider other factors, such as when the lead ballerina dances the character of Odette, she wears a white tutu. She is informally referred to as the *white swan*. The white swan is delicate, beautiful, and vulnerable: when she is captured by a hunter, Prince Siegfried, she struggles demurely, and then the two fall in love. They traverse the challenges of an inter-species relationship, experience magical transformations and betrayal, and then commit a love-pact suicide. Despite its implausible plot and troubling subject matter, *Swan Lake* is one of the most often performed ballets in the world.

The white swan, Odette, represents an archetypal white femme fatale. Beyond the physical and artistic requirements of the role, the dancer is expected to convey delicacy and vulnerability. So, how does the ballet teacher make casting choices when faced with a predominantly white student body, which might have several strong students of color? What considerations come to the forefront as we imagine the lead ballerina in a present-day US restaging of a Russian ballet from the late nineteenth century? Does authenticity matter in the given scenario? Do performances of historical European fairytales need to be racially accurate to accomplish their moral objectives?

Imagine a Black girl is bestowed with the opportunity to perform this archetypal role of white femaleness because she fulfills its technical and artistic requirements. How does she navigate the common opinion that the role was not created for young women who look like her? Does calling the character Odette instead of the white swan make a difference in the Black girl's experience? While she might imagine herself as Odette, can she easily see herself as the white swan in the context of American racial politics? Does the teacher who cast her believe the myth that a Black girl cannot play the role of the white swan? Moreover, if the teacher agrees with this assertion, why can white girls dance Odile, the *black swan*? What suspension of belief allows one student to be racially fluid and the other not? What accommodations are necessary for a Black girl to feel a sense of belonging? How will teachers and designers adjust costuming and lighting to accommodate a Black Odette? And if the casting is questioned, how will they protect and support the dancer?

Social Settings

Social settings outside the studio and stage, such as dressing rooms, hallways, and after-school activities—birthday parties, shopping trips, and meals—are often stressful for students of color in ballet. Here, they can be harassed about all aspects of their personhood. Too often, students' skin color, hair texture, facial features, weight, body shape, mannerisms, and cultural practices are critiqued and wrestled into compliance with white aesthetic standards. These challenges are exacerbated for Black girls and young women who are ghettoized, exoticized, and sexualized in dominant cultures.

Conclusion

So, what is the educator's role in dismantling ballet's racist system? What can teachers do to develop an antiracist teaching praxis?

Antiracist ballet teaching is a practice not dissimilar to training in ballet. It takes vigilant self-reflection, humility, identifying weaknesses and biases, hard work, discipline, and consistent practice. Reading this anthology is not enough because antiracist teaching is a lifelong commitment. It must stay at the forefront of educators' minds, and they must be prepared to be wrong, accept corrections, and do better. It is challenging and rewarding work that can improve young people's lives. Educators are part of the change ballet needs.

Notes

1 Kimberlé Crenshaw, "Demarginalizing the Intersection of Race and Sex: A Black Feminist Critique of Antidiscrimination Doctrine, Feminist Theory

and Antiracist Politics," *University of Chicago Legal Forum* 1, no. 8 (1989): 139–167.
2 Patricia Hill Collins, *Black Feminist Thought: Knowledge, Consciousness, and the Politics of Embodiment* (New York: Routledge, 2022), bii.
3 "Dancing: Dance at Court," Jane Alexander and Rhoda Grauer (ArtHaus Musik, 1993).
4 This School of Dance has a history of mistreating students: https://www.sltrib.com/artsliving/2021/11/16/ballet-alumni-demand/
5 Kwame Ture/Stokely Carmichael and Charles V. Hamilton, *Black Power: The Politics of Liberation in America* (New York: Random House, 1967/1992), 29.
6 "2021 Ballet Companies," *Dance Data Project*, https://www.dancedataproject.com/dance-data-project-announces-2021-largest-50-report-on-u-s-ballet-companies/
7 Douglas C. Sonntag, "Introduction," *National Endowment for the Arts: A History 1965–2008*. https://www.arts.gov/sites/default/files/nea-history-1965-2008.pdf
8 For more information about the imbrications of universities and white supremacy characteristics, see: https://brocansky.com/2020/08/why-higher-ed-cant-change.html
9 Scholar Safiya Umoja Noble has coined the term "technological redlining" to describe how digital decisions reinforce oppressive social relationships and enact new modes of racial profiling. See Noble, *Algorithms of Oppression* (New York: New York University Press, 2015), 1–14.
10 Ruha Benjamin, *Race after Technology* (Cambridge, UK: Polity Press, 2019), 80.
11 "Dancer of color" refers to a person's racial or ethnic identity. "Indigenous" or "Native American" dancer refers to a person's political identity because it describes an affiliation with a sovereign nation. Dr. Charmaine Nelson of McGill University notes, "We understand that under colonialism African and Indigenous people had very different experiences. To conflate everything in one is to erase, which is the very nature of genocidal practice." For more information, see Sandra E. Garcia, "Where did BIPOC Come From?" *New York Times*, June 17, 2020, https://www.nytimes.com/article/what-is-bipoc.html.
12 In contrast to Martin's dismissal of African American dancers in ballet, he consistently praised Hightower and Ono. See John Martin, "The Dance: Company Bow," *New York Times*, November 9, 1941, p. X2; John Martin, "The Dance: Third Season," *New York Times*, December 21, 1941, p. X2; Irene Hsiao, "Teach your Students about these Barrier-Breaking Asian-American Dance Artists," *Dance Teacher*, May 6, 2021.
13 "Karen Brown," https://www.joffreyballetschool.com/faculty/karen-brown
14 Brian Gibbs, "'Strange Fruit': Teaching the Present and Past of Racial Violence in the Rural South," *Equity & Excellence in Education* 54, no. 2 (2021): 174.
15 Please see Theresa Ruth Howard, Chapter 18.
16 John Martin, "The Dance: A Negro Art," *New York Times*, February 25, 1940, 114.

17 Martin, "Negro Art," February 25, 1940.
18 Lester A. Walton, "Music and the Stage: W. and W. Give Professional Matinee," *New York Age*, February 27, 1908.
19 Sarah Kaufman, "Harlem Lifted by a Ballerina," *Washington Post*, April 29, 1998. https://www.washingtonpost.com/archive/lifestyle/1998/04/29/harlem-lifted-by-a-ballerina/9e353d7b-d918-4ddd-8f7c-985fe07092da/
20 "Studio Visit: Debra Austin," *Southern Cultures*, https://www.southerncultures.org/article/studio-visit-debra-austin/
21 "The Psychology of Self-Doubt," *Hidden Brain*, https://hiddenbrain.org/podcast/the-psychology-of-self-doubt/
22 Dana Nichols, "I Am a Black Dancer Who Was Dressed Up in Blackface to Perform in La Bayadère," *Dance* Magazine, December 11, 2019, https://www.dancemagazine.com/black-face-in-ballet/
23 Kate Mattingly, "Moor for the Masses," *The Village Voice*, May 27, 1997, 53.
24 Anna Kisselgoff, "A Downtown Experiment has an Uptown Premiere," *New York Times*, May 26, 1997, https://www.nytimes.com/1997/05/26/arts/a-downtown-experiment-has-an-uptown-premiere.html
25 Dr. Josephine Lee, quoted on website *Final Bow for Yellowface*, www.yellowface.org.
26 Adanna J. Johnson, "Looks Could Kill: Understanding the Role of Racism-Related Stress & Trauma in Psychotherapy," Lecture/Seminar, 2017.
27 Brenda Dixon Gottschild, *The Black Dancing Body: A Geography from Coon to Cool* (New York: Palgrave MacMillan, 2003), 134.
28 Dixon Gottschild, *Black Dancing Body*, 134.
29 Adela Suliman, "Black Dancer Calls out Racism in 'Elitist' European Ballet World," *NBC News*, February 14, 2021, https://www.nbcnews.com/news/world/black-dancer-calls-out-racism-elitist-european-ballet-world-n1257141.
30 Suliman, "Black Dancer Calls out Racism," *NBC News*.
31 Gabe Stone Shayer, "American Ballet Theater Does Not See Me as I See Myself," *New York Times*, July 7, 2023, https://www.nytimes.com/2023/07/07/opinion/black-dancer-american-ballet-theater.html
32 S. P. Harrell, "A Multidimensional Conceptualization of Racism-Related Stress: Implications for the Well Being of People of Color," *American Journal of Orthopsychiatry* 70, no. 1 (January 2000): 42–57.
33 Johnson, "Looks Could Kill," Lecture/Seminar, 2017.

PART 1
Identities

1
TEACHING FOR TOMORROW
Antiracism in Ballet

Gabrielle Salvatto

Disclaimer:

The lived experiences of dance artists are shaped by their race, gender, sexual orientation, class, culture and other social and political identities. These unique intersectional identities are compounded by overlapping systems of marginalization and oppression. To end injustice for some, we must not perpetuate forms of oppression for others. While this chapter is primarily a focus on anti-Blackness within the ballet sector, we must actively work against misogyny, sexism, homophobia, transphobia, ableism, xenophobia, anti-Semitism, anti-Asian hate, colonization, and toxic capitalistic practices. It is crucial to be educated on the historical and lasting effects of colonization, imperialism, and enslavement imposed by the governing systems within the United States and Europe against Black, Indigenous, Latin, Asian, and Arab bodies.[1] If we are committed to actively understanding and dismantling racial inequity and injustice then we are on the right path. Wherever you find yourself on the spectrum of race and identity, please do not let the education and practice of antiracism trigger you. This is not meant to point the finger at any one individual or institution. We are all on our own personal journeys with antiracism, with varying levels of privilege, bias, and knowledge. If you feel personally threatened or defensive about antiracism work, take a breath and consider why.

DOI: 10.4324/9781003283065-3

It is a great honor to contribute to this anthology as an "amateur activist," dance artist, educator and writer. My life as a biracial female performing artist, as well as the shared experiences of marginalized artists in my communities, informs my insights. Artists of the global majority, particularly Black and Indigenous women, have not only been underrepresented in ballet (and beyond), but they have also been systematically excluded from studios, stages and leadership. The path to becoming a professional ballet dancer requires a level of sacrifice from everyone, but these communities have been disproportionately erased, dehumanized, and harmed by ongoing state sanctioned violence and inequity. Vicious cycles of oppression, historically and currently, force all of us to take a harder look at our experiences, and demand change with a new urgency.

Unfortunately, artists who advocate for antiracism and cultural competency in classical ballet are often met with transient acts of progress and solidarity. To make changes that are meaningful and sustainable, leaders must be determined to re-evaluate exclusive and harmful cultural practices in order to foster accurate and unbiased education, and to insist on diversity, inclusion, transparency, accessibility, and accountability in training and company settings. Centering the voices and experiences of those most affected by systems of oppression is essential to progress. This requires honoring our lives as intersectional human beings.

One aspiration of antiracist practices is the creation of diverse environments that prioritize inclusive decision-making. These practices are hindered by the white Eurocentric traditions and biases that exist in ballet settings. The performing arts, particularly ballet, operate within and through systems of classism, capitalism, and racism that benefit certain populations. The 2023 Dance Data Project Global Ballet Leadership Report analyzing the gender distribution of artistic leadership in over 198 ballet companies worldwide, 29% were directed by women, 71% directed by men.[2] There are also disparities in pay scales and ethnic identities. Given this preference for white and male leaders, ballet companies, consciously and unconsciously, perpetuate microaggressions, tokenism, sexism and discrimination.

Within the United States, artists of the global majority encounter a double-bind due to histories of anti-Blackness in this country. In *Caste: The Origins of our Discontents*, Isabel Wilkerson provides context for the anti-Black system that still governs the political, social, cultural, and financial equity of millions of people. Within ballet studios, these dance artists are asked to leave their unique identities at the door, even though these identities shape their lives and artistry. To dismantle these inequities, the Dancers Amplified Global Active Practices (GAP) document outlines equitable practices that are invested in diversity and provides initiatives for all members of an organization to invest in ballet's radically inclusive future. "It's ballet's politics that are of another era, not the form itself."[3]

Throughout my training and career in the United States, I experienced a range of institutional cultures and values that shaped my sense of belonging and empowerment as a dancer. I am grateful for the unique combination of my matriarchal family values and melting pot of culture and identities in New York City that, for a while, sheltered me from the complexities of institutionalized racism. Within dance institutions where ballet was not the central focus, I witnessed a palpable sense of equity and diversity. I observed that the hierarchical nature of ballet, with ascending levels in every setting, forces dancers to prioritize ballet above other hobbies. The closer I got to what some people call "success and prestige," the more my experiences were shaped by anti-Blackness and intersecting oppressions.

As many as 80% of white Americans embody unconscious bias against Black Americans, and in ballet settings these percentages are often higher.[4] These biases are upheld by exposure to and perpetuation of dehumanizing and stereotypical imagery and behavior. These biases are most pernicious in ballet studios where there are exclusive ideations of what a "ballet dancer" looks like. I have both experienced and benefitted from these biases due to the duality of my Italian/African American being. Body type aesthetics and colorism played in my favor when I could blend into white ideals, and I was offered opportunities that other marginalized dancers were not. I also experienced microaggressions about my hair and background, fetishization, stereotyping, tokenism and psychological abuse. This dichotomy slowly ate away at the sense of empowerment and belonging I felt in my early dance training, and transformed them into feelings of isolation, self-criticism and doubt. I retreated into a silence that robbed me, as well as other marginalized artists and our institutions, from believing in the merit of my dancing, my voice, and my ability to inspire change.

{Bare}

My early years in dance education were shaped by accessibility, diversity and inclusion. I was introduced to dancing at a local studio called the Bronx Dance Theater where I studied ballet, tap, jazz, modern, and Afro-Caribbean dance. I was surrounded by teachers and students of diverse ethnic and socioeconomic backgrounds. I experienced the same joy and liberation dancing in my first *Nutcracker* with Bronx Dance Theater, as I did while performing African techniques with my free-flowing curls and bare feet. I continued my studies at Ballet Hispanico where I fell in love with how rhythms and postures of Flamenco felt at home in my skin. Dance scholars and historians posit that the roots of flamenco are influenced by colonial ties and the trans-Atlantic slave trade.[5] I was still attending public school in the Bronx when I had the opportunity to join Ballet Tech, a school that provides ballet training for elementary through high schoolers. I was picked up in a yellow school bus with other black and brown children from the five boroughs and driven to 890 Broadway, a building where American Ballet Theatre also had studios. At Ballet Tech, we were provided free transportation, free training and dance and footwear if needed. Our dress code was either a leotard with bare legs or shorts and a t-shirt. Though I noticed a shift in the desired body types for ballet, I was not told to force my turnout or tuck my pelvis (although there was already a pronounced attention to my back curvature.) Our bare legs allowed us to embrace our unique identities and passions in a space where we felt represented and included.

{Flesh}

In the late 1990s I began training at Dance Theatre of Harlem with my older sister. Here we wore tights and shoes that matched our skin tones. We had to pancake our shoes, and some dancers even dyed their own tights with tea bags, because the revolution of the flesh-colored pointe shoes and dancewear was still two decades away. Pancaking our shoes was a tedious process that we shared with prima ballerinas of Dance Theatre of Harlem. In those early days of my training, I was inspired by seeing people who looked like me, and who were successful as ballerinas, educators, and administrators. My sister and I received full scholarships, and while there was a focus on classical ballet, we studied a variety of techniques. During summer programs we were shown historical videos and given hair tutorials for creating different styles, like French twists, with natural hair textures. Years later as a professional dancer with Dance Theatre of Harlem, I was able to dance on international stages with my curly hair, skin tone tights, and pointe shoes. Our tour schedule included international performances as well as local community events. I saw a similar twinkle in the eyes of the young dancers in Honduras and Turkey that I felt when I watched the dancers of Dance Theatre of Harlem, Ballet Hispanico, Complexions Contemporary Ballet and Lines Ballet. Representation matters and it needs to be reflected in classrooms, studios, stages, funding, casting, board rooms, and language.

{Pink}

When I started training at the School of American Ballet (SAB) our dress code in Girls Level Three was a pink leotard, pink tights and pink ballet shoes. In my final year in level C2, I wore a white leotard and the same pink tights and shoes. Initially I thought of the pink tights as just another kind of uniform, like the dark suntan Capezio tights I wore at SAB's inaugural community audition in 1998. I was offered a partial scholarship for most of my tenure, and a full ride my last year. Over the course of my eight years at the school I performed with the New York City Ballet (NYCB) on the David Koch stage, then The State Theater. I admired the artistry of inspirational performers but was wary of the lack of diversity. When I saw Aesha Ash, the only African American ballerina in the NYCB at that time and one of my idols, wearing pink tights onstage, I realized that pink was the skin tone choice. Within this prestigious institution, whiteness was both the majority and the standard. As I advanced through SAB's levels, I began to understand the ways that ballet culture isolated me, despite being treated well by my teachers and peers who were ALL white. I could not afford the same private lessons and summer programs as my classmates. Friends had chauffeurs and private tutors and I was riding the subway and splitting my time between academic classes at LaGuardia High School and ballet at SAB. My butt and thighs looked different in my white leotard. When I was, at times, asked to remove my ballet skirt, I felt ashamed of my body, even though I was thin and hypermobile. In my final years of training, I was the only female student of color left in my division. Parents of other dance students told my mother that it was possible I could claim the "ethnic spot" in NYCB with a hint of encouragement and jealousy. I was extremely conflicted about my potential as a classical ballerina, and when the opportunity presented itself to attend The Juilliard School I chose this path. There I realized that the exclusive nature of private institutions that focus on other codified techniques like Graham, Limón and Taylor, extend far beyond the confines of ballet.

Professional Journey

After receiving my BFA from Juilliard, I experienced life as a ballerina in a predominantly Black space, then in a majority white space, and now am fulfilling a dream of dancing in Europe. The culture shock I experienced while transitioning between companies in the United States was greater than the one I experienced when I moved abroad. Though I had been a Black face in a white space during my training, I needed more tools to analyze the ways institutionalized racism and unconscious bias were shaping my professional environments. I once had an artistic director ask me if I would like to wear skin tone tights and shoes for a soloist role in a popular classical ballet but remain in pink for my corps parts. The burden of purchasing materials and personally dying my shoes and costume straps fell on my shoulders, as they typically do for Black and Brown artists. The well-intentioned gesture of celebrating diversity was diminished by the preference for whiteness in the corps de ballet. As I reflect on this incident, I now insist that allowance for melanated skin cannot be dependent upon rank. Disruption of the white homogenous lines of the corps de ballet has been an excuse for hiring and casting decisions. I have personally experienced and witnessed other Black artists frequently relegated to athletic, modern, caricatured, and sexualized roles. Wilkerson notes, "Menial and comic roles were the chief ones allotted to Negroes in their relationships with white people... the images soothed the conscience and justified atrocities."[6] Ballet companies across the United States including the one mentioned here, now allow Black and Brown dancers to wear natural hair styles and skin tone tights. Two centuries after the invention of pointe shoes, some retailers are producing an array of shoes in different shades. Barriers still exist, most often coming from licensing orders by Trusts and powerful boards that prevent change. These gatekeepers insist on homogeneous stages, stereotypical cultural depictions including skin lightening for artists of the global majority, and roles that perpetuate yellowface and Blackface. Only when we interrogate personal biases can we begin to question the value of tradition and its impact on segregation and accessibility. Then we might be able to create new roles inspired by cultural competency and integrity.

Teaching for Tomorrow

Classical ballet history is often curated to leave whiteness unmarked and to remove Black and Brown bodies from its traditions. In contrast, ballet as a movement form is the result of collective influences and histories. While often promoted as the "top" of a hierarchy of dance techniques, or the "foundation" of all dancing, both statements are inaccurate. Alonzo King says, "Ballet is the Italian word for dance. The technical proper term would be Western Classical Dance. Every civilization has its classical dance forms. Classicism in a lot of Western minds, means white, based on racist superiority..."[7] Much of the language of white racial hegemony functions to minimize forms of art and expression created by people of the global majority. Scholar Jehbreal Muhammad Jackson challenges the notion that "...Baroque dances and their subsequent codifications into classical ballet are exclusively of Anglo-European construction..." Jackson's research reflects how cultural practices from al-Andalus and the Bukôngo religion (among others) influenced western classical dance as well as philosophies and sciences. Dance educators have a moral responsibility to continually investigate and seek accurate and inclusive history.

Present

Returning to Wilkerson's research, the anti-Black American racial caste system was manipulated by English, Irish, and other European immigrants' ability to blend into the general population of whiteness. When religious division proved unsuccessful, skin pigmentation allowed colonizers and enslavers to easily categorize and debase the value of human beings. In Europe, however, white-passing cultures are disseminated back into their unique ethnic identities, diluting some of the polarization between "white" and Black races. Though I have been subjected to toxic practices, my pervasive experience while abroad has been one of acceptance. My Blackness is still in the minority, but my identity is embraced. I perform contemporary and neoclassical repertoire, without restrictions on my hair and make-up, and flesh tone costuming. We are allowed to leave tattoos uncovered, and I work with a community of dancers who are empowered to advocate for their needs. The subservient inclinations of ballet settings I experienced in the States are nowhere near as pronounced. Although I am now living closer to the "origins" of ballet in the courts of France and Russia, I am enjoying less of the hierarchies and boundaries.

I follow the news coming from the States, especially the banning of books in schools, the misrepresentations of Critical Race Theory, the continued use of immigration cages, the infringements on the rights of women and LGBTQIA+ communities, the brutality of the prison-industrial-complex, the lack of accessible medical care, the lack of regulation to protect our environment, and the global crisis of COVID-19. People of the global majority are disproportionally affected by these crises, just as artists of the global majority have had to work twice as hard to access and pursue a career in ballet. This confluence of events has given us the impetus to demand reform and accountability. Dancers Amplified centers the needs of marginalized voices through community engagement events, resource sharing, and the GAP.[8] Our identities as artists and human beings are inseparable because WE ARE ALWAYS IN OUR SKIN.

Every individual has a critical role to play in working towards antiracism within ballet and within our communities. Recognizing the humanity of the whole dancer is the only way to create safe, inclusive and sustainable dance spaces. Artists are so much more than the perpetual boundaries of their racial and gendered constructs. Our advocacy must be driven by a moral framework of liberative justice, where our physical appearance or class plays no bearing on our treatment or value. In order to survive, ballet organizations, and all performing arts institutions, must be able to reflect the ever-evolving world we live in.

Notes

1 Black, Indigenous, Latin, Asian and Arab: These groups will henceforth be referred to as People of the Global Majority (PGM), as they represent upwards of 80% of the world's population. Language is integral to antiracist work and constantly evolving. We should move away from terms that centers Whiteness, are intentionally disempowering (ex: "minority")

2 "The 2023 Global Leadership Report," *Dance Data Project*, https://ddp-wordpress.storage.googleapis.com/wp-content/uploads/2023/04/13131540/Global-Leadership-Report-2023.pdf
3 Sarah Crompton, "William Forsythe: I want people to look forward to ballet, not endure it," *The Guardian*, March 13, 2022. https://www.theguardian.com/stage/2022/mar/13/william-forsythe-i-want-people-to-look-forward-to-ballet-not-endure-it
4 Isabel Wilkerson, *Caste: The Origins of our Discontents* (New York: Random House, 2020), 186–187. See also David R. William, interview by author, May 2, 2013.
5 K. Meira Goldberg's *Sonidos Negros: On the Blackness of Flamenco* (New York, Oxford University Press, 2019).
6 Wilkerson, *Caste*, 138.
7 Alonzo King, "Breaking Down Barriers of Race," September 26, 2019. https://www.youtube.com/watch?v=tj5rpArWTHQ
8 See Dancers Amplified: https://www.dancersamplified.com

2

PERSPECTIVE

Artistic Director of Ballet Tech

Dionne Figgins

Kate: Could you please describe the Jones Haywood School of Ballet and the vital role it has played in educating Black ballet dancers?

Dionne: Jones Haywood School of Ballet, now called Jones Haywood Dance School (JHDS), was started by Doris Jones and Claire Haywood over 80 years ago with the mission of introducing Black students to classical dance. During their time as founders and artistic directors, they trained Louis Johnson, Chita Rivera, Hinton Battle, Renee Robinson, Sylvester Campbell, Virginia Johnson, and my teacher and current Artistic Director of JHDS, Sandra Fortune-Green. At the time of its founding, there were no schools for Black ballet dancers, and there is much debate over whether this was the first Black ballet school in the country, or perhaps the world. They also founded the very first Black ballet company, the Capitol Ballet. Doris Jones was my teacher. By the time I had begun training, Miss Haywood had already passed away.

I grew up dancing in a single room studio built onto the rear of a house located on the corner of Georgia Avenue and Delafield Place in the historically black community of Petworth in Washington, DC. The studio had a wooden floor, and there was a grand piano in the corner. When we were lucky, we had live accompaniment for ballet class, but most often class was taught with classical albums on a record player.

DOI: 10.4324/9781003283065-4

There were two dressing rooms, one for girls and one for boys, and a ramp leading into the studio. On days when you weren't "acting right" or feeling well, you would sit on the iconic staircase leading to the main house. Upstairs, if you were lucky enough to go up there, was a pristine living room, and you would walk through it to head up the staircase to the top floor, where costume fittings were done, and life lessons were given.

Miss Jones, along with tap legend and friend Mary Chisholm, tailored all the costumes, holding a pin cushion and waiting to stick you because your "butt was in the way" of her pins. My mom, a seamstress by habit, sewed costumes from time to time to help pay for my tuition. I had opportunities to train at Rosella Hightower École de Danse in Cannes, France and Dance Theatre of Harlem (DTH) during the summers as a student of JHDS. All of my teachers were Black and all of them had performed professionally. Charmaine Hunter, principal dancer at DTH, was one of my first advanced level ballet teachers at JHDS, and of course, Sandra Fortune-Green, who in 1973 became the only African-American to ever compete in the Varna International Ballet Competition, was the teacher who I feared and revered the most, other than Ms. Jones herself.

JHDS was the light at the end of my training tunnel. By having so much exposure to professional dance training from such a young age from people who looked like me, there was never any doubt that I could be a professional dancer. I grew up at the Kennedy Center, watching my teachers perform with DTH, and seeing them gave me confidence that being a professional was possible for me too. It wasn't until I was an adult that I realized that other Black students were having a different experience.

All of my dance peers were Black, all of my teachers were Black, and it wasn't until I attended Rosella Hightower at the age of 12, that I ever experienced being a minority in a dance space. I realized, "Oh, my being here is not the norm." But at JHDS, there was nothing abnormal about someone like me training in ballet.

The other options for training in DC were the Washington Ballet, where there were hardly any students of color. I had a girlfriend who was training at the Kirov Academy, and her experience was completely different from mine. She was the only Black student training there at the time. She was such a beautiful dancer, but she was never encouraged to continue training in ballet. Instead, she was told that if she wanted to dance, her best option was to go to Alvin Ailey American Dance Theater—as if that is somehow secondary to a ballet company—because they felt she was more suited for modern dance. This is the experience of so many of my Black and Brown peers who attended predominantly white institutions for dance. At JHDS, ballet was always the first option, and Ms. Jones trained us like that was the only end goal, to be in a ballet company, despite the many obstacles she knew awaited us.

Kate: What is your current relationship with the Jones Haywood Dance School?

Dionne: Currently, I am a member of the faculty at JHDS and an active member of the Alumni Association. During the height of the pandemic, like many other organizations, classes were taught through Zoom. During the summer of 2020, Brandye Lee, longtime dance friend and fellow JHDS alumna and I produced the first ever online Summer Intensive to replace JHDS's annual summer intensive at Martha's Vineyard. I taught Contemporary Ballet, Broadway Jazz, and a class I've been developing for years, Acting for Dancers, which is the sister class to my long-standing class Movement for Actors. The program was so well received that Ms. Fortune-Green asked me to teach Contemporary Ballet, Broadway Jazz, and Acting for Dancers. Even with all the challenges of training through Zoom, I was able to choreograph, teach, and showcase—online of course—a contemporary ballet piece and a theater jazz piece, and each of my Acting for Dancers students learned and performed a monologue. During the 2021/22 school year, while in-person classes resumed, I continued to teach Acting for Dancers through Zoom. The contemporary piece, titled "New Dawn," choreographed through Zoom the year before, was presented in Spring 2022 by JHDS students as their competition group piece for the Youth American Grand Prix in Orlando. This was the first time since 1973 that JHDS dancers were competing in a dance competition. The piece was performed multiple times throughout the year, and eventually was performed as the finale piece at the annual Father's Day Concert in Summer 2022. At that same concert and for the first time in JHDS history, my Acting for Dancers students presented a short play conceived and written by them, and heavily edited by me.

In addition to my work on the faculty, I mentor and coach several students and young alumni of JHDS. I have choreographed students' college solos, provided training and career advice, and this past year, even had a student as an employee at my vintage store Couture du Jour. So, in essence, my relationship with JHDS serves to preserve the legacy and continue the mission, started by Doris Jones and Claire Haywood over 80 years ago, of providing access, support, and mentorship to Black students training in ballet.

Kate: Did your experiences of performing on Broadway and in television and film influence your perspectives, meaning make it possible to critique the culture of ballet?

Dionne: The dance space is a microcosm of the much larger society, with many of its systems stemming from white supremacy culture. These systems also exist in Broadway, film and television industries: obsession with appearance/youth, body dysmorphia, ageism, ableism, and racism. I think it's particularly rampant in ballet because dance artists are in a silent art medium, so they often do not have the tools or the training to speak up when they are faced with these challenges. My work as a Broadway, tv/film performer has allowed me to develop my voice, and therefore advocate in ways that are not always easy for dancers, who are frequently encouraged, if not outright expected, to remain silent and "go along to get along."

I have always been extremely outspoken, even as a student at JHDS. There were more than a few occasions when I even challenged Ms. Jones and other faculty. At the time, I was considered temperamental, perhaps even problematic, but in retrospect, what I was really challenging was the culture of ballet that requires dancers to maintain an unhealthy student/teacher dynamic which creates a dangerous power structure where the dancer is always in a subordinate position, even into adulthood. This structure that has dancers forever relegated to the obedient student has always been a challenge for me. My nature is to question everything, and this is not an admirable or even acceptable quality for a dancer to have. However, when I began doing more theater, I found my curiosity encouraged by creatives, who actually desire to work with artists willing to do their own exploration and investigation, and who are open to dialogue to arrive at the final product. I had finally found a place where I could fully express myself as an artist, and yet, I also mourned for dance artists who, even in the more commercial theatrical world, struggled to find their voices after years of being silenced.

I am hoping to help cultivate a more holistic approach to training and working with dancers, and it begins with teaching dance artists how to advocate for themselves. While the ballet world may not like to admit it, we encourage silence so our tried-and-true methods of training, no matter how toxic they may be, are not questioned and therefore, undone. When students are taught to be silent when they're young, it allows us, as dance educators, to pull and prod and touch them, for the sake of "correct" placement and proper alignment, even if they are uncomfortable. Sometimes, the silence which leads to a loss of a student's bodily autonomy, causes physical harm, particularly in the younger years when we are trying to train the body to hold poses that are often unnatural: turnout, extreme flexibility training, hyperextension of the knees. This silence is also what has led to many dance students experiencing sexual misconduct and abuse from teachers and other dance professionals. And while I have used my time as a Broadway, film, and tv performer to strengthen my voice, I also realize that even in those areas of entertainment, dancers are still very much at the bottom of the barrel.

Kate: I wonder if your role and presence as a Black woman has something to do with this kind of initiative where you nurture humans, authentic selves, and advocacy?

Dionne: I'm a humanitarian and I believe in the inherent value of every human life. I've watched people of all backgrounds being marginalized and minimized my entire life, and it has always, even before I understood the complexities of race, class, and gender, bothered me. Now, because I am a Black, femme presenting person, my experiences related to those constructs do allow me to relate to other people with similar backgrounds, but I don't think the constructs of my race and gender qualify me to exhibit these traits more than a person from a different background. I know Black women who uphold the tenets of white supremacy and patriarchy, and I know non-Black women who work diligently to make sure they are breaking down those same systems. I think the perception from others is that Black women are more suited to nurture because, historically, that's what we have been forced to do and brought to this country in chains to do. That's the Mammy trope that has Black women consistently relegated to taking care of others, but I do this because it is in my human nature to do so. It is also a response to my conditioning as a child, being the oldest sister of four. I don't like to get caught up in the web of racial and gender constructs because those same constructs are too often used to keep people in boxes created by a society that constantly upholds values that do not honor the humanity of people.

Kate: Do you think the approaches that you're taking will introduce a different path from Eliot Feld's role as director?

Dionne: Eliot is a choreographer. As much as the school was about giving access to New York City public school children, it was also about facilitating his work. I want to work with the kids in that capacity, as a choreographer, but my goal is to train them using a holistic approach, give them access to a comprehensive dance education with a focus beyond performative dance, and help them find their voice, through dance and in life. I'm in the unique position that I can partner with other organizations in a way that does not exist in the dance world because most training spaces of this type have companies that they are preparing the students to matriculate into. Ballet Tech doesn't have a company, so I'm trying to develop great relationships with other institutions to help facilitate my students finding a dance space that speaks to them as artists, where they feel they can grow and be nurtured into their full potential. And if they don't want to dance, that's fine too, because I also care about their overall education. Dance training has, typically, only placed value on performative dance, but there are so many lucrative careers in the dance and theater industry that students should be introduced to and educated about. In our midst could be the next great costume designer or Gyrotonics trainer or stage manager, so my aim is to open up the opportunities available to dancers from a much earlier age, so that students who may not excel in their dance training know that there are other options available to them.

Kate: How might your approach be contributing to antiracist ballet pedagogy?

Dionne: Nobody has benefited from the toxicity that exists in this current culture of ballet, not even the white people who it was created for. White ballet dancers experience the same struggles and issues that have been highlighted by Black people seeking to gain entry. Most white people do not fit the physical aesthetics required for ballet. Most white women have experienced some level of sexism in the space, from a lack of female choreographers to the preference for and favoritism of male dancers in the training and professional space. White people experience wealth disparity that create issues of access, though perhaps not as greatly as their non-White counterparts. And they also experience a loss of physical autonomy, and the ability to effectively advocate for themselves when they are uncomfortable with touch, theatrical intimacy, in pain, or injured. We do need to look at the politics of race when it comes to ballet, but in general, the toxic systems in the culture of ballet are problematic for everyone. So instead of flinging open the door, and inviting non-white people into an art form rife with inhumane practices to once again do the heavy lifting of having to point out the problems and also strategize and implement how fix them, the architects and gatekeepers of ballet should really be seeking to clean their own house, and support and elevate spaces, like DTH, that have had access, inclusivity, and equity as core tenets of their mission since day one. The same people espousing antiracist rhetoric and ticking off boxes of improvement will, in the same breath, argue that DTH does not belong in the same conversation as ABT. Opening doors to people and asking them to sit in your dirty house is not equity. Honoring the humanity and inherent value of every human life is innately antiracist, but most humans, including some of the Black ones, don't have the patience or tolerance to make that their daily practice.

This particular generation of children that is coming up, they're asking for us to do better and we're calling them entitled for requiring more of us, more from their education. They're asking to be seen and considered as whole people. And we're saying, "Oh no, only the ones that can take the abuse will make it." That sounds like slavery, not art. We have to begin from the place of wanting to see a reflection of the world around us, not just inviting Black people because it's trending and we can no longer hide the fact that they are beyond capable of excelling in ballet. The conversation around antiracism in ballet pedagogy is amusing because the technique is not racist. Either you can do the steps, or you can't. What needs to be addressed are the people who still think all the swans need to look the same for tradition to be upheld. And what I hope evolves is that people see the tradition of sameness in the ballet world as a people problem, not a pedagogy problem. Ballet is a perfect science, but the culture of ballet is about whiteness maintaining its identity as supreme and therefore in no need of change or reform.

3
PERSPECTIVE

Lourdes Lopez, Artistic Director of Miami City Ballet

Lourdes Lopez

Kate: Is there anyone who stands out in your training as a person who shifted how you saw yourself, or ballet, or yourself in ballet?

Lourdes Lopez: I was born in Cuba and raised in Miami, where I started my training. There were three main teachers here in Miami, two of them were women and Cuban and the other was a male Russian teacher. When I was 5 or 6 years old, I was in a children's dance class that was kind of playing around, nothing structured, nothing formal, but a very nurturing environment and we actually danced on stage in school recitals with costumes and all. The school was started and headed by two Cuban sisters and you went in and you followed other dancers in front of you and kind of did your own little thing to music. I was then moved to the Russian teacher, Alexander Nigodoff, when I was 8, for three years. It was really Mr. Nigodoff who taught me what ballet was: there were steps, and each step had a name. I wasn't really taught how to do them properly, nor that there was a right and wrong way to do them, but I was learning another language. He also showed me that there were ballets, stories and fairy tales: *Sleeping Beauty, Swan Lake*... All of a sudden, this world of ballet was opened up to me. Before, it was just moving around and now it's like, oh wow, there's a history and there's a structure.

DOI: 10.4324/9781003283065-5

I was moved to Miss Martha Mahr at the age of 11, when the School of American Ballet gave me a year-round scholarship and wanted to formalize my training. Miss Mahr was Argentinian, and she was your typical ballet teacher in those days. She had been trained at the National Ballet of Cuba, which has unbelievable pedagogy. I would say that she was the foundation of my technique, of my training, and it stayed with me my whole life. She was tough though, you know, she was that "Old World" teacher: You don't drink water during class, You arrive on time, and You stay late. You do more than what is expected of you. That shaped me and, like with many other teachers, there may have been a very tough exterior but inside, they are very caring and nurturing, in their way. They had gone through their own stuff, and those were my teachers in Miami.

Then I went to the School of American Ballet (SAB) and that was a whole world of teachers from every background and every style. We had Madame Tumkovsky and Madame Doubrovska who were Russians, and their classes were really hard! Everything was 32 counts or 64 counts, numerous jumps, and multiple turns. We also had Madame Danilova, and her teaching was fluid and lyrical, romantic, refined and very feminine. We also had Madame Stuart who was English and had been Pavlova's protégée. She had a very soft manner and taught us to use our upper bodies in a supple way and she was very expressive in how she would describe movement and body placement. Her approach to movement was very minimal: there was always an ease to how she wanted us to dance. We also had Stanley Williams, who taught Danish [Bournonville] technique. It was clear, simple, musical, and precise dancing. He gave simple combinations—nothing elaborate—and each class was pretty much structured the same, even the same combinations. It was really, I think, like getting a PhD in Dance. Every day, you walked into a different approach, a different personality, different combinations, different ways of asking you to do things, and you were expected to do it all. There was no modern dance or jazz classes, but you were expected to do all kinds of ballet. This, I think, created a very well-rounded dancer, and it's thrilling. As I say to my dancers, you have to do it all.

You know, I was always very curious and, when I got into New York City Ballet and was taking Mr. Balanchine's classes, there was a whole other revelation. Not only his specific steps, but also the timing he wanted, the accents and tempos. In his classes you learned how to dance, how to put everything together. Then, in the evening, you got another opportunity to do it again, but this time in his ballets. When I was in the company, in 1988, we did the American Music Festival [a 3-week festival to honor the company's 40th anniversary]. Peter [Martins, then the director] invited all these choreographers who had never worked at New York City Ballet. I remember doing the lead in a Lar Lubovitch work, called *Rhapsody in Blue* and I remember looking in the mirror and thinking, "I can't... this is all wrong for me...". Then one day I realized there was no right or wrong, it was about looking at your body differently, making different shapes, and thinking about dance differently. It was eye-opening, and felt freeing to me: like, this is still dancing, it's just not ballet.

What I think is so interesting about my generation of teachers at the School of American Ballet is that these were direct descendants of [Sergei] Diaghilev [director of the Ballets Russes, 1909–29]. Direct descendants of the 1920s when ballet was really exploratory and ballet was changing, shifting. [Bronislava] Nijinska was choreographing and there were mind-blowing things happening [collaborations with Stravinsky, Picasso, Matisse, Debussy, Satie, Ravel]. They were influenced by what they saw—and danced—and we were indirectly influenced as well. We were the beneficiaries.

Kate: Have you ever been in a ballet environment or had an experience with ballet that did not seem inclusive or equitable? Have you ever faced a barrier or obstacle?

Lourdes: You know, no. I think in many ways, I've always been in a bubble. I was with New York City Ballet and never danced with [American] Ballet Theatre. I've never danced for a European company. I would assume their ways of looking at dance and their ways of dancing are really very different. I don't know if that was a good thing for me, or not.

I see that, with dancers who now audition for Miami City Ballet, who come especially from Latin American or South American training, they come from their own cloistered environments as well. Some physically struggle with the quickness of steps, or with putting different steps together. The combinations are different. It's like cooking differently: there are different ingredients. What was so great about the training at SAB was that every day was different: somebody different was teaching, so you weren't doing the same thing. It's what I stress with dancers, and it's what I love about the repertory at Miami City Ballet. You experience it all, and the more experience a dancer has, the better the dancing, and the better artists you're going to be. You only have 20 years [as a professional ballet dancer] in which to do this, so this is not your whole life, right? You have to cram everything into about 15 years as a professional, and they go by very quickly.

Kate: Has your leadership role shifted your perspectives on ballet?

Lopez: I think it has broadened my perspectives: this year, for the first time ever, the company will perform a work by Martha Graham called *Diversion of Angels*. I did not know anything about Martha Graham, except that she was a dance pioneer and a female and that back in the 1930s, during the Depression, she started a dance company. We have to think about that, and what that meant at that time. I looked in on a rehearsal recently and I went, "Oh my God, this work is beautiful." I'm happy to see our dancers adapting to it so eagerly. I think there are things in it that I would not have appreciated ten years ago. Being an artistic director and making myself look at other work and making myself look at other choreographers, and ask the questions, "What do I bring to dancers and what do I bring to audiences to expand appreciation of this art form?" It's exciting to ask, "How can I engage dancers and audiences in this art form that, I think, speaks to everybody?"

When I was a kid, I would watch [American] Ballet Theatre performances in the summer in New York. This is where I first saw José Limón's *Moor's Pavane*, with dancers like Carla Fracci, Cynthia Gregory, and Royes Fernandez. These were massive ballet stars. It's a work that was in my mind, already. But it's another thing to bring in Graham's *Diversion of Angels* and *Moor's Pavane* and have the dancers do them on the same program. These are very different masterpieces. The dancers have said that *Diversion* is really hard, but they have loved the experience and the challenge. I think it's because we do so much, so many different works by different choreographers, that they have real respect for dance as an art form. It is part of their integrity: they want to understand what a choreographer and their work is about. They take full responsibility for the work they've been given and rise to it. In the end, it brings them great pleasure and I think they feel a great accomplishment and have a great time.

Kate: Why do you think there continues to be fewer women, especially women of color, in leadership roles in ballet?

Lourdes: There are so many entry points to that question, so it's not just one answer. I think one answer is role models. For many years, men had these positions. Then you ask, why men? I can't speak about European models, because I don't know that much about them, but I can speak to the American model [of supporting a dance company. For the most part, the board of directors tended to be men, and mostly, white men, with discretionary funds available to support a company. Women, I'm sure, formed part of the board, but if I had to guess, they were in the minority. These men and women wrongly assumed that only men could raise money and understand the business side of a ballet company, budgets, proposals, strategy, planning, governance, etc. I'm generalizing.

On the whole, it's the board of directors that determines the artistic director for any company. While you want someone with an artistic vision, you also have to have somebody with a business head. Somebody who can raise funds, inspire people to support, get their buy in, bring the company and staff together as a family, as a community, to get behind a vision and goals. Why this would only mean men, I don't know. It was like a rule everyone followed and someone had to break that glass.

I think that's what was so courageous about the Miami City Ballet board of directors a decade ago. I mean not only did they choose a woman, they chose a Latina woman. I understand this makes sense because we're in Miami, but I was someone who had never run a company, besides serving as executive director of Morphoses. I had never been in an artistic leadership position. What's interesting to me is that 10 years ago, nobody talked about the fact that they hired a Latina to lead a ballet company. There wasn't a single interview that I remember when I was named that asked me what it felt like to be a woman and Latin, running a ballet company. It wasn't at the forefront of our conversations like it is now, especially with Tamara [Rojo], Julie [Kent], and Susan [Jaffe]. But, you know, nobody ever talks about Monica Mason [artistic director of the Royal Ballet, 2002–2012] or Ninette de Valois [who established Sadler's Wells, predecessor of the Royal Ballet]. In the United States there was Boston Ballet [started by Virginia Williams] and Pennsylvania Ballet [started by Barbara Weisberger]. Why aren't they mentioned? The other visionary step that the board of directors took was that they asked the dancers to interview the candidates the board was interviewing for the artistic director position. At the time, that was highly unusual. So, it was not just a board decision.

I think if you don't build a narrative, a story around an event, people don't talk about it. You can start your little ballet company somewhere as a female of color, but unless people are talking about it, unless you tell that story, no one knows. Role models, I think, are important. I think narratives around those role models are critical. That is how mindsets start to shift, and obviously it's important to have a support system for them. Today, if someone at Miami City Ballet who is female says, "I wonder if I can direct a company?" They can say, well, look, Lourdes does. It becomes a possibility. Now, female dancers can be more aspirational.

Kate: Do you think there is a similar pattern with women imagining themselves to be choreographers?

Lourdes: With choreographers, I think it's something that more easily happens within the structure of a company. For the most part, I would say 90% of ballet companies and modern dance companies, have more women than men. In ballet companies, the women dance a lot more than the men. In *Giselle* it's men in the first act, and then only two men in the second act, right? The entire male corps de ballet goes home after first act. So I think we, as women, are in the theater a lot more. I'm making a gross generalization here. It's also the pointe shoe, which requires constant training [sewing them, breaking them in…]. I think women do not have the time that men have to experiment, and explore with your friends after class, or to work on other aspects of their lives. Time is not as readily available to female ballet dancers just because of the amount of time they are training, rehearsing, and dancing.

I feel another aspect is scholarship. Male empowerment is built into the dance world. Here, in the States, any male student, regardless of talent, financial need, or training gets a scholarship to dance, simply because of their gender. Female ballet students are constantly competing with hundreds of other female students for the scholarships, for acceptance into a prestigious ballet school, for a position in the company roster, etc. From very early on, because there's a scarcity, male ballet students are given a privileged position, and there is empowerment in this.

Kate: Would you describe your approach to leadership and pedagogy as "antiracist"?

Lourdes: I'm not sure why I would consider my leadership antiracist. I think maybe the conversation is, "Is ballet racist?" The way I've come to terms with this question is to define ballet, for me, as an art form. It's a step to music and it's a step that needs to be done a certain way. There's a structure, there's a right and a wrong way [to do a step]. In opera, there's a high C: you can tell right away when a singer doesn't hit it. So, ballet is an art form that has steps that need to be done a certain way to music.

Did this art form start in Europe? Yes. It's about 400 years old and the early works tell the stories of those times. That cannot be changed, right? It's in the past, and we can't change the past. There are barriers to access and inclusion, and there are a few critical things for me that need to change. Number one: unless a child who lives in an under-resourced community is brought to the ballet, or the ballet goes to them, they're not going to have access to it, right? They have to be able to look at a performance and say, "Gee, this is something that I want to do!" Number two: role models. If people look on that stage and there's someone that looks like them, even better! Then they say, wow, that person did it, so I can too. Access and role models.

The third thing that's important is a support system, that includes familial, or parental support, as well as financial support. Ballet training is a hard trajectory. From ages 8 to 17, there's a lot of stuff that happens to a growing child. It's also expensive, maybe not as expensive as equestrian training. But, you have to ask, how do we support young dancers? how do we support their families? All three are needed for any child to pursue a calling, for any child to become an artist.

Lastly, ballet is really young in the United States. It's not an old art form like opera, or theatre, or the visual arts, with a long evolutionary history. It's a relatively young art form that was brought in by Europeans, and it takes time to develop audiences and proper schools for training. I really take offense when people say ballet is racist. Ballet is an art form: it's a step to music. People need to differentiate its history, both in Europe and in the United States, from ballet itself.

I can take myself as an example: I was an immigrant, and my parents were poor and from Cuba. They couldn't afford ballet training, but at the age of 11, someone thought Lourdes was talented. From the age of 11, I had my classes in Miami paid for by the School of American Ballet. They paid for my leotards, tights, and pointe shoes. They paid for my flights from Miami to New York to study during the summer and then paid for my summer course and my studio apartment in NY. That was the only way Lourdes Lopez got to dance. And then, at the age of 14, they said, "You have to come live here and study with us full time, and they paid for that as well." They paid for half of my academics at the Professional Children's School, paid for my apartment, which was $110 a month in those years, and all of my tights, leotards, and shoes. Then I get into the company at age 16. Lourdes, a Cuban, becomes the first Latina principal dancer in the history of that company and continues to be the only Latina dancer that has reached the ranks of principal in NYCB history. Now, I am a female artistic director of color. It was access, role models, and support.

My parents took me to a performance, and I saw some Cuban dancers, like Lydia Diaz Cruz. At that time, some dancers came to Miami from New York: Royes Fernandez and Lupe Serrano. I went, "Oh my gosh, I'd love to do this." I want to do this, and then, a few years later, I'm under scholarship. It's hard but it can happen. The art form is not racist. It's the people around it that are, at times, myopic in their view of who can, or can't, do it.

Right now, in Latin and South America, these regions are really hurting economically. We did a conference through Zoom with teachers and directors from Latin America recently, representing ten different countries all interested in understanding how American [United States'] schools taught ballet. They had questions like, "How come your students dance so fast? How do they cover space the way you do?" During these classes, we either taught a class or gave students a combination and then talked about the combinations and why we give it and how we do it. Everyone was incredibly grateful because we had reached out to them. They had felt cut off, because of Covid and the state of the economy in their respective countries. All we did was reach out and connect to start a conversation, a friendship of sorts. Perhaps because of this, we will start hearing stories of young dancers who come to Miami, at the age of 12 or 13, because their teachers connected with Miami City Ballet. From my perspective, steps like these continue to diversify the art form.

Kate: I love that you've outlined this three-pronged approach in terms of access, representation, and support systems or networks. Are there more practical suggestions or recommendations that you could offer other teachers and leaders to ensure a future for ballet that is relevant and accessible?

Lourdes: There are sensitivities that, I think, we need to be aware of. Some of them are little things: if you have a costume, make sure that the elastics are the color of the dancer's skin. With young girls and boys of color who have afro-textured hair, it might be harder to put up in a certain style for class or stage. Help them. Things like that are just respectful, right? I think that we all had those teachers who said unfortunate things and you look back on and think, Oh God. Just because I survived, it doesn't mean that other people should be treated this way. It's about respect, about being respectful to everyone.

There are also other ways of using language and of delivering a message that is generous, thoughtful, and constructive. We have to bear in mind cultural sensitivities: when I got to the School of American Ballet, I spoke a different language, and I was different culturally. For example, I was used to greeting others by giving them a kiss and a hug, I mean I did this with everyone I met. I still do. That's just part of how I grew up. When I got to SAB, everybody was like, "No, we don't do that here." [Laughter]

I read a story once about traveling in Latin or South America and if you're on a bus and someone breaks out singing, the rest of the bus joins in. It's part of their culture. If you're on a bus in the United States and you break out singing, they ask you to step off the bus. This is about sensitivity to cultural differences, and I think that it's happening now in ballet classes and companies.

Something I wish to mention is about my heritage, about being Cuban. In 2018, when I got the *Dance* Magazine Award, during my remarks, I mentioned that I was the first Latina principal dancer in the history of New York City Ballet and continue to be the only Latina dancer that has reached the ranks of principal in that company. Some of the writers at the magazine didn't focus on this, which is fine, but they remarked that they never knew I was Cuban. You can imagine how hurtful that was to have spent 24 years dancing at Lincoln Center and to have people say, "I didn't know you were Cuban," when I've never hid it and it's in every program or bio.

This is what I mean by cultural sensitivity. Because Latinos and Latinas blend so easily, we are overlooked or not always highlighted for our achievements. About two years ago, someone said to me, "Well, you're white presenting." I thought, "What does that mean? Especially when I was born in Cuba?" Just because I don't speak with an accent, in either language, and spent a lifetime at Lincoln Center, I'm white-presenting? That comment shouldn't mean that people get to ignore where I was born. It was then I realized: it was not my problem, it was theirs.

4
NATIVE AMERICAN DANCING BEYOND SETTLER COLONIAL CONFINES

Kate Mattingly (white settler)

In 2022, Talia Dixon (Payómkawichum) showed me a photo by Cara Romero (Chemehuevi), an internationally acclaimed photographer whose work has appeared in the Metropolitan Museum of Art and on the pages of the *New York Times*.[1] The image Talia shared appeared on the cover of *Native American Art*, and foregrounded beauty, elegance, and connection: a dancer, balancing on her pointe shoe, gracefully lifts her arms like wings, about to take flight. The white feathers emerging from her head like a crown enrich this avian-esque image. She looks at the viewer with confidence and a hint of curiosity as her dark hair caresses her shoulders. Hand-cut abalone shells adorn her neck and shine like the sun-speckled sky behind her. More white feathers decorate her bodice, and a copper-colored grass skirt ends just above her knees, suggesting a tutu. Her pointe shoes are painted with red ochre, complementing the copper of the grass strands. She bends one leg, so her knees touch and the arch of her foot aligns with the horizon of the ocean, a relationship that emphasizes harmony with her environment, her surroundings, and the sand that is her stage.

This photo by Cara Romero of dancer Crickett Tiger (Muscogee Creek/Cochiti), in a dress designed by Leah Mata-Fragua (Northern Chumash), is a stunning testament to Native American artistry. As a ballet historian, I also sensed resonances with legendary dancers like Maria Tallchief, a member of the Osage Nation, acclaimed for her

DOI: 10.4324/9781003283065-6

FIGURE 4.1 "Gaea" photograph by Cara Romero of dancer Crickett Tiger (Muscogee Creek/Cochiti) on the California Coast wearing Leah Mata-Fragua's all-Indigenous dancewear.

creation of the lead role in *Firebird*, choreographed by George Balanchine. Tallchief was not the only Native American dancer who significantly changed the history of ballet during the 20th century. In 1962, Yvonne Chouteau created the dance department at the University of Oklahoma, which still emphasizes ballet training. Chouteau was a member of the Shawnee Tribe and joined Tallchief and other Native American ballet dancers for a performance called "Four Moons" at the Oklahoma Indian Ballerina Festival in 1967, honoring five acclaimed Native American dancers: Chouteau, sisters Maria and Marjorie Tallchief, of the Osage Nation, Rosella Hightower

4
NATIVE AMERICAN DANCING BEYOND SETTLER COLONIAL CONFINES

Kate Mattingly (white settler)

In 2022, Talia Dixon (Payómkawichum) showed me a photo by Cara Romero (Chemehuevi), an internationally acclaimed photographer whose work has appeared in the Metropolitan Museum of Art and on the pages of the *New York Times*.[1] The image Talia shared appeared on the cover of *Native American Art*, and foregrounded beauty, elegance, and connection: a dancer, balancing on her pointe shoe, gracefully lifts her arms like wings, about to take flight. The white feathers emerging from her head like a crown enrich this avian-esque image. She looks at the viewer with confidence and a hint of curiosity as her dark hair caresses her shoulders. Hand-cut abalone shells adorn her neck and shine like the sun-speckled sky behind her. More white feathers decorate her bodice, and a copper-colored grass skirt ends just above her knees, suggesting a tutu. Her pointe shoes are painted with red ochre, complementing the copper of the grass strands. She bends one leg, so her knees touch and the arch of her foot aligns with the horizon of the ocean, a relationship that emphasizes harmony with her environment, her surroundings, and the sand that is her stage.

This photo by Cara Romero of dancer Crickett Tiger (Muscogee Creek/Cochiti), in a dress designed by Leah Mata-Fragua (Northern Chumash), is a stunning testament to Native American artistry. As a ballet historian, I also sensed resonances with legendary dancers like Maria Tallchief, a member of the Osage Nation, acclaimed for her

DOI: 10.4324/9781003283065-6

FIGURE 4.1 "Gaea" photograph by Cara Romero of dancer Crickett Tiger (Muscogee Creek/Cochiti) on the California Coast wearing Leah Mata-Fragua's all-Indigenous dancewear.

creation of the lead role in *Firebird*, choreographed by George Balanchine. Tallchief was not the only Native American dancer who significantly changed the history of ballet during the 20th century. In 1962, Yvonne Chouteau created the dance department at the University of Oklahoma, which still emphasizes ballet training. Chouteau was a member of the Shawnee Tribe and joined Tallchief and other Native American ballet dancers for a performance called "Four Moons" at the Oklahoma Indian Ballerina Festival in 1967, honoring five acclaimed Native American dancers: Chouteau, sisters Maria and Marjorie Tallchief, of the Osage Nation, Rosella Hightower

(Choctaw), and Moscelyne Larkin (Peoria Eastern Shawnee). When the University of Oklahoma celebrated the Five Moons Dance Festival in 2021, organizers hoped to feature female choreographers from underrepresented populations and to generate greater awareness of Native culture. One of the featured choreographers, Jenna Smith LaViolette (Osage), presented her choreography of *Wahzhazhe: An Osage Ballet*. [2] She told *Dance Teacher* Magazine that when she created this project in 2012, she was "hard pressed to find any Indigenous professional dancers, let alone Osage dancers."[3]

Discussions of barriers to training in ballet have tended to center experiences of Black and African American dancers, and Indigenous dancers are often overlooked in dance courses and "diversity" discussions. At the root of this erasure is settler colonialism and its logics permeate most educational settings in what is called the United States, relegating Indigenous peoples to a historic and disappearing past. The genocide committed against Native Americans by settler colonial nations, and the dispossession of Indigenous peoples from their lands, is the origin story of the United States. Sarah E. K. Fong (Chinese American) states, "The accumulation and dispossession of Indigenous territories provides the ground on which to develop extractive and racialized economies in the Americas."[4] This chapter takes a critical look at how ballet pedagogies are imbricated in these extractive and racialized economies, and how the formation of individuated liberal subjects, which undergirds racial-colonial subjugation, is also present in ballet training.[5]

More specifically, this chapter departs from conversations about "diversity" or "inclusion" to foreground the significance of responsibility, reciprocity, and sovereignty in any discussion that attempts to address equity in dance education. I contribute this chapter to this anthology as a call to move from "rights" to responsibilities, from settler colonialism to #LandBack, and to foreground reciprocity in educational settings. Cara Romero's photograph, titled *Gaea*, conjures the pulls between restriction and flight, between scarcity and abundance, while making visible Indigenous philosophies and epistemologies. Romero states that her work seeks to "critically explore what it means to live on someone's ancestral sacred land" and her intention to move "beyond a land acknowledgment to #LandBack."[6] As a white settler, I seek to highlight the importance of sovereignty, defined by Tria Blu Wakpa (Filipina, European, and tribally-unenrolled Native ancestries) as "Native expressions of agency and authority—rooted in Indigenous worldviews, languages, narratives, experiences, and practices—that relate to human and/or more-than-human collectives and promote Native well-being and futurities,"[7] and to place Romero's image alongside historical and current representations of Native American dancers. Ultimately this chapter seeks to challenge the erasure and misrepresentation of Native American artistry and redirect priorities in dance education.

Reparations: Foreground #LandBack

Dance in university settings presents an intertwined relationship between the techniques required in a curriculum and histories taught in lecture/seminar courses, which are often designed to honor and amplify the techniques and lineages taught in studios.[8] History courses tend to validate techniques taught in studio courses and reinforce settler colonial values by centering white artists like Isadora Duncan, Martha Graham, and Anna Halprin, often heralded as innovators, and downplaying their appropriation and erasure of Indigenous practices, perspectives, and peoples. Some of the most egregious examples occur in analysis of Graham's performance, yet, in dance history courses, this appropriation and erasure are rarely discussed. In 1935 Graham created a solo called *Frontier* that has been analyzed by Arabella Stanger (white), using the framework of Glen Sean Coulthard (Yellowknives Dene), as a prime example of "democratic individualism," a euphemism for "possessive individualism" that upholds "the ideological apparatus of slave-holding settler colonialism."[9] In choreography and performances of *Frontier* and *Appalachian Spring* (1944), Graham literally presents a narrative of settlers dominating land that is available for her taking, and in *Appalachian Spring*, she names a character "Pioneer Woman."[10] The word "pioneer" reinscribes the settler fallacies of "unoccupied" land available for the taking, as well as people who are the "first" to settle in a region.

Canonical choreographers promote settler colonial values that are reproduced and affirmed through the study and restaging of their choreography. In university courses, these aspects of settler choreographers are often ignored, perpetuating the possessive individualism that drives the theatrical dance canon and overlooking history teachers' complicity with Indigenous dispossession. In Stanger's analysis, she notes similarities in settler approaches to choreography by both Graham and Balanchine that obscure the "dispossessions bound up with the idea of space as availability."[11] Scholar Kim Tallbear (Sisseton-Wahpeton Oyate) exposes the hubris of these artists' aspirations as indicative of a distinct approach: "white bodies and white families in spaces of safety have been propagated in intimate co-constitution with the culling of black, red, and brown bodies and the wastelanding of their spaces."[12]

Far too often, conversations about equity in dance education do not address settler colonialism and fail to interrogate whiteness as a strategy that protects settler colonialism. One of the characteristics of white supremacy cultures theorized by Tema Okun (white) is "individualism," which persists in white supremacist organizations through the valorizing of competition over cooperation, individual recognition and credit over cooperation and supporting networks, and entitlement or "rights" over responsibility. In ballet classes and professional settings, I frequently observe these elements through a lack of consideration for different perspectives or needs, a squelching or censoring of alternate views, a lack of curiosity about privileges, identities, and barriers to access, and a refusal to consider any feedback concerning a teacher's or leader's presumed authority.

Educational settings are incubators for enforcing values that undergird racial-settler capitalism, and Sarah E. K. Fong analyzes how the curricula and daily routines of industrial boarding schools were a form of "cultural warfare intended to dissolve Native nations as political, social, and landed entities. Upon arrival at school, for example, Native students were forced to dress in 'citizens' clothing' and cut their hair."[13] While it would be incongruous to compare the lethal actions of boarding school administrators to ballet teachers, there are similar tactics that seek to strip a person of identities and values in the name of "character building." Fong examines this term as a euphemism for industrial-moral training that serves racial-settler capitalism:

> The purpose of character building thus surpassed the fulfillment of late-nineteenth-century labor demands. Rather, school authorities sought to craft workers driven to labor by the force of their own wills; to train laborers who not only could work but also whose internal ethics told them they must work. Thus, even as good character is advanced by manual labor, it exceeds embodied labor itself. School authorities constructed good character as a sign that students had internalized a moral orientation towards labor that would oblige them to work without external compulsion.[14]

Boarding school curricula also enforced settler colonial approaches to domesticity as "an indication of good character." Fong writes, "Female students were required to take courses that prepared them to become housewives and domestic laborers, such as domestic arts and sciences, physiology, and hygiene."[15] Racial-settler capitalism depends on blurring industrial and moral training, through the acquisitive logics of "character building," to cultivate individualism and extractive relationships between labor and land.

Images, poems, and articles were used by boarding school newspapers to instruct students on "character building,"[16] and, in a similar fashion, historical images of dancers like Maria Tallchief reveal how whiteness in ballet manages to reassert itself, even while engaging with Indigenous dancers and worldviews. Thomas F. DeFrantz (African American) describes how whiteness in ballet "snaps back," meaning reconfigures any conversation or action to reassert its supremacy, evoking the image of a rubber band that stretches to accommodate a new object while retaining its elasticity, its traction, and its extractive properties.[17] Paying attention to ballet settings that empower settler colonialism brings a nuanced view to how Indigenous dancers like Maria Tallchief navigated predominantly white spaces of ballet.

Maria Tallchief and "American" Ballet

While Maria Tallchief is often heralded as a Native American ballerina, less attention is brought to the confluence of events that afforded her this career path. In her autobiography, Tallchief writes that "overnight" the Osage tribe became rich when oil was discovered:

> I felt my father owned the town. He had property everywhere. The local movie theater on Main Street, and the pool hall opposite, belonged to him. Our ten-room, terra-cotta-brick house stood high on a hill overlooking the reservation.
>
> When my father was a young man, he married a young German immigrant and they had three children... They were little children when their mother died. Later, when Ruth Porter, my mother, came to Fairfax to visit her sister, who worked as a cook and housekeeper for my Grandma Tall Chief, Daddy was Fairfax's most eligible bachelor. Mother must have arrived tired and dusty from

her long journey, but from what I'm told there was an instant attraction between them.

Mother was born in Oxford, Kansas. A determined woman of Scots-Irish blood, she was beautiful, with light brown hair, gray eyes, and delicate features. My tall and lanky father and my tiny mother made an odd couple physically, but they were very much in love.[18]

The "delicate features" of Tallchief's mother contributed to Maria's proximity to whiteness. In addition, the Tallchief family's wealth, acquired through the settler colonial dispossession and redistribution of Native land, made it possible for Maria and Marjorie to train in Los Angeles with Bronislava Nijinska and David Lichine.

These anomalies of Tallchief's upbringing expose the complexity in Tallchief's narrative, as well as how "success" for Native dancers in ballet relies on access to exceptional circumstances. Not only is ballet training enormously expensive, if not out of geographical reach for Native dancers, but also definitions of dancing as an aesthetic activity and one that depends on possessive individualism run counter to Indigenous epistemologies.

During Tallchief's career, critics praised her ability to evoke and become the title role of Balanchine's *Firebird*, and emphasize her approach to dancing as more than steps or shapes. *New York Times* critic John Martin wrote, "Her movements are sharp and quick and clean, and we are always aware that the air is her true milieu."[19] Tallchief, like Hightower and Chateau, understood the significance of dancing as a form of communication, as well as a technique that is about precision and alignment. A student who worked with Tallchief at Chicago Lyric Opera Ballet in the 1970s recalled that her dancing seemed to be propelled by the idea, "I dance therefore I feel."[20]

Tallchief made significant contributions to George Balanchine's choreography, notably through roles she developed in narrative ballets, especially her embodiment of these characters, that attracted national and international fans. She is a pivotal artist in both the formations of "American" ballet and the survival of ballet as an art form. In 1951 *Time* magazine wrote, "Maria is America's ranking classical ballerina."[21] She appeared on the cover of *Newsweek* on October 11, 1954 with the caption: "The Ballet's Tallchief: Native Dancer," contributing to discourses of both ballet as an "American" (as opposed to European or Russian) art form and Native Americans as "American," significant during this Tribal Termination Era.²² Scholar Rebekah Kowal (Jewish-American settler) describes Tallchief's performances in *Firebird* (1948) as her "breakout role," adding that "her persona and her dancing fueled the development of [Balanchine's] creativity and the New York City Ballet."²³ Critics also praised her performances in *Swan Lake* as Odette and Odile: John Martin described her dancing as "a stunning performance,"²⁴ and "genuinely appealing,"²⁵ noteworthy given Martin's campaign against Black and African-American dancers in ballet throughout the 1940s and 1950s.²⁶

In *Playing Indian*, Philip Deloria (Dakota) examines notions of "American" culture, character, and practices that both rely on and remove Indigenous peoples: Maria Tallchief's contributions to the creation of "American" ballet vivify these erasures. As Deloria notes, "the practice of playing Indian," meaning white people adopting characteristics of Indianness, emerges post-World War II as people grapple with post-industrial realities: Indian play is used to "encounter the authentic amidst the anxiety."²⁷ Via proximity to Tallchief, Balanchine, like Graham, appropriates and capitalizes on aspects of Indianness to reinforce notions of authenticity and simplicity. In her scholarship, Shannon Toll (white settler) astutely describes Tallchief's navigation of these settler spaces, "Tallchief was an active agent not only in her career as a dancer but in her construction of her image for public audiences (balletic and literary alike) as a 'postindian princess.'"²⁸ When President William J. Clinton (white settler) honored Maria Tallchief with the National Medal of the Arts in 1999, he said, "Maria Tallchief took what had been a European art form and made it America's own—how fitting that a Native American woman would do that."²⁹ While the President intends this to be a compliment, Deloria's "playing Indian," meaning extracting from Indigenous cultures to create American identities, is explicitly revealed.

Alongside this interpellation of Native artistry into ballet, Tallchief herself had to navigate Othering, such as the headline following her 1947 appearance at the Paris Opera Ballet, "The daughter of an Indian Chief dances at the Opera!" Toll explicates the settler colonial stereotypes of Native American women as daughters of chiefs and princesses, which renders "them passive and submissive in the public consciousness."³⁰

In 1952, when Tallchief appeared on the cover of *Holiday* magazine, the image removes her upper body and head, featuring only her legs, balancing on pointe in a fourth position. Placing this cover alongside

Cara Romero's photograph of Crickett Tiger, the differences are striking: by cropping out Tallchief's face, the *Holiday* cover removes her distinct identity and persona. By only including legs and feet, clad in tights and a tutu, the cover dissociates these body parts from Tallchief's personal and cultural histories, and by extension, amplifies the exclusive homogeneity of ballet, namely whiteness.

Cara Romero, Crickett Tiger, and Leah Mata-Fragua

Artist Leah Mata-Fragua, who designed the dress Crickett wears in the *Gaea* photograph, says she foregrounds the personal as well as the political in her collaborations with photographer Cara Romero. Leah says:

> If the first visual experience you associate with this dress is ballet, then you look more deeply and you realize there's a lot more going on, a lot more to unpack: 1. The visibility of Indigenous people, not just in dance, but in everything. 2. The materials that I use, that we make or that we use in our Northern Chumash dance dresses. 3. I wanted to see what putting these elements together could show us about climate change, about the lack of diversity in ballet, and about the materials that we use for our dresses that are now endangered.[31]

She explains how her materials amplify both awareness of environmental injustices and the dynamism of Native practices, which are continually evolving. Scholar Yve Chavez (Tongva) has detailed how "coastal peoples collected abalone and other mollusks, which were a staple of their diet. They also carved the shells to make beads, fishhooks, and polished pieces to inlay in other objects."[32] Today overexploitation and climate change have drastically impacted the availability of abalone. Similarly, the Migratory Bird Treaty Act, created in response to rampant hunting, requires that people apply for a permit to use feathers of migratory birds.[33] Leah explains how this impacts the "top-knot" on Crickett's head:

> It's not normally what we would have worn, in terms of the feathers, because we can't use migratory birds. So, I used white dove. This also speaks to climate change, endangered habitats, and migratory birds.

Each feather is hand-shaped and hand-sewn. I cut all the abalone shell in this sequence, all of these tiny shells, I cut by hand [holds a shell that has been shaped in a circle, less than an inch in diameter] And now abalone is on the endangered list, which means I can find a diamond at a jewelry store more easily than I can get abalone. People are unaware that there's pretty much no more abalone. And why is a diamond more precious than an abalone shell? Right now, I can go buy diamonds at a Kay Jewelers or any other billion places, and there's no abalone. Who sets that value? What culture sets that value? Why are we taught that diamonds are more valued than abalone?

Reciprocity: Redistributing Resources and Priorities

The depletion of feathers and shells mirrors the scarcity of Native peoples in university settings, as well as leadership positions across the arts and education.[34] Just as ballet as an art form ossifies without a vibrant diversity of artists and choreography, so too our educational environments must honor the distinct knowledge of Native dancing and dancers.

In 2018, Colorado Ballet brought attention to the ongoing presence of Native Americans by commissioning Fancy Shawl dancer Keya Clairmont (Sicangu Lakota/Sisseton Wahpeton Dakota/Taos Pueblo/Meskwaki/Leech Lake Ojibwe) to create a performance with the dancers of Colorado Ballet's Studio company. In a trailer about the choreographic process, one of the ballet dancers says, "I didn't know there was Native dancing. I had no idea there were different styles of Native dancing."[35] The statement reveals the lack of awareness of Native artistry among dancers and exposes an often-insular approach to ballet training. Clairmont explains that Fancy Shawl dancing emerged as a response to Men's Fancy Dancing and is incredibly fast-paced, athletic, and challenging. Clairmont adds, "We wanted to show that women could dance to these super-fast songs and make it look incredibly graceful."[36] Watching Clairmont dance is captivating. Her fast footwork maintains a steady rhythm with the drum, and there's a rebounding quality similar to the ballon of a petit allegro combination, as each jump fosters energy, resilience, and momentum. Clairmont acknowledges the shared ethos of the dancing: "We're all artists and we have to train very hard, and we love what we do."

Scholar Tria Blu Wakpa describes "the inextricable linkages" among sovereignty, survival, futurity, and even freedom: "In the Indigenous context, the focus on 'traditions' implies bodies and movement forms and the overlapping temporalities of past, present, and future, which may depart from Eurocentric constructs of time."[37] In other words, dancing is a form of activation that connects ideas and actions, humans and more-than-humans, futurities and traditions, as well as the past and the future. In many Indigenous understandings of time, the past is not divided from the present and future, but rather understood as ever-present.

In 2021, when the *Gaea* photo was featured on the cover of *Native American Art*, the image attracted widespread acclaim. The Facebook page for the magazine has 11,000 followers, and the 2021 post about the *Gaea* cover was shared more than 180 times. When I wrote to *Pointe* magazine in 2022 asking if I could interview the Native artists and highlight the project, the non-Native editor replied, "This was done in 2021. Is there anything that's new?" Here again, the insistence on the "perpetual new" denies people's values and the significance of spiraling time as antidote to division and separation. This dismissal of Romero's photo was especially painful given the lack of access Native American artists have to predominantly white platforms, like *Pointe* magazine, and the abundance of photos and performances by white dancers highlighted by the predominantly white writers and editors.

While chronological order presupposes a "progression" of time, Indigenous temporalities tend to emphasize cyclical or spiraling relationships. These values contrast sharply with ballet education and performances, historically and currently, that insist on hierarchical, individualistic, and Anthropocentric structures. These separations form the core of the harm and violence of settler colonialism, which relies on division and Othering. In contrast, Native dancing foregrounds connections among movement, sensorial awareness, and existing in balance with surrounding environments.

Cara Romero's approach to photography amplifies Native artistry rather than attempting to capture or trap Indigenous cultures, as seen in photography by white settlers like Edward Curtis (1868–1952) or Jack Hillers (1843–1925). Romero's emphasis on connection is evident in her description of *Gaea*:

> The photograph is a celebration of Mother Earth, women of color dancers and Indigenous futurism aesthetics in classical dance. Leah and I, both California Native women, living and working in Santa

Fe, often come together in cultural exchange to co-create images that are rooted in our shared histories and experience to bring critical visibility to California First Peoples through our respective arts.[38]

The collaborators' attention to details, materials, and colors enriches connections between the ocean setting and dress design. The importance of honoring connections among people and places is made vivid.

From Rights to Responsibilities: Foreground Native Epistemologies

Leah Mata-Fragua, designer of the dress Crickett wears, researched dancers of color in ballet and found that access to training is "different" for Native communities:

> If I wanted to take ballet classes, I would have had to drive an hour each way, so 2 hours, or 50 miles each way, so that's paying for 100 miles of gas and then paying for the lessons so it's a no-go for me. So many young children often have that fantasy of being a dancer, right? I can't think of any kid in my neighborhood, when you're in kindergarten, first grade, second grade: everybody wants to be a professional dancer. Plus, we tend to come from larger families, and the current poverty rate of urban Native Americans is high. If you've got five kids, paying for ballet lessons for that many kids is just not happening, and it's not going to happen. And it's unfortunate because a lot of our people enjoy ballet.[39]

Leah identifies multiple obstacles in these sentences, all of which result from settler colonialism. The objective of settler colonialism is for settlers to make "a new home on the land, a homemaking that insists on settler sovereignty over all things in their new domain."[40] To do so, the US government has attempted to annihilate Indigenous peoples and cultures, most visibly by creating reservations and boarding schools that detrimentally impact Native well-being and epistemologies, as well as imposing bans on Native dancing and ceremonies.[41] Settlers feared these rituals and gatherings as attempts to overthrow their unjust regime.[42] Until the 1970s, tribal groups around the country were banned from and criminalized for the engagement of any ceremonial doings or dance practices.

While there are some Native American people who belong to federally recognized tribes, and there are 574 recognized nations in what is called the United States, many Indigenous people continue to exist without this affiliation. As a result, the term Native American is complicated: to be independent governing bodies, nations need to conform to policies dictated by a genocidal, settler government.

Conclusion

Native artists emphasize connections between knowledge and sensorial engagement, between humans and-more-than-human relatives, as well as through past, present, and future time. Centering Indigenous peoples and knowledge means centering the vital and ongoing innovations and contributions of Native dancing, and the scarcity of Native dancing in university settings is glaring.

Tria Blu Wakpa highlights the significance of Native peoples' authority to "represent themselves spiritually, individually, and relationally with humans and more-than-humans, and in ways that contribute to human and more-than-human healing."[43] As a white settler who has worked in university settings for two decades, I can only think of a handful of occasions when Native dancers, or Native artist/scholars, have visited a dance course or spoken about their research and dancing. Rather than focus on Native American dancers in ballet, a more vital question may be, How are dance educators, especially white settler educators, supporting Native dancing and innovation? How are white settlers in universities leveraging resources to support and compensate Native American artists? Are your department's dance performances and choice of repertory undergirding settler colonial values by restaging canonical pieces that deny Indigenous artistry and epistemologies, especially the inseparability of dancing and living? How often are you hiring Indigenous artists for tenure-track positions with job security and a living wage or paying Indigenous artists to meet with and educate students and faculty? How versed are white settler faculty in Native studies, especially scholarship by Blu Wakpa, Coulthard, Deloria, and TallBear?

Notes

1 Holland Cotter, "At the Met, Protest and Poetry about Water," *New York Times*, July 4, 2022, C1. https://www.nytimes.com/2022/07/03/arts/design/native-american-art-norby-water.html

2 "Wahzhazhe: An Osage Ballet," *Smithsonian*, March 26, 2013, https://www.si.edu/object/yt_ipwe0Jluhpo.
3 April Deocariza, "Osage Ballet Teacher Jenna Smith Violette," *Dance Teacher*, November 5, 2020, https://dance-teacher.com/osage-ballet-teacher-jenna-smith-laviolette-tallchief-oklahoma/.
4 Sarah E. K. Fong, "Racial Settler Capitalism: Character Building and the Accumulation of Land and Labor in the Late Nineteenth Century," *American Indian Culture and Research Journal* 43, no. 2 (2019): 30.
5 Saidiya Hartman, *Scenes of Subjection: Terror, Slavery, and Self-Making in Nineteenth-Century America* (New York: Oxford University Press, 1997), 116.
6 Cara Romero, https://www.cararomerophotography.com/tongvaland.
7 Tria Blu Wakpa, "From Buffalo Dance to Tatanka Kcizapi Wakpala, 1894–2020: Indigenous Human and More-Than-Human Choreographies of Sovereignty and Survival," *American Quarterly* 74, no. 4 (December 2022): 895–920.
8 Kate Mattingly, *Shaping Dance Canons* (Gainesville: University of Florida Press, 2023).
9 Arabella Stanger, *Dancing on Violent Ground: Utopia as Dispossession in Euro-American Theater Dance* (Evanston: Northwestern University Press, 2021), 64.
10 For analysis of *Appalachian Spring* see Kate Mattingly, "Modern and Postmodern Dance: War and Choreography in the 20^{Th} and 21st Centuries," *Milestones in Dance History* (New York: Routledge, 2022), 108–133.
11 Stanger, *Dancing*, 64.
12 Kim TallBear, "Making Love and Relations beyond Settler Sex and Family," *Making Kin Not Population* eds. Adele E. Clark and Donna Haraway (Chicago: Prickly Paradigm Press, 2018), 145–166.
13 Fong, "Racial Settler Capitalism," 32.
14 Fong, "Racial Settler Capitalism," 35.
15 Fong, "Racial Settler Capitalism," 38.
16 Fong, "Racial Settler Capitalism," 36.
17 Please see Chapter 20 in this anthology
18 "Maria Tallchief," *California Indian Education*, https://www.californiaindianeducation.org/famous_indians/maria_tallchief/
19 John Martin, "City Ballet Scores a New Firebird," *New York Times*, November 28, 1949, 11.
20 Jennifer Homans, "Maria Tallchief: The Osage Dancer who took Paris by Storm," *New York Times*, December 21, 2013, https://archive.nytimes.com/www.nytimes.com/news/the-lives-they-lived/2013/12/21/maria-tallchief/
21 "American as Wampum, *Time* Magazine, February 26, 1951, 76–77.
22 Rebekah Kowal, "Indian Ballerinas Toe Up: Maria Tallchief and Making Ballet 'American'" *Dance Research Journal* 46, no. 2 (August 2014): 73–96.
23 Kowal, "Indian Ballerinas," 79.
24 John Martin, "Dance: Full Recovery," *New York Times*, December 5, 1955, 35.
25 John Martin, "Ballet: 'Swan Lake'," *New York Times,* January 7, 1957, 29.

26 See Kate Mattingly, *Shaping Dance Canons* (Gainesville: University Press of Florida, 2023).
27 Philip Deloria, *Playing Indian* (New Haven, CT: Yale University Press, 1999), 7. *Playing Indian*, 7.
28 Shannon Toll, "Maria Tallchief, (Native) *America's Prima Ballerina*," *Studies in American Indian Literatures* 30, no. 1 (Spring 2018): 52.
29 "Maria Tallchief," *California Indian Education*, https://www.californiaindianeducation.org/famous_indians/maria_tallchief/
30 Toll, "Maria Tallchief," 51.
31 Leah Mata-Fragua, Interview with the author, 2022.
32 Yve Chavez, Indigenous Artists, Ingenuity, and Resistance at the California Missions After 1769. Dissertation, UCLA, 2017.
33 "Migratory Bird Treaty Act," *US Fish and Wildlife Service*, https://www.fws.gov/lab/featheratlas/feathers-and-the-law.php
34 In Canada, there is now a First Nations dancer who is Ballet Kelowna's first artist-in residence. For more information see "Tla'amin ballet star brings cultural stories to the Kelowna stage," *Vancouver Sun*, December 26, 2022.
35 "Moccasins en Pointe," *Colorado Ballet*, March 16, 2018, https://www.youtube.com/watch?v=AhuIXU4ZESU
36 "Moccasins en Pointe," *Colorado Ballet*, March 16, 2018, https://www.youtube.com/watch?v=AhuIXU4ZESU
37 Blu Wakpa, *Buffalo Dance*, 899.
38 Cara Romero, "Gaea," *Cara Romero Photography*, https://www.cararomerophotography.com/editions/gaea.
39 Leah Mata-Fragua, Interview with the author, 2022.
40 Eve Tuck and K. Wayne Yang, "Decolonization is not a metaphor," *Decolonization: Indigeneity, Education, & Society* 1, no. 1 (2012): 1–40.
41 Tria Blu Wakpa, "Challenging Settler Colonial Choreographies during COVID-19," *Critical Stages* 23 (June 2021), https://www.critical-stages.org/23/challenging-settler-colonial-choreographies-during-covid-19-acosia-red-elks-powwow-yoga/.
42 Kathy Weiser, "The Ghost Dance—A Promise of Fulfillment," Legends of America, February 2020, https://www.legendsofamerica.com/na-ghostdance/.
43 Blu Wakpa, "Buffalo Dance," 900.

5

REFLECTIONS ON QUARE DANCE

Ballet and Black, Queer, Fem(me)inist Aesthetics

Alyah Baker

Quare Dance: Fashioning a Black, Queer, Fem(me)inist Aesthetic in Ballet is an ongoing creative praxis that imagines and embodies new possibilities for ballet. Employing an intersectional lens that considers race, gender, and sexuality, this praxis decenters the white, cisgender, heteronormative epistemologies prevalent in ballet discourse. Instead, *Quare Dance* moves to chart new pathways and amend incomplete ballet histories by centering the often-overlooked experiences of Black Queer Ballerinas. This work draws from dance and performance studies, Black feminist theory, and queer studies to animate the concept of *quare*, as defined by scholar E. Patrick Johnson. Quare, a variant of queer, specifies "one for whom sexual and gender identities always already intersect with racial subjectivity."[1]

My interest in the relationship between identity and ballet stems from a desire to understand my experience as a Black Queer Ballerina. Since ballerinas rose to prominence in the 19th century, they have been synonymous with an idealized and elusive standard of beauty. Even as ballet technique evolved, the ballerina archetype remained narrowly defined as cisgender, heterosexual, thin, and white. As a dancer, I fail to achieve the archetype on many levels. Still, I identify as a ballerina and know there are others like me. Finding community was a crucial first step in this praxis. This community of Black Queer Ballerinas helped to reflect and contextualize my experience. They serve as a means to

DOI: 10.4324/9781003283065-7

combat the erasure and isolation that results from raced and gendered ballet norms.

Ballet companies, with few exceptions, continue to have racial diversity issues. The lack of Black ballerinas is particularly apparent. Often Black dancers exist as token members of white institutions.[2] While tokenism and a lack of diversity can be found globally, my research is heavily informed by ballet culture and white supremacy in the U.S. context. Centuries of discrimination have deemed the Black dancing body unfit for ballet. Furthermore, the significant influence of Black culture and the immense contributions of Black dancers have been systematically omitted from dominant ballet narratives. The scholarship and advocacy of Brenda Dixon Gottschild, Theresa Ruth Howard, Adesola Akinleye, Misty Copeland, Nyama McCarthy Brown, and others are changing this norm.

In terms of gender and sexuality, it is apparent that ballet has historically subscribed to binary thinking. Men and women are held to distinctly different standards, while little, if any consideration, is given to genders beyond this binary. Generations of queer men have found acceptance, community, celebrity, and even power within the world of ballet. In *A Queer History of Ballet*, Peter Stoneley writes at length about the interests, desires, and aesthetics of gay, primarily white, men that have shaped ballet.[3] The presence and influence of a relatively diverse fraternity of queer men can be found throughout ballet histories and within the ranks of many present-day institutions. Yet, even when they achieve a certain level of safety and comfort in ballet spaces, queer men are often still beholden to binary gender norms. Being perceived as effeminate or soft can impact opportunities for promotions and leading roles. When performing "male" roles dancers are expected to exude strength, power, and control as the hypermasculine counterpoint to the delicate ballerina.

Mirroring broader American culture, the presence, interests, and desires of lesbian and queer women, non-binary, and trans dancers in ballet have largely been ignored. Artists and scholars like myself, Adriana Pierce, Katy Pyle, Ashton Edwards, Lauren Flower, Gretchen Alterowitz, and Maxfield Haynes are advocating for greater representation and recognition in the mainstream. *Quare Dance* collaborators, Cortney Taylor Key, Audrey Malek, and Kiara Felder represent important voices at the intersection of race, gender, sexuality, and ballet.

Compared to other art forms, ballet has been slow to change, and archaic practices, ideals, and repertoire persist. An injection of modernity is needed to bring the form into the 21st century. Such moves are urgent because the grip of white, cis heteronormativity has nearly immobilized the corps de ballet, keeping the form stagnant and threatening to make it obsolete. Maurya Kerr, a choreographer, poet, and former dancer with Alonzo King LINES Ballet, states:

> Ballet actually needs you. The form needs people of color. It needs people of different body types. It needs people with different experiences, so it doesn't remain this out-of-touch, elitist form that no one wants to see. It is a dying form because it is catering to a very elite, old, dying, white society.[4]

A graduate school professor, Sarah Wilbur, was the first to ask me if *Quare Dance* might constitute an antiracist praxis. I take this opportunity to reflect on the type of interventions *Quare Dance* proposes. I will consider how these interventions resist the white cis heteronormativity of dominant ballet discourse and offer a glimpse of alternative realities and possibilities for the form. To analyze how *Quare Dance* represents an antiracist approach to ballet, a working definition of antiracist is needed.

Ibram X. Kendi defines antiracist as "one who is supporting an antiracist policy through actions or expressing an antiracist idea."[5] Drilling down further, he writes, "An antiracist idea is any idea that suggests the racial groups are equals in all their apparent differences—that there is nothing right or wrong with any racial group. Antiracist ideas argue that racist policies are the cause of racial inequities."[6] The text details how race, racism, and the resulting ideas and policies intertwine with social constructs including gender, and sexuality producing complex and layered forms of oppression. For Kendi, working against oppression and discrimination based on gender and sexuality is a crucial part of an antiracist practice. Intersectional thinking that acknowledges the necessary and "productive overlap" of antiracism with feminist, queer, and other civil rights movements builds on the contributions of Audre Lorde, The Combahee River Collective, Kimberlé Crenshaw, and others.[7]

Quare Dance takes up intersectional thinking and moves to expand the conversation on race, gender, sexuality, and ballet. Applying Kendi's definition, to be antiracist is to be in action, to move beyond the passive and complicit stance of "not racist." Antiracism must be enacted on individual, interpersonal, and institutional levels. Operating in an antiracist paradigm is always personal and collective work.

As interest in antiracist praxis has increased in the wake of the deaths of Ahmaud Arbery, Breonna Taylor, and George Floyd, there has been a proliferation of resources that propose where to start and what steps to take. Examining a range of sources, a pathway through which to enter and understand antiracist praxis starts to emerge. Common themes include self-education and reflection, understanding unconscious bias, centering those most impacted by oppression, revising histories and practices to avoid reproducing racial inequalities, consistently implementing these practices, and co-creating environments for mutual learning.[8]

To develop *Quare Dance* I took cues from practices rooted in Black queer feminist movements, somatics, improvisation, liberation, and joy which align with antiracist frameworks. Bhattacharyya et al. remind us that "recent remakings of anti-racist thought reveal the deep influence of black feminism and, increasingly, the analytic insights of black queer activism."[9] With this knowledge and my lived experiences, I moved forward.

Quare Dance is a communal and collaborative endeavor, yet as with any antiracist praxis, the real work started with deep self-investigation. Long before graduate school, I was curious to understand how my Blackness and queerness shaped my career. After years in pre-professional and professional ballet realms, I had drifted towards modern and contemporary dance spaces which felt much easier to inhabit. My beloved ballet, while always present in my body, took a supporting role. I began to ponder, "Why did I love ballet? What was challenging? Where were the other Black Queer ballerinas? What would a ballet praxis that reflected my fullness look like?" Even as an avid student of the form, there were gaps in my knowledge, particularly around Black and queer artists and their contributions to the form.

I continue to find archival information and texts that reshape and expand my understanding of ballet. Take, for example, Josephine Baker's and Katherine Dunham's relationships with and influence on George Balanchine or the story of ballet dancer turned queer activist Angela Bowen. From these fragments of history, I am piecing together an alternative ballet narrative that includes and celebrates Black, queer artists, and their contributions.

In addition to amending ballet histories, enacting new possibilities for the form is an important aspect of my work. The desire to "infuse my dance practice, heavily informed by many years of ballet, with a Quare Fem(me)inist sensibility" guides my creative work and was the impetus for *Quare Dance*.[10] Through months of experimentation that included improvisation, reading, writing, and many conversations, a framework for a quare, fem(me)inist approach to exploring ballet emerged. Amidst the rethinking of all aspects of life prompted by COVID-19, I rolled this framework out to an intimate group of collaborators. Together we began the process of imagining and embodying the antiracist ballet world of our dreams. In what follows I share an excerpt of *Quare Dance: Fashioning a Black, Queer, Fem(me)inist Aesthetic in Ballet*, edited for brevity and clarity, that details and reflects on an antiracist praxis in motion.

Quare Dance: Engaging Collaborators

In October of 2020, Kiara Felder of Les Grands Ballet Canadiens de Montréal, Audrey Malek of Washington Ballet, Freelancer Cortney Taylor Key, and I gathered for the first time to dream *Quare Dance* into existence. Due to the pandemic, our entire creative process unfolded over Zoom. Even though we did not meet in person and varied in age, location, and dance experience, our group felt instantly connected. Deep bonds were forged over shared Black, Queer/LGBTIA+ identities, experiences of womanhood, and a love of ballet.

By design, our process was flexible and meant to evolve with the needs, desires, and schedules of the group. Over the course of six months, we participated in a series of group and one-on-one conversations, reflective journaling exercises, and solo movement improvisation with the goal of (re)connecting with aspects of ourselves that are often unwelcome or ignored in traditional ballet settings. Although I initiated this project and was responsible for guiding the process, the creative content generated for *Quare Dance* is the embodiment of the hopes and dreams of four different dancers spread across the US and Canada.

Quare Dance: Key Components

Discussion, witnessing, self-reflection, and improvisation were key components of our methodology. While I intentionally selected each of these components based on previous creative processes, proven

choreographic methods, COVID constraints, and theoretical interest, each element's importance became more apparent as the weeks progressed. Suprisingly, discussion emerged as one of the most important pieces of the puzzle.

In my experience, discussion is not always a part of the creative process, especially in a dance context. Time to create and rehearse is often limited and expensive, so learning and generating movement is prioritized. On occasion, a choreographer or director may relay a theme, story, or background information, but there is rarely time to engage in robust discussion. By contrast, discussion figured prominently throughout the *Quare Dance* process. Each Zoom session began with one to two hours of discussion, and topics ranged from dance and identity to personal relationships, favorite books and songs, and how we were navigating the pandemic. Prioritizing dialogue allowed us to develop the comfort necessary to be vulnerable while exploring personal issues like race, gender, and sexuality. Conversation also allowed us to combat the isolation of the pandemic, work against socio-cultural forces that silence Black and Queer folks, and build a community rooted in care. In many ballet spaces, there is a culture of silence that penalizes dancers who speak up. For scholar Patricia Hill Collins, dialogue amongst community and an ethic of care are necessary components of a Black feminist epistemology.[11]

Witnessing, another key component of our process, was also part of establishing an ethic of care. I define witnessing as an engaged, responsive, participatory way of seeing. This way of seeing is experiential and embodied, denoting an exchange between subjects rather than an audience-object relationship. Our creative process and the resulting installation invited multiple types of witnessing. On one level, folks who attended the installation were able to spend time with and witness a piece of each artist's story. As participants, Kiara, Cortney, Audrey, and I learned from and witnessed each other. Getting a front row seat to the inner and outer expressions of my collaborators was a gift. In each of them, I saw elements of my story reflected. Most importantly, each artist had the opportunity to witness and reflect on their own identity, movement, and experience.

From the outset, each collaborator was asked to critically reflect on the role that race, gender, and sexuality play in their life and ballet career. Several strategies were employed to facilitate this process of self-reflection including journaling, building vision boards, and documenting our process through photos, video, and voice recordings. Time to think deeply about how our identities shape the ways we move our bodies was crucial to this project's success.

Quare Dance facilitated a moment of integration, a space to put our lived experience as Black, Queer folks in dialogue with what we do for a living. Reflecting on this, I am reminded of Collins' articulation of lived experience as a crucial part of a Black feminist epistemology.[12] José Esteban Muñoz's theory of disidentification is also relevant to frame the process of claiming and making sense of seemingly conflicting identities like Black, Queer, and ballerina.[13] Centering self-reflection allowed us to give more weight to our internal voice and deprioritize the dominant discourse.

Through improvisation, a similar process unfolded with movement. Each collaborator was invited to move in the style that felt most authentic. While our discussions centered around ballet, the goal for improvisation sessions was to move towards pleasure and discovery. Improvisation plays an important role in the creative process for many dancers and choreographers. Within ballet, William Forsythe's "Improvisation Technologies," which builds on the work of Laban, is one of the most well-known methodologies.[14]

Forsythe's interest seems to be geometric, and shape-based, extending and manipulating lines and curves by modifying various spatial planes and dynamics. In this instance, my approach to improvisation was not bound by a particular movement methodology. I was interested in mining our individual movement inheritances and desires. To communicate this to the collaborators, I referenced ideas and imagery from Black vernacular creative praxis. Improvisational quilting, jazz music, and collage are specific influences. I encouraged Kiara, Audrey, and Cortney to let their movements be guided by sensations, feelings, and thoughts. What might it look like to dance as ourselves? How do we like to move? What feels good?

I have come to understand improvisation as an act of recovery, rediscovery, and response: the recovery of subjugated ways of moving trained away by codified technique, rediscovery of pleasurable ways of moving, and response to an emotion, physical site, song, or idea. At its best, improvisation feels like a practice of self-actualization and liberation. On several occasions, we noted that engaging in a regular improvisational movement practice enhanced our ability to bring increased richness, nuance, and joy to ballet. This anecdotal and experiential evidence [re] affirms my interest in investigating how to fully embody complex identities within ballet.

Conclusion

Identifying as a Black Queer ballerina does not make my dance praxis inherently antiracist. Yet, my lived experience has engendered a desire to challenge and dismantle oppressive structures. *Quare Dance* proposes and enacts multiple interventions that align with antiracist praxis, in an effort to edit, reimagine, and expand ballet. When we decenter white cis heteronormativity, unacknowledged possibilities are revealed. An intersectional lens allows us to see and do ballet differently.

Ballet praxis can encourage dialogue instead of silence, prioritize autonomy over authority, value difference rather than homogeneity, and invite belonging versus exclusivity. For Black and Queer ballerinas our identity and lived experience can finally be recognized and embraced as an asset instead of a liability. And ballet benefits. The form is expanded, enriched, and transformed by artists that embody alternative realities and exist beyond false binaries. These artists are manifestations of what is possible, an equitable and inclusive future for ballet.

Notes

1 Patrick E. Johnson, Johnson, "'Quare' Studies, or (Almost) Everything I Know about Queer Studies I Learned from My Grandmother." *Text and Performance Quarterly* 21, no. 1 (2001): 1–25.
2 Gia Kourlas, "Where Are All the Black Swans?" *The New York Times*, May 6, 2007, https://www.nytimes.com/2007/05/06/arts/dance/06kour.html; Jennifer Fisher, "Ballet and Whiteness: Will Ballet Forever Be the Kingdom of the Pale," *The Oxford Handbook of Dance and Ethnicity*, Anthony Shay and Barbara Sellers-Young, eds. (New York: Oxford University Press, 2016).
3 Peter Stoneley, *A Queer History of the Ballet* (New York: Routledge, 2007).
4 Maurya Kerr, "Maurya Kerr: On the Intersectionality of Dance and Social Change," *Medium*, January 10, 2017. https://medium.com/@sabrinassellers/maurya-kerr-on-the-intersectionality-of-dance-and-social-change-9b55cec3ca8e.
5 Ibram X. Kendi, *How to Be an Antiracist* (New York: One World, 2019), 13.
6 Kendi, *Antiracist*, 20.
7 Clare Croft, "Introduction," *Queer Dance* (New York: Oxford University Press, 2017), PG.

8 Thema Bryant-Davis and Edith Arrington, *The Antiracism Handbook: Practical Tools to Shift Your Mindset and Uproot Racism in Your Life and Community* (Oakland, CA: New Harbinger Publications, 2022).
9 Gargi Bhattacharyya, Satnam Virdee, and Aaron Winter, "Revisiting Histories of Anti-Racist Thought and Activism." *Identities* 27, no. 1 (2019): 1–19.
10 Alyah Baker, "Quare Dance: Fashioning a Black, Queer, Fem (me)inist Aesthetic in Ballet." MFA Thesis. Duke University, 2021.
11 Patricia Hill Collins, *Black feminist thought: knowledge, consciousness, and the politics of empowerment* (New York: Routledge, 2015).
12 Hill Collins, *Black feminist thought*.
13 José Esteban Muñoz, *Disidentifications: queers of color and the performance of politics* (Minneapolis: University of Minnesota Press, 1999).
14 William Forsythe, Christine Bürkle, Noah Gelber, Thomas McManus, Crystal Pite, and Roslyn Sulcas, *William Forsythe improvisation technologies: a tool for the analytical dance eye (Hamburg:* Hatje Cantz, 2010).

PART 2
Pedagogies

6
CLASSICAL PERSPECTIVES
Performance, Pedagogy, and (Changing) Cultures

Anjali Austin

My life in classical ballet began in the 1960s when my family relocated from Tallahassee, Florida to San Francisco, California, where I was exposed to new artistic and cultural experiences. I was asked what I wanted to study. My answer was specific, "Ballet." My mother enrolled me in the San Francisco Ballet School (SFBS), which became my stepping stone to a career in dance. I trained there for eight years, studying with Harold Christensen (brother of respected ballet teachers and choreographers, Lew and Willam), Zelda Mortimore, Jocelyn Vollmar, Richard Gladstone, and others. The school provided me with solid ballet training, and I performed children's roles in SFB's seasonal *Nutcracker Suite* and was also cast for the role of Mohammed in the San Francisco Opera's *Der Rosenkavalier*. These were my earliest experiences that eventually lead me to pursue a successful career as a performing artist.

I later found out that my mother, Ms. Mary Lee Hill, had been approached by some of my teachers who spoke with her about my talents and suggested that I also take modern dance. In that moment and still today, I wonder how often she may have had those types of conversations. In retrospect, I recognize that she was effectively shielding me from comments that might have influenced my artistic objectives. I am perplexed as to why my teachers were guiding me to include modern dance in my training. At best it was their misguided attempt to protect me from future disappointments; and at worst—whether it was conscious or not—they were continuing the practice of trying to exclude young Black ballet students from an area that was normally reserved for white bodies. The latter results in a terrible waste of creativity and talent. As scholar and curator Theresa Ruth Howard reminds us in her discussion of Delores Browne:

> Browne was determined to endure and she did. However, the career she had was a bittersweet consolation for the one she was truly built for, and had she been white, she would no doubt have obtained. When you have the talent, do the work, follow all the rules, and you are denied solely because of your race, it creates wounds that are hard to heal and tend to keloid.[1]

My family returned to Tallahassee, Florida in 1974. Mother realized my commitment to ballet and found a teacher for me to train with. Mrs. Helen Salter had previously been a dancer in George Balanchine's Ballet Society, a precursor to New York City Ballet. Few people outside of my family knew about my ballet training, and by the time friends found out, I was already performing with the Tallahassee Civic Ballet. As a high school junior, I enrolled in ballet classes at the Department of Dance at Florida State University (FSU), where I studied with Maria de Baroncelli, a former member of the world-renowned Ballet Russe de Monte Carlo. Even in a small southern town, away from larger cities where ballet flourished, I had excellent teachers.

In 1975, FSU Department of Dance Chair, Dr. Nancy Smith Fichter, whose familial heritage was grounded in social and political activism, brought Arthur Mitchell in to teach master classes for dance majors. Mitchell was the first African-American dancer to become a member of George Balanchine's New York City Ballet, where he performed from 1955 to 1968. He and Karel Shook co-founded the Dance Theatre of Harlem (DTH) in 1969. His school and company have nurtured the careers of many artists, and by 1975, his company was internationally recognized. Fichter invited me to take his class, and her generous gesture opened new opportunities that impacted my career.

In 1978, I became a member of DTH, a company that included people of color from around the globe. One of our common experiences was that most of us had come from schools where there were only a few, if any,

Black students. In those environments, each of us had received comments, both subtle and overt, that encouraged us to focus on professional directions that were "more appropriate," like those that had been suggested to my mother. Even though we were taught classical ballet roles, many of us understood that we would never perform them on stage, in those environments. Our experiences as members of DTH confirmed our convictions that there was a place for Black artists in the world of classical ballet. The company created an environment where we could discuss these matters with each other and understand them on the most visceral level.

Dance Theatre of Harlem

At various times during my thirteen years with the Dance Theatre of Harlem, the company numbered between 30 and 75 professionally trained Black ballet dancers. Our visual presence disrupted the perception that people of color were not suited for European classical ballet, and it opened minds in ways words could not. Our repertoire consisted of classical, neo-classical, contemporary, and dance theatre pieces, including *Le Corsaire, Pas de Dix (Raymonda Variations), Square Dance, Dougla, Les Noces, Fall River Legend, Creole Giselle, Allegro Brillante, Frankie and Johnny, Voluntaries, Doina, Concerto Barocco, Troy Games, Sylvia Pas De Deux, Les Biches, A Streetcar Named Desire,* and *Flower Festival.*

We performed nationally and internationally, touring to Japan, Israel, Australia, France, Argentina, and Egypt. One significant tour found us in the Soviet Union for five weeks, performing in the cities of Moscow, Tbilisi, and Leningrad, now known as St. Petersburg. The media buzz before and after this tour was incredible. In the September 1988 issue of *Ebony* Magazine there was a five-page spread on DTH's Soviet Union tour titled, "Dance Theatre of Harlem Wows Russia." Author Renee D. Turner wrote:

> The New York troupe wins critical acclaim in the land where classical ballet was perfected... the predominantly Black troupe triumphed. Russians shouted "Bravos" and rose in a rare standing ovation... The Dance Theatre of Harlem's Soviet tour was the first in 13 years by an American dance company. Among its most enthusiastic fans was Raisa Gorbachev, wife of the Soviet leader

[Mikhail Gorbachev]. She was so enamored that she attended a second performance of the company after the opening night in the Kremlin's Palace of Congresses...Women in gowns hoisted themselves through boiler room windows after being locked out of the packed Paliashvili Theatre in Tbilisi...It was unbelievable...[2]

Dance Theatre of Harlem had been accepted in the country that was known as the home of classical ballet.

Mr. Mitchell and his staff nurtured us and encouraged us to fulfill his vision of the artist as a complete human being. We were smartly attired, courteous, and well-spoken. Our expectations of ourselves were higher than those that mainstream society might have had for us. We were empowered by our high visibility and our acclaim, and that came with responsibility. It also came with the recognition that we were performing before audiences that might view us differently than we viewed ourselves. To some, we might have been foreign beings who represented the exotic fantasies of individuals who had few—if any—encounters with Black people. Those were some of the thoughts that ran through my mind, as I reflected on my feelings in a diary entry after one of my performances in 1979:

> Dublin, Ireland is really very beautiful. They do not, however, see a lot of Black people here. Today we had an 11:00 AM call. After class we spaced *Serenade, Four Temperaments* (George Balanchine), *Manifestations* (Arthur Mitchell) and *Troy Games* (Robert North). The performance went alright. It was funny though, as soon as the curtain went up I felt very uncomfortable. I guess, to me, knowing that they do not see many Blacks here I felt more as though they were examining our body(ies) to see if we were the same.

Teaching Ballet in Academia

My career path shifted in 1995 when Dr. Fichter invited me to join the faculty of the Dance Department at FSU. Her mentorship prepared me for the new challenges I encountered with dance pedagogy in academia. Generally speaking, training a dancer at any age, or at any stage of their development, is a very personal process, because the teacher is engaging with the student's physical instrument—their body. Moreover, dealing with young adults at the university level may present challenges that are different from those at a private studio or a school attached to a professional ballet company. Most university dance departments offer non-major classes for students who may be participating in their first dance class experience. These older students are well along in their anatomical development, which makes it more difficult for them to adapt their bodies to the demands of classical ballet technique. At the same time, these students are adults engaged in academic study and often bring questions and insights into ballet classes that can be compelling and inspiring. At many universities, there are also ballet classes for students who have been training since childhood. The teacher's approach must be flexible enough to address the capabilities and goals of these different students.

The most important influences on my approach to teaching was my prior training in Pilates and the GYROTONIC EXPANSION SYSTEM®. These somatic methodologies enabled me to understand my physical instrument, its strengths and weaknesses, and gain a more extensive technical command of my body. My instructor in Pilates was Kathleen S. Grant, an African-American ballet dancer whose career had ended due to a debilitating knee injury. Grant rehabilitated her knee by training with Joseph Pilates and she became one of his earliest and most revered teachers. In Gyrotonic, I studied under and worked with its co-founders, Juliu Horvath, a former dancer with the Romanian National Ballet Company, and Hilary Cartwright, former soloist with the Royal Ballet in England. I continued to study these methodologies and eventually focused on Gyrotonic, where I became an instructor and among the first group of Specialized Master Trainers certified to conduct Teacher Training.

Representation, Advocacy, and Mentorship

I have continued to refine my pedagogical approach over the years. Drawing on my training in Gyrotonic, I prioritize being aware of each student's unique physique and physical ability. This is especially true when teaching young adults whose prior experiences with ballet may range from none to several years of training. From this baseline, I teach students to understand the importance of anatomical alignment in all of their work. I make sure that they understand how to apply basic concepts like abdominal engagement in ways that enable them to achieve anatomical connectivity. I strive to instill in students a sense of freedom of movement that they can apply as they broaden their technical skill-sets in regard to exercises at the barre, at center-floor, and during larger combinations of movement that fully explore ballet's rich movement vocabulary. Each student is taught to sense their body in all of these situations and in relationship to an understanding of their flexibility, strength, and musculature. In these ways, I am teaching students how to *know their bodies*. Moreover, I stress the idea that the final goal of developing expertise in ballet technique is to synthesize physical capability with artistic expression.

I also am aware of the value of teaching ballet in university settings because these students could be future audience members and supporters of ballet and other art forms. Additionally, the university students I teach, from beginners to advanced dancers, may go on to have children and make a decision to place them in ballet classes, based on their experiences in my classes. This reinforces my teaching philosophy: exposure to sound, anatomically safe, and inspiring pedagogies may be essential to the future sustainability of ballet.

My path to becoming a professor has revealed that there is important work to be done within the studios and classrooms of academic institutions. I believe in maintaining the highest level of instruction in classical ballet technique classes, while attending to the specific needs of a spectrum of students. I am particularly aware of underrepresented students whose experiences in predominately white institutions have sometimes included the detrimental impact of specious notions of Black inferiority. I have grown to understand that *developing the whole person* necessitates addressing the denigrating approaches a student might have endured during their prior dance experiences.

As a faculty member at FSU, I realize the impact that my presence and my caring has had on these students. For example, early in my career, an African-American graduate student approached me after a ballet class and said, "I am so glad you are here, because now I see how ballet can look on my body." Her poignant statement revealed that she had been receiving signals that her body—like my own—was not considered to be an ideal body for a classical ballet dancer. With me as a role model, she could see that the prior comments about her physical shortcomings were misguided. Within my class, she was free to explore her full potentialities, and free to discard those negative insinuations. In view of situations like hers, I realized that my role as a teacher could include being an advocate for students who might, otherwise, not have one. It has also driven me to include underrepresented students when setting choreography—restaged and original classical, neo-classical, and contemporary works—to provide them with opportunities to perform works they may never have been given the opportunity to perform before.

In retrospect, I can see how my experiences with DTH influence my university teaching in numerous ways. Similar to how DTH's senior dancers were role models and mentors for the younger dancers, I now see myself as a mentor and guide for university students. I am a role model as well as a teacher who is in a position to help Black dancers envision futures that are full of possibilities. I know these dancers can succeed in an artistic field that few have been encouraged to enter. My greatest joy is seeing students realize their dreams, and this is what fuels my determination and dedication.

My ongoing journey in ballet performance, pedagogy, and cultural change has taken me around the world. I have danced in major theaters and opera houses, as well as in studios and lecture halls. The lessons I have learned along the way have taught me that classical ballet is a bodily discipline that is meant to be shared with a diverse range of people. It is capable of shaping and strengthening the human body to become an instrument that explores the full range of our potential. When ballet is approached as a path to cultivating and enriching the life of an individual, it becomes an exceptionally powerful tool for developing the artist-citizen. I have witnessed these transformations for almost three decades at FSU, and look forward to welcoming future artist-citizens into the studio.

Notes

1 "Delores Browne," *Memoirs of Blacks in Ballet*, www.mobballet.org/Tree/phone/browne.html.
2 Renee D. Turner, "Dance Theatre of Harlem Wows Russia: The New York troupe wins critical acclaim in the land where classical ballet was perfected," *Ebony Magazine* 43, no. 11 (September 1988): 38–42.

7

DEAR BALLET TEACHERS, LET'S TALK ABOUT RACE

Ilana Goldman and Paige Cunningham

We are two white professors of ballet technique in higher education writing for ballet educators in both academia and dance studio settings, who are deep in a process of reconsidering white dominant attitudes, affects, expectations, and aesthetics in the ballet class environment. In tackling the subject, we draw upon anti-racism educator, artist, and poet Tema Okun's article, "White Supremacy Culture,"[1] making ties between white supremacy cultural characteristics and classical ballet. In this context, we (and Okun) are not referencing the characteristics of extremist, hate groups, but rather "the dominant, unquestioned standards of behavior and ways of functioning embodied by the vast majority of institutions in the United States."[2] These cultural practices are normalized, making them hard to see.[3] Our premise is that characteristics of white supremacy culture manifest in the ballet studio through Eurocentric ideals, practices, aesthetics, and a privileging of the white body.

We will start with one characteristic identified by Okun: "Worship of the Written Word." We see a parallel between the unrelenting devotion of ballet instructors toward codified ballet techniques and the way that whiteness often worships the written word (particularly in the context of academic spaces), with little acceptance of physical or oral ways of knowing. Ballet practitioners often say "classical" ballet technique to signify the highest quality. How does the term "classical," when applied to ballet technique, create "superiority to a very limited body of knowing and being, consigning other ways of knowing and being as 'less than' while rarely recognizing other cultural and community-based ways of knowing"[4] ballet? Specific codified ballet techniques are seen as "the law" with little acknowledgement of alternative experiences. We posit that ballet vocabulary (its written word) does not have to be exclusionary, but an enforcement of rigid cultural traditions within codified systems can be. Contemporary ballet educators and choreographers like Alonzo King utilize ballet vocabulary without adhering to an orthodox interpretation of that language, incorporating diverse and progressive cultural influences.

We imagine a transition away from a rigid interpretation of ballet, toward an embrace of approaches filled with care for our students AND a rigorous class experience that challenges dancers in healthy ways. These approaches, which are part of a broader movement of more inclusive ballet pedagogy, come from our teaching and students, as well as our experiences as students in ballet, contemporary, and modern dance classes, and as dancers in professional modern, ballet, and contemporary ballet companies. We present ballet pedagogy as a constant work in process, acknowledging that not every faculty member feels as though they are in a position of power to implement practices that relinquish their authority in the classroom because of rank, race, or gender. To borrow from ballet scholar Theresa Ruth Howard and her *12 Steps to Ballet's Cultural Recovery*, we "admit that we don't have the answers and commit to trying to find them."[5]

We focus on five of Okun's characteristics, grouping them according to how they may show up in a ballet studio. We offer strategies/invitations for ways to counteract these characteristics along with more specific examples/suggestions. The strategies and examples we provide are merely guideposts and not comprehensive; they are meant to spark reflection as we seek new models, unlearn unhealthy habits, and ensure that we are creating an optimal learning environment for the 21st century with the students who are in the room with us. As part of an ongoing practice, these shifts are not meant to be implemented all at once, but progressively. As dance educator/scholar Nyama McCarthy-Brown states, "Changing your classroom culture is similar to changing your diet. It cannot be done in one day and would be overwhelming to do even in one school year."[6]

I Perfectionism

Okun: "The conditioned belief and attitude that we can be perfect based on a standard or set of rules that we did not create and that we are led to believe will prove our value."[7]

Studio Translation: The teacher holds students to a standard of an "ideal ballet body" without consideration for a diversity of bodies, and only points out the student's mistake with no tangible steps given to improve upon said mistake and no appreciation for the student's strengths.

The ballet teacher overcompensates to be perfect herself. In our experiences, this can often play out as the "nice, white" ballet teacher, giving up on challenging students the moment discomfort or stress arises and leaving the burden of holding students accountable to BIPOC teachers.

Strategies/Invitations:

(A) Acknowledge student excellence by developing a class ritual: snapping, clapping, or some other gesture (practices often used in African diasporic cultures).
(B) Normalize mistakes:
   1. Remind students to view their classwork as a laboratory. Can a challenging petit allegro/small jumps cultivate what Modupe Akinola calls the "stress mindset?"[8] Avoid backing down from a difficult combination because students are instantly unsuccessful. Be both empathetic and help students understand that "Struggle helps us learn better. There is a sweet spot between what you already know well and what seems impossible. That middle zone is productive struggle."[9]
   2. "Be vulnerable when encouraging students to take risks. Bring personal experiences into the classroom. Take the first risk."[10]
   3. Ask students to journal about what "taking a risk" in ballet class means to them and to reflect on risk-taking at the end of each week. Ask students to determine one risk they will take for a particular combination.
   4. At the end of class, invite students to name one high and one low moment from class.

(C) Separate the student from the mistake. When offering feedback, start with what the student did well, and follow through with tactical steps for improvement.[11] For example, "You took a real risk in that pirouette/turn. What happens if you commit to a straight back leg on that preparation and push off the back foot a little more?" Have students immediately try whatever approach you are offering. If successful, ask them to try again so that they are encoding successful completion of the pirouette and experiencing what success looks like in this instance. Practice does not make perfect. Practice makes permanent.[12]

(D) Discourage judgment:
   1. Face students away from the mirror, focusing on movement sensation over image.
   2. Cue what students should do or feel, not what their bodies look like: "Lift the front of your pelvis" instead of "Your bottom is sticking out."
   3. Celebrate incremental victories and recognize the skills students bring to class.
   4. Begin with a body scan, set an intention, and whisper it aloud. A reflective start mollifies the desire to press forward hastily, bringing attention inward and reducing external comparisons.

(E) Do not equate raising difficult issues (like addressing where a student is struggling) with being impolite. Notice when we, as instructors, are complaining about a student with our colleagues without ever being clear and direct in our concerns with the student. Employ a "radical candor" approach: "feedback that's both kind and clear, specific and sincere."[13]

II Denial & Defensiveness

Okun: "The habit of denying and defending against the ways in which white supremacy and racism are produced and our individual or collective participation in that production."[14]

Studio Translation: The ballet instructor does not acknowledge any of the inequities within, or harm caused from, ballet's traditions, aesthetics, or teaching practices.

Strategies/Invitations:

(A) Acknowledge the harm that comes from upholding hurtful traditions and aesthetics within ballet, and your role in those systems. Reimagine ballet's potential. For instance, sit in a circle with students to discuss both historical and current discriminatory practices in ballet and ways to create change. If students feel comfortable, share personal stories in small groups.
(B) Deliver the content of your class and engage with students in a way that aligns with your intent to uphold equitable and antiracist practices. "[P]rofessors may attempt to deconstruct traditional biases while sharing that information through body posture, tone, word choice, and so on that perpetuate those very hierarchies and biases they are critiquing."[15]

1. Apologize when you inflict a microaggression and openly talk about it.
2. Ask someone you trust to observe your class, giving feedback specific to the way your classroom choices may unintentionally affect students.
3. Are the policies within your ballet syllabus "supportive and not punitive or deficit thinking?"[16] Invite students to wear tights and shoes that match their skin tone. Allow students to wear hairstyles other than a bun as long as it is secured.
4. Provide time at the end of class for students to show off their skills, improvise, and cheer each other on (a common practice in African diasporic dance forms).
5. Create opportunities for students to speak while they are dancing, literally and figuratively nurturing their voices, and dispelling the stereotype of the silent, powerless dancer.

III Paternalism

Okun: "Those holding power control decision-making" and there is "little, if any, value around sharing power."[17]

Studio Translation: Students have no say in how the ballet course is administered.

Strategies/Invitations:

(A) Cultivate student leadership by including power-sharing in your course.[18] "Professors don't have to be dictators. One can teach without reinforcing existing systems of domination... Making the classroom a democratic setting where everyone feels a responsibility to contribute is a central goal of transformative pedagogy:"[19]

1. Review the syllabus and invite students to add a learning objective of their own.
2. Co-author community agreements with students.[20]
3. On the first day of the semester, form small groups to discuss the kind of culture the class hopes to engender. List five "rules for engagement" amongst students and the instructor to uphold this culture.
4. Invite students to state their goals for the semester, how the course can support those goals, what they think your expectations of them should be, and their expectations of you (giving personalized feedback, ending on time, etc.).
5. Divide students into pairs to watch each other and share feedback.
6. Ask a student to lead a combination in class, building leadership and teaching skills while promoting deeper understanding of class content.

(B) Solicit feedback on your teaching. One approach is to distribute an anonymous, mid-semester survey where students describe which strategies are facilitating and/or impeding learning thus far, and what they would change for the remaining semester, keeping in mind that students also bring biases into the classroom.

(C) Recognize power hierarchies among faculty and the implications of power sharing with students. The "nice, white" ballet teacher approach does not always "balance inclusive and equitable efforts for students with inclusive and equitable efforts for instructors."[21] Faculty from marginalized groups may not have the same privilege to yield control and are more apt to have their legitimacy questioned.

IV Individualism

Okun: "Our cultural story that we make it on our own, without help, while pulling ourselves up by our own bootstraps, is a toxic denial of our essential interdependence and the reality that we are all in this, literally, together."[22]

Studio Translation: Ballet class is a place for individual practice; no sense of community is fostered and student support of one another is lacking.
Strategies/Invitations:

(A) Create opportunities for students to connect:
  1. Encourage students to make eye contact while performing combinations facing each other.
  2. Invite students to come to the front of the studio to watch their peers perform a combination, acknowledging the efforts of the group.
  3. Devise opportunities for students to share something personal with each other. For example, when dividing students into two groups for center combinations, tell them to find a partner and share their middle name, favorite song, or fun personal fact. Then tell them, "Whichever is alphabetized first is in the first group."[23]
(B) Encourage ensemble building by choreographing shifting spatial formations for combinations so that students must stay aware of each other.[24] Or, create a showcase for sharing class choreography at the end of the semester.[25]
(C) Experiment with check-ins and check-outs to acknowledge our collective humanity. During roll call, ask students to share a word to describe how they are feeling, and then share another word at the end of class.[26]

V Either/Or & The Binary

Okun: "Reduces the complexity of life and the nuance of our relationships with each other and all living things into either/or, yes or no, right or wrong in ways that reinforce toxic power."[27]

Studio Translation: The instructor believes that a student's execution is good/bad or right/wrong.
Strategies/Invitations:

(A) Accept that there are many ways to get to the same goal:
  1. Discuss that certain steps can be done differently depending on the dance form or style. For one class, try pirouettes

preparing with a straight back leg and straight front arm, and another day turn with a rounded front arm and two bent knees in fourth position.
2. Encourage students to create their own cues that will facilitate the incorporation of feedback.
3. Ask students to share what they were thinking about when they executed a certain movement well.

(B) Decenter ballet learning objectives that focus solely on the good/bad binary. For instance, assessment can be approached with learning-progression language like "beginning, developing, applying, and extending."[28] Create space for students to see their ballet practice as a continual process that is always in progress.

(C) Acknowledge that ballet is a cultural form.[29] Recognize that you have a teaching point of view that has been shaped by your teachers and the dance traditions that you grew up in and this affects how you teach, what you teach, and the feedback that you give:
1. At the beginning of the semester, give students a brief explanation of your personal ballet lineage. Were you trained solely in the Cecchetti method for example? Are you assuming your students know what that is?
2. Discuss the values, aesthetics, and practices of ballet that you and the students would like to see change, especially those upholding racist ideologies, and what you would like to maintain.
3. Provide an instructor's statement in the syllabus that discusses your priorities within ballet technique.

(D) Recognize that students are not blank slates. Applaud students for making bold choices and provide moments during class for improvisation.

(E) Learn about your students' cultures. For example, when working with recorded music, ask students to send you music that they listened to as children and create a class playlist. Ask them to share something about the music that was contributed.

(F) Interrogate your ballet biases by cultivating an environment that foregrounds research and inquiry:
1. For courses with learning management systems, like Canvas or BlackBoard, include an "In Ballet News" column where

students can contribute articles, podcasts, videos, and recommend books about current ballet research.
2. Create an information sharing resource for ballet faculty at your institution.

(G) Rethink representation. What canon, whose canon, are you representing? Who is representing ballet excellence in your visual examples?[30]

Conclusion

In closing, we offer one last strategy: a contemporary ballet approach can be another way to demonstrate commitment to progressing the form. Quick shifts of weight, off-center balance, and use of improvisation may be ways to awaken curiosity and encourage process over product. By including contemporary ballet methods in a ballet class, instructors subvert a strict adherence to codified ballet systems as they seek to evolve beyond classical ballet, valuing aspects of its methodology while also reimagining the form. If including contemporary ballet vocabulary in a ballet class is outside an instructor's wheelhouse, viewing works by contemporary ballet choreographers who continue to revere the form while simultaneously disrupting its archaic practices and aesthetics may be a valuable alternative. In transitioning away from rigid interpretations of ballet instruction, we open spaces to jettison racist or discriminatory practices and values within the training. When students see their instructor embracing an evolution of ballet and not strictly following an inflexible dogma, they may see the ballet studio as a more inviting and accepting place.

Notes

1 Tema Okun, *White Supremacy Culture*, https://www.whitesupremacyculture.info/.
2 "Glossary," *Racial Equity Tools*, https://www.racialequitytools.org/glossary.
3 "Glossary," *Racial Equity Tools*, https://www.racialequitytools.org/glossary.
4 Tema Okun, "White Supremacy Culture – Still Here," https://www.dismantlingracism.org/uploads/4/3/5/7/43579015/white_supremacy_culture_-_still_here.pdf
5 "Episode 19: Theresa Ruth Howard Calls the Ballet World to Action for Diversity," *Margaret Mullin*, June 10, 2020, http://www.margaretmullin.com/episodes/episode19-theresa-ruth-howard.

6 Nyama McCarthy-Brown, "The Need for Culturally Relevant Dance Education," *Journal of Dance Education* 9, no. 4 (October 2009): 124.
7 Tema Okun, "Perfectionism," *White Supremacy Culture*, https://www.whitesupremacyculture.info/one-right-way.html.
8 "#373. Optimizing Your Stress | Modupe Akinola," *Ten Percent Happier*, August 25, 2021, https://www.tenpercent.com/podcast-episode/modupe-akinola-373.
9 "How to Make Struggles More Productive," *Coaching for Leaders*. February 28, 2022. https://coachingforleaders.com/podcast/make-struggles-more-productive-sarah-stein-greenberg/.
10 bells hooks, *Teaching to Transgress: Education as the Practice of Freedom* (New York: Routledge, 1994), 21.
11 "SciDance 7: Self Talk and Goal Setting with Paul Doyle" *Backtracks.Fm*, https://backtracks.fm/discover/s/scidance/ca9beb96cf372a05/e/7-self-talk-and-goal-setting-with-paul-doyle/d49406af21e7e94e.
12 Doug Lemov, Erica Woolway, and Katie Yezzi, *Practice Perfect* (San Francisco: Jossey-Bass, 2012).
13 Kim Scott, *Radical Candor* (New York: St. Martin's Press, 2017).
14 Tema Okun, "Denial & Defensiveness," *White Supremacy Culture*," https://www.whitesupremacyculture.info/denial–defensiveness.html.
15 hooks, *Teaching to Transgress*, 141.
16 Hossna Sadat Ahadi and Luis A. Guerrero, "Decolonizing Your Syllabus, an Anti-Racist Guide for Your College," *Academic Senate for California Community Colleges*, November 2020. https://www.asccc.org/content/decolonizing-your-syllabus-anti-racist-guide-your-college.
17 Tema Okun, "One Right Way: Paternalism," *White Supremacy Culture*, https://www.whitesupremacyculture.info/one-right-way.html.
18 Sydney Mosley, "Dismantling White Supremacy within Dance Institutions – A Response," *The Dance Union* (June 15, 2020). https://www.youtube.com/watch?v=NbziQLsv2DA&t=4676s.
19 hooks, *Teaching to Transgress*, 18 and 39.
20 "#NotRacistOSU Archives," *Koritha Mitchell*, http://www.korithamitchell.com/category/notracistosu/.
21 "231. Include Instructors in Inclusive Instruction," *Tea for Teaching*, https://teaforteaching.com/231-include-instructors-in-inclusive-instruction/.
22 Tema Okun, "Individualism," *White Supremacy Culture*, https://www.whitesupremacyculture.info/individualism.html.
23 From Brenna Monroe-Cook's technique class.
24 From Carolyn Adams's technique class.
25 Attributed to The Dance Center of Columbia College Chicago.
26 From Sophie Lehman, Florida State University undergraduate.
27 Tena Okun, "Either/Or & The Binary," *White Supremacy Culture*, https://www.whitesupremacyculture.info/eitheror–the-binary.html.
28 Jennifer Gonzalez, "Introducing the HyperRubric: A Tool That Takes Learning to the Next Level," *Cult of Pedagogy*, August 22, 2021, https://www.cultofpedagogy.com/hyperrubric/.
29 Mosley, "Dismantling White Supremacy."
30 *First Day First Image*, https://www.firstdayfirstimage.com.

8
MAKING SPACE
Inclusive and Equitable Teaching Practices for Ballet in Higher Education

Alana Isiguen

My pedagogical approach to ballet is rooted in different embodied knowledges. I am Filipina, Cuban, and Russian and began dancing as a child with my family in the kitchen, feeling that joy of moving my body to the rhythm. When my parents sensed this joy within me, I was fortunate they had the resources to enroll me in classes at a local studio. I felt at home in jazz and tap classes. I was often the only brown girl at the ballet conservatory, yet I excelled at Balanchine's repertory, connecting to the embedded Africanist aesthetics[1] and jazz elements: the polyrhythmic 5s over 4s, use of the pelvis, coolness, and sense of play. I especially relished the high-affect juxtaposition, contrariety of movement qualities, changing on a dime from smooth to sharp, melting to suddenly explode. Alongside ballet, I continued to study jazz with my African American male teacher. However, as I moved through different schools and institutions, I observed how ballet and modern were prioritized over dances of the African diaspora. This hierarchy, meaning valuing certain appearances, backgrounds, and demeanors over others, is something I aim to challenge in my own teaching.

Ballet has a reputation for being strict, classist, elitist, and white. This is visible in the professional ballet world as well as in pop culture. These references influence, and are influenced by, the teaching and learning of ballet. Some examples include ballet instructors who are often associated with authoritarian methods, and students of ballet

DOI: 10.4324/9781003283065-11

who are associated with a specific thin body type. While there have been inklings of change, those identifiers mostly remain. I feel fortunate to have had teachers who challenged these ideas and provided examples of different paths to shaping transformative, thought-provoking experiences in the studio.

As a teenager, I worked one-on-one with a teacher to unravel habitual patterns created by forcing my structure into ballet shapes for years. She did not identify as "a somatic practitioner" yet her beliefs and teaching style aligned with the idea that every individual's body is unique. She valued understanding sensations from a student's perspective, encouraging me to listen to my inner dialogue about body pathways. To have this experience with someone who fostered mutual respect was incredibly influential for me as a student and young teacher.

In my undergraduate studies, I began to understand the strength of letting go, both muscularly through understanding my own anatomy, and mentally, in terms of relinquishing preconceived notions. It was my first introduction to the field of somatics, and though it was in a modern dance class, my teacher supported us to find connections to other forms of movement and personal experiences. He taught with humanity, care, and a sense of humor. With his guidance, I was able to rehabilitate a severe back injury safely and holistically. In addition, he was my first model of a dancing Filipinx body similar to mine, a powerful and formative experience in my life.

For the first time out of an institution, I continued to build the strength to trust myself, to take risks, and to believe in my own embodied knowledge. I studied with a teacher who put students in the driver's seat. We had clear autonomy. She challenged ballet's traditions in many ways, from designing distinct class sequences to constructing her studio without mirrors. She pushed us to explore a meaning behind the steps, as she examined and questioned standards or singular ways to come to a conclusion. With her poetic and highly articulate guiding words, I drew connections between the studio and the world beyond.

Each experience, in dance and in life, influences how I embody movement and ultimately how I teach. I am the same human in a ballet class as I am in an underground club; the same teacher who coaches professional dancers refining subtle nuances and also helps stroke patients learn how to walk again. As a performer, educator, and choreographer, I have culled together experiences to inform my practice;

this makes for a broader perspective and more ways to connect with fellow dancers, students, and colleagues.

My experiences will inevitably be different from my students'. What began as a way to aid students in preventing injuries and undoing inefficient movement patterns in ballet, prompted deeper research into somatics. What I have found to be powerful and timely in the use of a somatic approach within a ballet class is the agency that emerges in students through the process of self-sensing. By listening to their bodies, students develop an internal dialogue that leads to self-knowledge and trust that goes beyond understanding their anatomy and biomechanics. The ability to express themselves in unique and individual ways strengthens with the practice of self-trust.

Inclusivity, equity, integrity, and humanity are vital aspects of my teaching, but I do not label my class "somatic ballet" or "antiracist ballet." Such a label would presume that ballet taught somatically is an exception or that racism is a fundamental part of ballet. Instead, my teaching foregrounds self-examination, investigation, and intentional, educated actions that promote equity. When speaking about connecting to students and building understandings of deep culture, educational specialist Dr. Sandra Duval writes, "The diversity of our students challenges us to be honest about this 'othering'; understand the impact of *our own cultural understandings on our teaching*; and explore the complexities of the cultures, histories, and experiences of our students."[2] As a teacher, I must start with my own self-examination because my identity, experiences, and knowledge influence how, what, and why I teach. I do not make assumptions or "should" statements about students: each student has a unique background with different experiences and understandings. Contrary to historical and authoritative styles of teaching ballet, I do not believe students are empty vessels to be filled, that they are only bad habits to undo, or bodies to be broken down and built back up again. Each student brings different information and associations that make for a richer classroom environment for all.

Many cultural norms in higher education—professionalism, perfectionism, and competition—also historically underline ballet training. When speaking about antiracist pedagogy, Dr. Rachel Stauffer points out that these cultural norms reinforce cycles that disproportionately advantage white students in educational settings. She goes on to note that students who have had more access to elite educational experiences are privileged, due to concepts that are implicit in these situations.³ Dismantling these cycles is essential to teaching in a way that is conducive to learning. In a ballet class, I do this in different ways; some are more visible than others, yet all have the intention of creating space for each student to be seen and for each unique experience to be recognized as valid and useful information.

As a teacher, I build an environment that values community over competition: students learn from me, from one another, and from themselves. Having the space to build trust in this idea of *learning in the round* allows the reciprocal 'give and take' of teaching and learning to exist. I reconfigure the space, literally and figuratively, aiming for an environment that is open, welcoming, and supportive. I often change facings and have students observe from non-traditional "fronts." Turning away from the mirror not only encourages kinesthetic sensing, non-reliance on the mirror, and less judgement based on image, but also a chance to question: Who is this for? What is the intention? How am I connecting to the music, to the space and those around me?

I utilize partner work not only for tactile and kinesthetic feedback, but also for community building and interpersonal learning. When guiding students through hands-on cuing, I encourage them to discuss ideas with classmates, listen to others' thought-processes and consider their own. Depending on each person's unique learning style and experiences, what may click for some, may not for others. Therefore, I direct students to search out other sources of information instead of relying only on the instructor's feedback. This shakes up the traditionally silent, strict, and solitary study that is often found in ballet classes.

To support this non-traditional class environment, I attend to the volume in the room oscillating between a focused calm and boisterous play. It is important to promote students' motor learning, self-study, and musicality by not narrating every moment and not speaking over the musician. In other instances, however, I find it necessary to bring in ideas from jazz and social dance, such as verbal affirmations and partner dialogue to show support and build a sense of community. Pointing out moments to tap into the joy of movement or the groove of the rhythm, as well as creating levity using my own sense of humor softens challenging moments. I welcome laughter and find it, as well as partner- and group-dialogue, to be helpful in breaking from the intensely serious, and at times, negative self-talk within students. This in turn creates a more supportive environment overall.

From written student reflections and one-on-one meetings, I hear from many students that they are trying to heal their relationships with ballet. They have a love-hate relationship, explaining it is something they love to do yet were told they were never good enough, their bodies weren't the ideal shape, or they weren't the right look. They felt they didn't have a place in the room. Students question how to continue practicing the form and how to let go of deeply rooted beliefs they are confronted with each time they walk into class.

I strive to make space for students to come as they are, to ask questions without feeling like they should already know the answer, or they will be judged for not meeting an opaque expectation. I demonstrate with my own body to challenge assumptions of what ballet "should" look like, as I am muscular, brown, and without 180 degrees of turnout. I explicitly state the studio is a laboratory for experimenting and exploring different choices, not for repetitive perfection. I ask for students' ideas and thoughts, offer various options to workshop with one another, and explain that we will all connect to movement differently. Each day will be different. Exploring these various approaches helps to fill dancers' experiential toolboxes with richer insights and information.

To expose students to varying perspectives, I teach excerpts of repertory from choreographers who push against what ballet has been and who it is for, and I actively seek out choreographers who are women and people of color. Focusing on process rather than product, my intention for the students is not that they perfect a style to perform or showcase, but rather to explore specific movement languages, to experience known vocabulary in new ways, and to discover different voices within themselves. Students begin to draw their own connections between dance and what is relevant to them.

Learning students' reasonings behind pursuing ballet in a college setting has supported both my pedagogical approach and the students' learning. Through written self-reflections, I encourage students to question what is interesting to them and what they would like to investigate further. By directing students to think about their intentions, I am able to establish some common ground. I utilize feedback in class not only to help with technical execution, but also to aid them in making connections to different styles of dance, to their other studies in math or social work, and to their interests beyond dance. As students continue to study dance, their abilities to notice details are heightened. They gain a lens that is applicable outside the studio, strengthening their kinesthetic knowledge and broadening their understanding of cultural diversity.

Considering somatic concepts within ballet

The writings of Brodie and Lobel have been helpful in distilling overarching somatic concepts to apply into a dance practice, specifically the use of breath, self-sensing, connection, initiation, and intention.[4] An aspect of somatics that is often overlooked is the fact that different populations require varied approaches. When integrating somatic concepts into ballet pedagogy, a common intention is to find neutral alignment of the spine and pelvis to aid efficient movement. I explain to students that each individual body will have a different "neutral" just like each body's 5th position will be different. Everyone will not feel "ease and efficiency" the same way. We do not all have the same experiences or associations. Glenna Batson writes, "[S]omatic studies need to be viewed through the lens of a multi-cultural world. Personal body practices are grounded in specific sociological, cultural, and class contexts that are neither universal nor 'neutral.'"[5]

Turning up the volume on first-person kinesthesia promotes autonomy, and it is also a form of self-care. Self-sensing is a learning tool that shifts power from instructors to students. Giving students the opportunity to reflect on what's happening inside their own bodies, and to choose the path forward, is quite radical in ballet. I ask students to "make choices" and "modify what you need," with the aim to amplify students' inner voice. I remind classes "wherever you are today, meet yourself there: what are your intentions for the rest of class?" Some will apply this to exploration of personal artistry, dynamic qualities and musicality. Others will attend to their wellness and self-care, taking note of injuries, their state of mind, and how much they need to push in this moment.

Concepts like time-taking (meaning taking the time to move slowly and to listen to our bodies), and decision-making (meaning students come forward to offer their thoughts), will be acknowledged differently with different populations. Students who already feel out of place or that ballet is not for them, often do not feel comfortable speaking up, trying new things, or taking risks for fear of embarrassment or punishment.

Students who have been trained in schools where strict discipline equates to ignoring injuries or being criticized for resting, may find that self-care feels odd, uncomfortable, or not rigorous enough. When I ask students to take risks, be it standing on one leg or expressing their thoughts aloud, the environment created must allow them to do so.

Overlaps

An important connection that I have made in my research about teaching ballet comes from, simultaneously, teaching jazz. In *Rooted Jazz Dance*, authors discuss the importance of always identifying Africanist aesthetics, with their cultural sociopolitical, and historical contexts, as the primary source for jazz dance: "To truly see jazz, the entire continuum from its roots to today, is to see racism in America."[6] Equity work starts with identifying and naming things, especially those voices historically left out. In teaching and practicing ballet, I confront the inequities of where this form came from and who it is intended for, both performer and audience. I do not teach the form to uphold an unattainable standard of historical value. Rather, I continue to teach ballet to explore the joy in intricate and powerful movements, the play of melody and rhythms, and the creativity in artistic expression. I teach from my place of lived experience, bringing in overlaps from jazz, modern, and social dance forms.

While the following excerpt refers to jazz, I find it simultaneously applies to ballet:

> Investing in improvisation and individuality opens the door to holistic creative processes and classroom environments, and uniting music, rhythm, and movement together inspires a potentially transcendent experience.[7]

Ballet class can be a place for creative process that is relevant. As a teacher, it is imperative to understand the historical context of ballet and where it is going, but also allow space for the unrecognizable and the yet-to-be. Utilizing resources such as live streams across the globe, current publications, embodied research, and dialogue with colleagues in various fields, helps me create an environment where students feel empowered to find their own voice. They are able to improvise on set material to find new ways of moving, collaborate with our live musician, and challenge what has been the "standard." Throughout this supportive space, I have observed students grow in their ability to take risks and express themselves.

Last thoughts

I recognize that classes, courses, departments, and institutions have specific missions and goals. Many BFA programs aspire to create dancers ready to enter a professional world that still carries traditions of hierarchy, elitism, and perfectionism. It is a system that is slow to change because of funding, the role of performing arts in society, structural racism, and many other factors. Students, however, are the next generation of performers, directors, choreographers, and arts patrons. Therefore, I encourage students to question, to seek out what is not visible, and to trust their voices. Even the tiniest seeds of ideas about different environments and possibilities provide paths towards ballet spaces that are shifting and relevant. As I tell my students, change is a continuous process, and we won't know the possibilities until we try exploring something different.

Notes

1 Brenda Dixon Gottschild, "Stripping the emperor: the Africanist presence in American concert dance," *Looking out: perspectives on dance and criticism in a multicultural world* (New York: Schirmer Books, 1995).
2 Sandra Duval, "Antiracist Practices: Strengthening Students' Sense of Self to Promote Hope and Confidence for Student Success," *Teachers as Allies: Transformative Practices for Teaching DREAMers and Undocumented Students* (New York: Teachers College Press, 2018), 52. Emphasis added.
3 Rachel Stauffer, "Creating an Antiracist Pedagogy of the Oppressed," *Slavic and East European Journal* 64, no. 4 (Winter 2020): 597.
4 Julie A. Brodie and Elin E. Lobel, *Dance and Somatics: Mind Body Principles of Teaching and Performance* (Jefferson: McFarland & Company, Inc, 2012).
5 Glenna Batson, *Somatics Studies and Dance*. IADMS Resource Paper, 2009.
6 Lindsay Guarino, Carlos R.A. Jones, and Wendy Oliver, "Introduction," *Rooted Jazz Dance: Africanist aesthetics and equity in the twenty-first century* (Gainesville: University Press of Florida, 2022), 5.
7 Guarino et al., *Rooted Jazz Dance*, 6.

9
DISMANTLING ANTI-BLACKNESS IN BALLET

Pedagogies of Freedom

Maurya Kerr

As educator, author, and speaker Catrice Jackson wrote in 2020, "Becoming anti-racist is a marathon. Don't expect to be coddled; in fact expect to be unnerved. If you don't have an anti-racism plan, you plan to be racist."[1] Her words exhort us to be intimately involved in antiracist praxis, not just theory.[2] Instead of optical allyship or "wokespeak" utterances of #BlackLivesMatter, we must each personally ask ourselves, *what am I doing to actualize a reality where Black lives actually do matter?* Because for 500+ years Black lives have never mattered in America, despite our nation's willful historical amnesia. In the words of writer Ta-Nehisi Coates, "In America, it is traditional to destroy the black body—it is heritage."[3]

Just as we diligently, often from childhood, train to become dancers, we must likewise diligently train to become anti-racist, to uncolonize our minds and spheres of influence. (A note that I am deliberately using "uncolonization"[4] in place of "decolonization" because the latter literally means the ceding and rematriation of stolen land back to its Indigenous peoples. Decolonization is not metaphorical.)[5] A lifetime indoctrinated in the calculated structures of white supremacy will not be undone by reading an article or a book or accepting a few Black students into your dance program.[6] Because racism is so purposeful and conscious, so must our responses be to destroy it. Because racism is an exhaustive, bodily, entrenched praxis, so must anti-racism be a radical, experiential, transformative enactment. We must acknowledge our privileges—thinking something isn't a problem because it's not a problem *to you personally* is a part of privilege— and commit to being anti-racist as an unwavering way of being in the world and within ourselves. As Jackson indicates, that journey will be unnerving as we discover the ways in which we have advanced white supremacy—consciously or not, owning that impact outweighs intent— and continue to cause harm.[7] And because few white people voluntarily grapple with their unearned skin advantage, intentionality is requisite to disseminate, process, and activate what is, for many, such foreign and disquieting information. Author Ibram X. Kendi teaches that those who insist they're "not racist" are hiding behind a fictional neutrality because there is no neutrality in the battle against racism: "The opposite of 'racist' isn't 'not racist.' It is 'anti-racist'."[8] It's important to really let the magnitude of that either/or paradigm sink in—*either* you're actively fighting racism, *or* you're racist.

Antiracism is not about equality, racial diversity, being nicer, or reading Black authors (particularly only when they write about race). It is about explicitly calling out and dismantling white supremacy, disestablishing hierarchies of violence, and refusing to be complicit in the normalization of whiteness, its privileges, and concomitant marginalization of minoritized bodies. It is about understanding the intersectional oppressions of racism, misogyny, classism, size-ism, heteronormativity, and trans- and homophobia perpetuated in our classrooms. It is about spotting "moves to innocence," or attempts to deny culpability for systems of domination.[9] It is about moving from actor to ally to accomplice,[10] racism enabler to racism confronter, white voyeurism to white traitor.[11] It is about actively critiquing the white supremacy culture embedded in our art form.[12] And we need white people to do that work—whiteness birthed those systems, so it's white people's responsibility to abolish them. In the words of educator Dwayne Reed, "White supremacy won't die until white people see it as a white issue they need to solve rather than a Black issue they need to empathize with."[13]

I believe the body is a site of liberation. I love ballet as a form of movement that has the potential to assist us in that liberation. I also actively denounce ballet's authoritarian pedagogic traditions, its self-proclaimed throne as the foundation of dance, and its contempt of otherness. Scholar Adesola Akinleye writes that the forms of oppression that have been nurtured and clung to in ballet culture collapse "into the way ballet classes and rehearsals are conducted, the way bodies are addressed, valued, starved and dismissed, and the subject matter of the stories mainstream ballet portrays."[14] Where is the space for Blackness in the drown of ballet's whiteness? Room for a young Black student to overpower the dominant imagination and envision themselves as prince or swan? I hold on to bell hooks' belief in "education as the practice of freedom."[15] So if we recognize both education and the body as potential sites of liberation, the promise for some kind of emancipatory embodied learning is revolutionary and boundless. In my own body and artistic practices, I am always trying to "get free"—acknowledging that our individual, subjective liberations are dependent upon our respective, complex amalgams of marginalization and power—and am likewise invested in inviting others of the global majority into that self-research and untethering. Historian Stephanie Camp wrote, "For people... who have experienced oppression through the body, the body becomes an important site not only of suffering but also (and therefore) of resistance, enjoyment, and potentially, transcendence."[16] Can we "get free" and locate transcendence amidst dance practices anchored in white supremacy? Can we discover and then transmit subversive techniques of freedom? Can we help students view themselves, as James Baldwin said, as "living, at the moment, in an enormous province,"[17] and then do the counter-hegemonic work necessary to make that their lived truth?

Bodies are political. We live in a white supremacist, capitalist heteropatriarchy founded on the genocide of Indigenous bodies and the enslavement and forced labor of Black bodies. Because dance deals so intimately with the body, the classroom spaces we cultivate, or neglect to cultivate, are likewise profoundly political. Scholar Rebecca Chaleff writes, "Artistic spaces are activated by the bodies that inhabit them."[18] Inversely, artistic spaces are deadened because of the absence of certain bodies. Marginalized bodies are generally subjected to either hypervisibility or invisibility, or both simultaneously, and the fungibility of Black students, or more bluntly, Black *bodies*, in dance spaces is evident. White supremacy socialization teaches us all how to view, and live in, our bodies, but Black children especially are "taught their bodies."[19] Engaging students within an imagery- and sensation-based pedagogy can arm them with the tools needed to get bigger than their bodies via an imagination-fueled physical vastness, and also bigger than what society has dictated their racialized and gendered selves to be.[20] *Port de bras* means "carriage of the arms," but arms are wings and wings are flight and flight is freedom. Coates writes that the violent praxis of white supremacy is meant, "first and foremost, to deny you and me the right to secure and govern our own bodies."[21] Dance training can no longer collude in the historical destruction of racialized bodies for the purposes of those lives forced into subordination and obedience.[22]

So many of the young, racialized dancers I teach feel, and are, ostracized from ballet. Particularly for those who don't "speak ballet" as a first language, coming into the form, its institutions, and what Judith Butler coins "annihilating norms,"[23] can be terrifying. Number one on the list of scholar Peggy McIntosh's article, "White Privilege: Unpacking the Invisible Knapsack"—which identifies the privileges whiteness confers that are "invisible" precisely because of said privilege—is, "I can if I wish arrange to be in the company of people of my race most of the time."[24] Imagine yourself as the only one of something in a room: the only Black person in a sea of whiteness, the only woman in a room of men, the only queer person in a room of "straight-time." We must become sensitive to how lonely, alienating, and unwelcoming it must be for young dancers from historically disinvested communities to enter rooms of whiteness. And we must empower their entry not just to survive, but to thrive. In her article "Recognizing Systemic Racism in Dance," dance artist Alicia Mullikin writes that "Equality is NOT sufficient to combat systemic racism."[25, 26]

To compound feeling "uncomfortable, exposed, visible, different…"[27] young dancers of the global majority are often told that they, and their bodies, are "unfit," the tacit meaning being *unfit according to colonial aesthetics*. To them I say, *Ballet desperately needs you and your Black selves; it needs your lived experience inside your Black bodies; it needs a multi-cultural, heterogenous expansiveness. You are entitled to claim ballet as your own. In other words: you are a gift to this form; believe in yourself as such.* White saviorism would suggest that white institutions are doing racialized students a favor by accepting them into their programs, but nothing could be less true. As Aboriginal artist and activist Lilla Watson said, "If you have come here to help me, you are wasting your time. But if you have come because your liberation is bound up with mine, then let us work together."[28] *All* of our freedoms are inexorably linked.[29]

In *Citizen: An American Lyric*, Claudia Rankine writes, "How to care for the injured body, / the kind of body that can't hold / the content it is living?"[30] To ensure that you are not bringing racialized students into further injury, further harm, it is necessary to move beyond a mere racial diversity framework toward one of active concern and support regarding their experiences once they have "desegregated" your studio space. And how students are offered, or denied, entrance into ballet programs needs to account for barriers to access, perhaps allowing time for a student to improvise in order to see their potential outside of the circumscribed, exclusive ballet paradigm. Any conversation about talent and meritocracy must also engage with circumstantial privilege.[31] Whiteness and its privileges are inherited—one person's unearned advantages are grievously dependent on another's unearned disadvantages.[32] How is your organization actively acknowledging the fact that Black families in particular have been excluded from building intergenerational wealth?[33] (In 2019 the typical Black household's wealth was $24,100, compared to a typical white household's $188,200.)[34] It's important to remember that some students may not have familial financial support and thus may be working nights and weekends in addition to their full days of training. Perhaps they need empathy around early mornings, an excused day off, or an anonymously given gift certificate for groceries or dancewear.

Primarily white institutions need to ask themselves, both personally and organizationally, *who is missing from this space? And now that I'm implicated in upholding this racial exclusivity, what are my action steps beyond guilt?* Or better expressed by activist Rachel Cargle, "What are the values that have been celebrated and perpetuated that have led to exclusion of Black people?"[35] But as you work towards a more racially equitable space, be careful to not tokenize racialized bodies or use them as "proof." Building a more racially diverse student body is not enough. In his article "21 Signs You or Your Organization May Be the White Moderate Dr. King Warned About," writer Vu Le notes, "You help marginalized people... survive and compete in inequitable systems instead of working with them to dismantle those systems."[36] No matter what you do, there will never be adequate reparations. America's debt to Black and Indigenous people is incommensurable. Thus, antiracism efforts should never be a source of pride,[37] but the most basic form of activism.[38]

I believe our task as educators is to be of service, share knowledge, and lead by example, in and out of the classroom. My hope is that whatever dance practices we engage in with students will lead them towards a more courageous, empathetic, and selfless personhood; that they leave our care above all as better citizens, well-armed to be in service to their art, each other, and the world; and that they understand that how they dance and how they live are deeply connected—how we approach our dancing has the power to transform our minds and therefore our entirety. As educators we have the power, and consequently the duty, to reinvigorate the dance studio as a place for social, political, cultural learning and transformation. Instead of the charge to foster professional dancers, let's invest in their autonomy and assimilation of what they've learned to therefore manifest it in the world, in whatever form that takes. Toni Cade Bambara wrote, "The job of a writer is to make revolution irresistible,"[39] and I would hope that our work, as dance educators, is to likewise make revolution, within oneself and in the world, irrepressible and unavoidable.

I am moved and encouraged by students with a beautiful work ethic. And by that I don't mean "ethic" within a capitalistic framework which measures progress and success by bigger, better, more- and I'm not referring to students with talent as prescribed by colonialist aesthetics. I mean "ethic" as a way of working, an intentionality of devotion, curiosity, humility, a willingness to transform, and love; that requires that as a teacher I come in reciprocally, engaging students with intentionality, devotion, curiosity, humility, a willingness to be transformed, and love—an orientation, for both student and teacher, of "learning to become."[40] Picture the kind of student you want to teach, find joy in teaching—will you commit to becoming that kind of student of an anti-racism education?

I want to nurture and participate in pedagogical and artistic practices that embolden and shape us towards more revolutionary, compassionate, creative, and patient versions of ourselves. Educational consultant Jamilah Pitts writes, "There has to be a complete shift that recognizes that to teach well is to emancipate, heal, resist, and love…"[41] If we are indeed invested in setting up our classrooms as spaces of emancipation, healing, resistance, and love, how can we ourselves not be transformed? But cultivating those spaces requires "persistent self-awareness, constant self-criticism, and regular self-examination."[42] An engaged, emancipatory, and empathetic pedagogy emphasizes well-being,[43] but an unwell, unconscious teacher cannot lead a student toward wellness. We can't expect to "teach well" or embody anti-racism in the classroom if we're not committed to first unearthing our own internalized white supremacy and then purposefully dismantling its manifestations within. It's about self-actualizing, and then cultivating that space for students. One issue

I've had to face is that a deep part of me wants to police and punish (although I didn't have such precise language until recently with my increased awareness of prison abolition movements). I have to actively work to abolish the carceral state that lives within me. Artist and activist Marc Bamuthi Joseph points out that Black youth are already "constantly having to police themselves before they get policed,"[44] so that is a legacy I cannot, must not, perpetuate against students of any race.

Most ballet classes, and I imagine other techniques as well, are taught within a hierarchy of importance, where steps are assigned value—*grand battement* more important than the fifth position that precedes or follows it; *piqué arabesque* more important than *faille*; the power of my legs more important than the technique and generosity of my *épaulement*. People snap and clap for multiple pirouettes and high extensions but too often fail to see the potency of a deeply-imagined-full-of-sensation tendu. Locate that to the expectations and strictures placed on certain bodies and how we assign importance, or insignificance, to those bodies in society and in dance. Are we immune, or blind, to the poetry of certain bodies? Are you stirred only by the lush waltzing sweep of a thin, white woman with long flowing hair? Impressed only by physical pyrotechnics as opposed to the virtuosity of nuance and meaning making? As teachers we can strive to teach a non-hierarchical thoughtfulness where nothing gets left behind, where no detritus exists. We can strive to teach in such a way that students understand that everything they do in class is within their purview and agency; that everything is a choice; that not making a choice is a de facto choice; and that they have the power to illuminate the invisibilized. I believe that artistry and mastery are found when the transitions are just as important as the arrival, and when the artist, through their intelligence and choice-making, brings the previously unnoticed into luminosity. Those could likewise be mandates of an anti-racist, ethical pedagogy. Consider, as artist Jessica Sabogal notes, that "whiteness remains invisible to those who reap its benefits,"[45] ergo the actions of upholding white supremacy likewise remain invisible and inconspicuous, like the mechanisms of breathing. In the words of poet Kyle "Guante" Tran Myhre, "white supremacy is not a shark; it is the water."[46] Can we pledge ourselves, and embolden students, to bring white supremacy into the light and expose it as the poison that we all live, breathe, swim, and die in?

One aspect of that coming into light is an absolute refusal to fall into the negligent swap of the names of the racialized students in your class. The defensiveness of *I'm just bad with names*, or, *I call them by their correct names most of the time*, is an example of whiteness denying its privilege, prioritizing intent over impact, and choosing to ignore the exhausting, painful legacy of "But They All Look The Same To Me."[47] Let's call it what it is, racist, instead of the easy convenience of falling back on a commodified phrase such as *it's just my implicit bias* (which many scholars believe should be renamed as "complicit bias,"[48] a semantic switch that calls one into action instead of exoneration). Professor Meera E. Deo writes, "Language has a direct connection to subordination, and therefore anti-subordination."[49] As educators, learning students' names, which often requires a little extra work outside the classroom, is a minimum investment toward making sure that everyone in the room feels seen and held. The absence of that nominal care is a form of subjection and linguistic violence.

To be clear, I don't think that engaging students with pedagogies of freedom is a free-for-all. I believe in form and the rigor of training as things of deep beauty and value, if "taught well." Embodied knowledge of technique is essential toward understanding how to depart from form, but form cannot be the end point—across disciplines it is always a means to an end. Poet Denise Levertov believed that "Accuracy is always the gateway to mystery."[50] If we consider form as a bowl, the bowl itself is not the objective, but instead the space and delineation for content the bowl provides. Similarly, personal freedom cannot be the end point; as Toni Morrison says, "the function of freedom is to free someone else."[51]

So, what might a classroom immersed in antiracism and pedagogies of freedom look like? Beyond what I've already spoken to, here are a few more possibilities that I know now (and that will continue to evolve as I learn more): it centers the needs of those most adversely impacted by white supremacy, those on the bottom rungs of the ladder of what social justice activist Sonya Renee Taylor coins "the ladder of body hierarchy;"[52] it is uninterested in white people's comfort and unmoved by white tears;[53] it allows space for marginalized students to not trust you— they shouldn't; it supports the reclamation of bodily autonomy, in part by encouraging students to respectfully state their bodily needs, instead of asking permission to safeguard and attend to their injuries; it considers class as an open-ended question, thus honoring unknowing[54] and the unknown; it interrogates colonizer body mores in order to disrupt the authority of "the ideal body;"[55] it proposes the primacy of embodied sensation and imagination over a mirror-based affirmation of "this is what it's supposed to look like"—the infinity of arabesque looks blessedly different on every single being; and it acknowledges that alterity is truth and creative lifeblood,[56] its dearth the collective death of bloom and vision. As for how it feels? Let's find out together with the students we are privileged to have in our care.

Notes

1. Catrice Jackson, "If you don't have an anti-racism plan, you plan to *be* racist" *Harper's Bazaar*, June 8, 2020, https://www.harpersbazaar.com/uk/culture/a32781443/catrice-jackson-anti-racism-action/
2. "...theory's cool, but theory with no practice ain't shit"—from a speech delivered by Fred Hampton, deputy chairman of the national Black Panther Party.
3. Ta-Nehisi Coates, *Between the World and Me* (New York: Spiegel & Grau, 2015), 103.
4. Tanya Rodriguez, "Decolonization, A Guidebook For Settlers Living On Stolen Land." *Unsettling America*, April 3, 2021, https://unsettlingamerica.wordpress.com/2021/04/03/decolonization-a-guidebook-for-settlers-living-on-stolen-land/
5. Eve Tuck and K. Wayne Yang, "Decolonization is not a metaphor," *Decolonization: Indigeneity, Education, & Society* 1, no. 1 (2012), 1–40.
6. While aware that ballet has historically excluded all marginalized peoples, for the purposes of this paper I am focusing specifically on anti-blackness.
7. Jackson, "If you don't have."
8. Ibram X. Kendi, *How to Be an Antiracist* (New York: One World, 2019), 9.
9. Tuck and Yang, "Decolonization is not a metaphor."
10. Jonathan Osler, "White Accomplices," *Opportunities for White People in the Fight for Racial Justice*, https://www.whiteaccomplices.org/
11. In "The 8 White Identities," Barnor Hesse defines White Voyeurism as "Wouldn't challenge a white supremacist; desires non-whiteness because it's interesting, pleasurable; seeks to control the consumption and appropriation of non-whiteness; fascination with culture (ex: consuming black culture without the burden of blackness). White Traitor is defined as "Actively refuses complicity; names what's going on; intention is to subvert white authority and tell the truth at whatever cost; need them to dismantle institutions."
12. Heath Schultz, "Disrupting White Vision: Pedagogic Strategies Against White Supremacy" *Journal of Cultural Research in Art Education* 36, no. 3 (2019): 59-73.
13. Dwayne Reed, Twitter post, June 4, 2020, @TeachMrReed.
14. Adesola Akinleye, "Introduction" (*Re:)Claiming Ballet* (Bristol, UK: Intellect, 2021), 1–8.

15 bell hooks, *Teaching to Transgress* (New York: Routledge, 1994), 4.
16 Stephanie M. H. Camp, "The Pleasures of Resistance: Enslaved Women and Body Politics in the Plantation South, 1830–1861." *The Journal of Southern History* 68, no. 3 (August 2002): 533–572.
17 James Baldwin, "A Talk to Teachers," *The Saturday Review*, December 21, 1963. (originally delivered as a speech on October 16, 1963, entitled "The Negro Child – His Self-Image.")
18 Rebecca Chaleff, "Activating Whiteness: Racializing the Ordinary in US American Postmodern Dance," *Dance Research Journal* 50, no. 3 (December 2018): 71–84.
19 Phillip Atiba Goff and Matthew Christian Jackson, Brooke Allison Lewis Di Leone, Carmen Marie Culotta, and Natalie Ann DiTomasso, "The Essence of Innocence: Consequences of Dehumanizing Black Children," *Journal of Personality and Social Psychology* 106, no. 4 (2014): 526–545.
20 Sharon J. Todd, "'Bringing more than I contain': ethics, curriculum and the pedagogical demand for altered egos," *Journal of Curriculum Studies* 33, no. 4 (2001): 438. The quote continues: "'…receiving beyond the capacity of the I' that learning strives to achieve…"
21 Coates, *Between the World and Me*, 8.
22 Brenda Dixon Gottschild, "Ballet beyond boundaries: a personal history," in *(Re:)Claiming Ballet*, ed. Adesola Akinleye (Bristol, UK: Intellect, 2021), 108.
23 Judith Butler, "Gender is Burning: Questions of Appropriation and Subversion," *Bodies That Matter: On the Discursive Limits of Sex* (New York: Routledge, 2011), 84.
24 Peggy McIntosh, "White Privilege: Unpacking the Invisible Knapsack," *Peace and Freedom* (July/August 1989).
25 Alicia Mullikin, "Recognizing Systemic Racism in Dance," *Seattle Dances*, June 19, 2020, http://seattledances.com/2020/06/recognizing-systemic-racism-in-dance/. See also "What is meant by Diversity, Equity, and Inclusion?" https://apo.ucsc.edu/diversity.html:
26 "As opposed to equality, where everyone receives the same support regardless of circumstance… Equity acknowledges structural issues and barriers such as racism, sexism, homophobia, bullying, and sexual harassment that have prevented the full participation of individuals from marginalized groups."
27 Sara Ahmed, "A Phenomenology of Whiteness," *Feminist Theory* 8, no. 2 (2007): 157.
28 Lilla Watson, Speech delivered at the United Nations Decade for Women Conference, Nairobi, 1985.
29 Nia Wilson, quoted in "The Cut," *New York* Magazine, August 2018. Full quote: "I want to be free. I want you to be free. And you aren't free until I am. Spend your privilege, and just when you think you've spent enough, spend some more," https://www.thecut.com/2018/08/nia-wilson-spend-your-privilege.html
30 Claudia Rankine, *Citizen: An American Lyric* (Minneapolis: Graywolf Press, 2014), 143.
31 McIntosh, "White Privilege."

32 McIntosh, "White Privilege."
33 Christian E. Weller and Lily Roberts, "Report: Eliminating the Black-White Wealth Gap Is a Generational Challenge," *American Progress*, March 19, 2021, https://www.americanprogress.org/article/eliminating-black-white-wealth-gap-generational-challenge/. Full quote: "The persistent Black-white wealth gap is not an accident but rather the result of centuries of federal and state policies that have systematically facilitated the deprivation of Black Americans. From the brutal exploitation of Africans during slavery, to systematic oppression in the Jim Crow South, to today's institutionalized racism—apparent in disparate access to and outcomes in education, health care, jobs, housing, and criminal justice—government policy has created or maintained hurdles for African Americans who attempt to build, maintain, and pass on wealth."
34 Natasha Hicks, Fenaba Addo, Anne Prince, and William Darity, "Still Running Up the Down Escalator: How Narratives Shape our Understanding of Racial Wealth Inequality," *Insight Center for Community Economic Development*, 2021.
35 This question has been attributed to Rachel Cargle on social media, alongside: "I want to invite you to think critically about the idea of 'brining [sic] in color' & 'offering a seat at the table' into workplaces and organizations that haven't invested in interrogating and dismantling the racist systems that brought them to even need to consider 'DEI'. What are the values that have been celebrated and perpetuated that have led to exclusion of Black people? What internal biases were upheld that disregarded the voices and expertise of the Black community? How have the voices of Black people, the realities of Black existence been dismissed and held in less regard to those that are white/white adjacent (i.e., Are only the Black people who talk, dress and act like white people given respect?) How have long standing stereotypes of blackness given you 'excuses' to downplay the lack of inclusion you have? (Recent example is execs stating there 'aren't enough Black people in the field'— which more times than not isn't true). How have you been tokenizing the one/few Black people that are in your space to dissolve your own notion of possibly being racist/perpetuating racism. What do you say to yourself to complete the sentence 'I'm not racist because _____' and consider if that is truly fighting a racist system or simply soothing your own guilt. What knowledge, empathy and action must take place by everyone in your organization to ensure the Black people in your space feel heard, respected, valued and safe. We are not here to simply bring Black people into harmful organizations for the sake of 'diversity and inclusion'— the world is dismantling the systems that have traditionally existed in and thrives under the ideas, stereotypes and biases of racism and white supremacy."
36 Vu Le, "21 signs you or your organization may be the white moderate Dr. King warned about," *Generocity*, January 18, 2021. https://generocity.org/philly/2021/01/18/vu-le-mlk-white-moderate-nonprofits/
37 Sara Ahmed, "The Nonperformativity of Antiracism," *Meridians* 7, no. 1 (2006): 104–126.

38 bell hooks, "Love as the Practice of Freedom," *Outlaw Culture* (New York: Routledge, 2006), 289-298.
39 Toni Cade Bambara, in *Black Women Writers at Work*, ed. Claudia Tate (New York: Continuum, 1983).
40 Sharon Todd, "'Bringing more than I contain': ethics, curriculum and the pedagogical demand for altered egos," *Journal of Curriculum Studies* 33 (4), 2001, 431–450.
41 Jamilah Pitts, "It's time to Move Beyond Buzzwords and Radically Reimagine Schools," *Education Week*, June 16, 2020, https://www.edweek.org/leadership/opinion-its-time-to-move-beyond-buzzwords-and-radically-re-imagine-schools/2020/06
42 Kendi, *Antiracist*, 23.
43 hooks, *Teaching to Transgress*, 170.
44 Marc Bamuthi Joseph, "The Just and the Blind," https://www.celebrityseries.org/productions/the-just-and-the-blind/
45 Jessica Sabogal, "Whiteness Remains Invisible," https://www.pathway-art.com/jessica-sabogal
46 Kyle "Guante" Tran Myhre, "How to Explain White Supremacy to a White Supremacist," *A Love Song, A Death Rattle, A Battle Cry* (Minneapolis: Button Poetry, 2018), read by Kyle "Guante" Tran Myhre here: https://guante.info/2016/03/17/how-to-explain-white-supremacy-to-a-white-supremacist-new-video/
47 "Leslie Cuyjet and Angie Pittman are not the same dancer," *critical correspondence*, March 26, 2021.
48 Jules Holyrod, Robin Scaife, and Tom Stafford, "Responsibility for implicit bias," *Philosophy Compass* 12, no. 3 (March 2017): 1–13.
49 Meera E. Deo, "Why BIPOC Fails," *Virginia Law Review* 107, no. 115 (2021): 119.
50 Dujie Tahat, "Hoa Nguyen's *A Thousand Times You Lose Your Treasure*," *Poems.com*, https://poems.com/features/what-sparks-poetry/dujie-tahat-on-hoa-nguyens-a-thousand-times-you-lose-your-treasure/
51 Dan and Steve Fouts, "The Function of Freedom," *Teach Different*, https://teachdifferent.com/podcast/the-function-of-freedom-is-to-free-someone-else-teach-different-with-toni-morrison-responsibility/
52 Sonya Renee Taylor, *The Body is Not an Apology* (Oakland: Berrett-Koehler Publishers 2018), 93.
53 Alison Phipps, "White tears, white rage: Victimhood and (as) violence in mainstream feminism," *European Journal of Cultural Studies* 24, no. 1 (2021): 81–93.
54 Michalinos Zembylas, "A Pedagogy of Unknowing: Witnessing Unknowability in Teaching and Learning" *Studies in Philosophy and Education* 24 (2005): 152.
55 Jessica Zeller, "'Can you feel it?': Pioneering pedagogies that challenge ballet's authoritarian traditions," in *(Re:)Claiming Ballet*, ed. Adesola Akinleye (Bristol, UK: Intellect, 2021), 175.
56 Audre Lorde, "Master's Tools," *Sister Outsider: Essays and Speeches* (Berkeley: Crossing Press, 2007), 111.

10
RECENTERING THE STUDIO
Ballet Leadership and Learning Through Intersectional and Antiracist Approaches

Renée K. Nicholson and Lisa DeFrank-Cole

Girls in leotards and tights, boys in tights and crisp white T-shirts, file in and take their places at the barre. The teacher enters and the class begins with guided warmups, pliés, tendus, and so on. There is no ambiguity regarding who runs the class: the teacher has prepared exercises, sets the musical tempos for them, and gives the corrections. Except for the music and the voice of the teacher, the studio remains mostly silent. The ballet teacher is the authority, regardless of the age or level of the students. However, ballet teachers have an opportunity to become leaders both inside and outside the studio. As leaders, ballet teachers can deliver and provide more inclusive approaches to instruction, working with students to develop an all-embracing relationship with the artform, and promoting it to ensure ballet's relevance in the future.

Dance historian Jennifer Fisher makes a powerful case for access to quality ballet instruction: "Ballet is not a way to escape life; it's a way to negotiate life by learning a valuable practice, by offering complexity, depth, and beauty."[1] These qualities should be available to anyone who seeks instruction, from those who will go on to professional ranks to those whose training is purely recreational. While Fisher's aspirations for instruction apply to ballet technique, they also extend beyond technical acquisition of ballet's vocabulary. What a student absorbs in the studio can set a foundation for a love of ballet well past the execution of any particular step. Therefore, providing the right setting for learning creates

DOI: 10.4324/9781003283065-13

future dancers and instructors as well as a devoted and informed audience, and lifelong supporters of ballet and ballet institutions.

Much can be said for the influence of famous dancers and beloved dance teachers, which extends beyond the walls and mirrors of the dance studio. Christiane Vaussard, who taught at the Paris Opera Ballet's school, said, "We are obligated as teachers to pass on the good ideas we were given by our own teachers."[2] Suki Schorer published a book about George Balanchine and her take on Balanchine's technique. He was not only her artistic director and teacher, but a mentor as well:

> I believed in Balanchine. Seeing and dancing in his ballets made me believe in his aesthetic...in my teaching, in my lectures, in my writing, and in my videos on the technique, I have tried to convey not only his aesthetic, but also his beliefs about how to work, how to deal with each other and how to live.[3]

Schorer's words convey Balanchine's imprint on her teaching, first as an instructor and later as director of the School of American Ballet (SAB). Balanchine's influence on the landscape of ballet is unrivaled and, too often, unquestioned. When Schorer asserts that she tried to address "how to live" as part of the framework that Balanchine gave her, she is teaching well beyond the strictures of pure technique. Her teaching has influenced generations of dancers trained at SAB, as well as those who have been influenced by her writings and videos.

While Balanchine's approach to technique is widely discussed and circulated, less attention has been brought to the enormous financial support he received that was not available to others. Lauren Erin Brown writes, "Any conversation about ballet training mid-century must acknowledge George Balanchine's relationship with the Ford Foundation."[4] While Schorer codified Balanchine's teachings, the powerful influence of the money the Ford Foundation provided Balanchine ensured his outsized influence: "the Ford Foundation would strengthen the School of American Ballet (SAB) as a national school, raise the local training standards while providing scholarships to outstanding students to study at SAB, and strengthen selected companies."[5] Compared to other dance leaders and their institutions, Balanchine's support was unparalleled, making the Ford Foundation complicit in setting up SAB as the preeminent school: "Ford's grant solidified Balanchine's fate at the top of the dance world, anointing his views and preferences as an American template."[6] These providers did not examine Balanchine's limited aesthetics— ethereal features and lily-white skin—nor his approach to leadership, and the impact of his aesthetics and leadership extended far beyond SAB's walls. As a result, leadership in ballet in the United States became small, select, and insular. Insular leadership is defined as "the leader and at least some followers minimize or disregard the health and welfare of 'the other'—that is, those outside the group or organization for which they are directly responsible."[7]

If society today supports and mandates more attention to diversity, equity, and inclusion, Balanchine's preferences belong to an antiquated era. Balanchine, a Russian immigrant and white man, had tremendous biases. Brown writes, "[B]y the mid-to-late-1960s and early 1970s the definition of a ballet body, by virtue of the predilection of one man and his company, proved increasingly complicated—mainly for the bodies left out."[8] Fisher echoes this perspective when she writes, "On some days, in some places, ballet is everything evil that people imagine it to be—elitist, exclusionary, and impossibly old fashioned. Just ask young black dancers how welcoming the ballet world has been."[9] For dancers of color, the requirement to assimilate to Eurocentric body types, dress codes, and casting takes a heavy toll on self-esteem and psychological well-being. Whether subtle or blatant, academies and companies convey harmful messages of a lesser-than status to many dancers of color. Tobin James exposes this approach, "Non-white students become increasingly aware of attitudes and behaviors that suggest a lesser membership in classes and through ballet organizations."[10]

Even today, a specific white gaze causes students of color to feel ignored, to be spoken of in disapproving tones, and to be told to smile in classes, among other indignities.[11] Later, if students of color go on to become professional artists, their casting is often limited, with the argument being that ballet audiences prefer to see the homogeneity of a corps of white bodies. Often, dancers of color are siphoned off into roles of servitude, or roles that are exoticized, eroticized, and otherwise othered. James writes, "Classical ballet institutions have been strongholds of elitist and exclusionary practices, consistently positioning barriers of the inclusion of non-White communities."[12] This exclusionary approach is also evident in *Suki Schorer on Balanchine Technique* where only one of seven models is a dancer of color: Jock Soto, a principal dancer with New York City Ballet of Puerto Rican and Navajo descent. All the others are white.

Furthermore, when Schorer writes about dancers who inspired her own ideals, they are predominately white, and she uses descriptors for them like "delicate," "nuanced," "elegant," "slightly cool," "doll-like," and "incandescent." In contrast, when she writes about Maria Tallchief of the Osage Nation, she uses different vocabulary, "It never occurred to me to try to emulate the powerful, dominating presence of Maria Tallchief, but I surely tried to incorporate her many useful suggestions—for example, how to walk and run when on stage."[13]

Words matter, especially when they are used to describe human bodies and to signal difference and othering. If Schorer tried to emulate those white, elegant, delicate, and doll-like dancers, how do these personal preferences influence her leveling and promotion decisions for current students? Her publication presents a clue: "Mr. Balanchine's classes had only one purpose: to prepare us to dance his ballets better and more in keeping with his aesthetic."[14] While SAB recently brought in former New York City Ballet dancer Aesha Ash as an instructor, and quickly promoted her to the position of Associate Chair of Faculty in June 2022, it is important to note the decades of white gatekeeping at SAB, and the performative aspects of tokenizing instructors of color.

While increased attention has been brought to leadership in ballet organizations, mostly due to the work of Theresa Ruth Howard, more attention must be brought to the impact of teachers. Many ballet instructors exert power over students, and influence their technique, diet, and life-choices. Peter G. Northouse writes, "People have power when they have the ability to affect others' beliefs, attitudes, and courses of action."[15] Examining power, research by John R. P. French and Bertram Raven offers five different approaches—reward, coercive, legitimate, referent, and expert—that align with pedagogical approaches.[16]

First, with reward power, a teacher may give a coveted role to a student. Second, coercive power is evident in dancers being penalized for undesirable behavior by being told to practice and exercise repeatedly. Third, legitimate power is demonstrated by formal job authority and any teacher may possess this type by simply being introduced as the instructor. Fourth, referent power is displayed when a student is fond of the instructor and their admiration causes them to follow instruction. Lastly, expert power describes teachers who are acclaimed in the field, as performers, directors, or instructors. For school directors, it is vital to pay attention to the criteria used to hire ballet teachers (Does a reputation as a famous dancer necessarily equate with great teaching?), and for students it is wise to notice how certain teachers wield power and the impact of their behavior.

The paths from teacher to leader or company director also need to be examined. In insular leadership, as seen at SAB, a director appoints people who best emulate desired aesthetics and behaviors. Using a critical perspective and looking at a variety of structural inequalities, we can think about who benefits from such systems.[17] Historically in ballet, white bodies with thin and delicate shapes were preferred over those with darker skin and curves. We need to be aware where "structural domination and inequalities" exist and work to change them.[18] Those in leadership should understand "the flow of power in society, how this contributes to the social stratification, and ways in which we can create more democratic and just social arrangements."[19] In other words, teacher-leaders need to advocate for a more diverse group of students to practice the art form.

Embracing cultural humility is one path toward dismantling the deleterious effects of the white gaze. Cultural humility can be defined as "a lifelong process of self-reflection and self-critique whereby the individual not only learns about another's culture, but initially starts with an examination of her/his own beliefs and cultural identities."[20] Future ballet leaders need to build awareness of and aptitude for navigating cultural intersections that better reflect changing demographics. As dancer, choreographer, and activist Phil Chan asks, "As a new generation takes the reins at performing arts institutions around the world, what are we repeating, and why?"[21] Jane M. Alexandre has created a theory of dance leadership that would benefit anyone thinking about what should be incorporated as we move into the future.[22]

Teachers, leaders, and administrators who work in the ballet industry would also benefit from an active understanding of intersectionality, a term coined by Kimberlé Crenshaw in 1989, that allows us to see how various social identities intersect to disadvantage an individual.[23] Lisa DeFrank-Cole and Sherylle J. Tan write, "These identities, specifically race, class, and gender, when combined demonstrate how those who are deemed less powerful or marginalized are disadvantaged by overlapping oppressions."[24] What are the specific intersections of people who do not fit the Balanchine mold? How might these voices inform the creation of more intentionally inclusive and diverse studios and teaching? Demonstrating cultural humility and being vulnerable in leadership is about giving up on *knowing it all* and inviting the perspectives of others to enhance the system.

Economic barriers, such as audition fees and audition locations, need overhauling to create a pedagogy of equal access. Rethinking what we ask students to wear to class is important and can improve students' feelings of being welcomed and included. James writes, "Another outdated Eurocentric tradition is the required uniform of pink tights and shoes, which clashes with the complexion of students of color and does little to enhance their classical line."[25] Being able to see the body clearly to offer meaningful corrections that support proper technique is quite different from insisting on a homogenous color palette.

When teachers understand their roles as leaders, the impact of their classes can create a ripple effect. For example, in your classes, which artists are referenced and referred to as models and innovators? The platform, Memoirs of Blacks in Ballet, created by Theresa Ruth Howard gives immediate access to anyone with an internet connection and device.[26] As barriers decrease, these resources create a larger context outside the technique class for dancers to explore diversity. A small library of material can be curated on even a modest budget, allowing students and their family members to enrich their learning, and autobiographies by dancers such as Misty Copeland, Michaela DePrince, and Georgina Pazcoguin can form its foundation.

Jennifer Fisher writes, "I critique ballet, I always say, because ballet can take it, and because ballet needs it."[27] Ballet's current leaders hold the potential to make transformational changes in how the next generation of dancers, of audiences, of funders and other stakeholders are fostered and encouraged. Each of these communities will influence what ballet will become. According to James, we already see some changes happening, "Students expect a dance training environment that transcends societal prejudice."[28] Good leaders ensure that changes are thoughtful and thorough. This moment of cultural humility is also an opportunity to grow classroom participation as well as expand audiences. Doesn't ballet know how to show us the value of embracing challenge and nurturing possibility?

Notes

1 Jennifer Fisher, *Ballet Matters: A Cultural Memoir of Dance Dreams and Empowering Realities* (Jefferson: McFarland and Company, 2019), 1.
2 Gretchen Warren, *The Art of Teaching Ballet: Ten Twentieth-Century Masters* (Gainesville: University Press of Florida, 1999), 9.

3 Suki Schorer and Russell Lee, *Suki Schorer on Balanchine Technique* (New York: Knopf, 1999), xiii.
4 Lauren Erin Brown, "'As Long as They Have Talent': Organizational Barriers to Black Ballet." *Dance Chronicle* 41, no. 3 (2018): 371.
5 Brown, "As Long as They Have Talent," 372.
6 Brown, "As Long as They Have Talent," 373.
7 Barbara Kellerman, *Bad Leadership: What It Is, How It Happens, Why It Matters* (Boston, MA: Harvard Business School Press, 2004), 45.
8 Brown, "As Long as They Have Talent," 374.
9 Fischer, *Ballet Matters*, 5.
10 Tobin James, "Calling for Cultural Humility in Ballet Academies and Companies: A Complementary Construct to Diversity, Equity, and Inclusion Initiatives." *Journal of Dance Education* 20, no. 3 (2020): 133.
11 James, "Calling," 132.
12 James, "Calling," 132.
13 Schorer and Lee, *Balanchine Technique*, 4.
14 Schorer and Lee, *Balanchine Technique*, 5.
15 Peter G. Northouse, *Leadership: Theory and practice* (Thousand Oaks, CA: SAGE Publications, 2019), 9.
16 John R. P. French, Jr. and Bertram Raven, "The Bases of Social Power," *Studies in Social Power*, Dorwin Cartwright, ed. (University of Michigan: Research Center for Group Dynamics, Institute for Social Research, 1959), 155–156.
17 John P. Dugan and Natasha T. Turman, "Renewing the Vow, Changing the Commitments: The Call to Infuse Critical Perspectives into Leadership Education," *National Clearinghouse for Leadership Programs Concepts and Connections: A Publication for Leadership Educators* 22 no. 2 (2018): 5.
18 Bradley A. Levinson, "Exploring Critical Social Theories and Education," *Beyond Critique: Exploring Critical Social Theories and Education* (London: Routledge, 2015), 2.
19 John P. Dugan, *Leadership Theory: Cultivating Critical Perspectives* (San Francisco: Jossey-Bass, 2017), 32.
20 Melanie Tervalon and Jann Murray-Garcia qtd. in James, 132.
21 Phil Chan and Michele Chase, *Final Bow for Yellowface: Dancing Between Intention and Impact* (Brooklyn: Yellow Peril Press, 2020), 9.
22 Jane M. Alexandre, *Dance Leadership: Theory Into Practice* (London: Palgrave Macmillan, 2017).
23 Kimberlé Crenshaw, "Demarginalizing the Intersection of Race and Sex: A Black Feminist Critique of Antidiscrimination Doctrine, Feminist Theory and Antiracist USA Politics," *University of Chicago Legal Forum* (January 1989): 139–68.
24 Lisa DeFrank-Cole and Sherylle J. Tan, *Women and Leadership: Journey Toward Equity* (Thousand Oaks: SAGE Publications, 2022), 4.
25 James, "Calling," 133.
26 "Memoirs of Blacks in Ballet," https://mobballet.org/.
27 Fisher, *Ballet Matters*, 5
28 James, "Calling," 133.

11
CREDIBILITY AND EXPERTISE
Black Women Teaching Classical Ballet

Monica Stephenson

Doris Jones (1913–2006), a renowned and beloved teacher, opened the Jones Haywood School of Ballet with Claire Haywood in 1941. The school is in the nation's capital and is now known as the Jones Haywood School of Dance. Currently, Sandra Fortune-Green serves as director and continues the distinct tutelage of Ms. Jones. Dancers who studied with Ms. Jones between 1933, when she began teaching, and 2006, pursued successful careers on Broadway and in professional companies such as Dance Theatre of Harlem and Alvin Ailey American Dance Theater. More significantly, Ms. Jones' students became remarkable citizens and excelled in endeavors and careers beyond ballet.

This chapter traces the unconventional journey of Ms. Jones into classical ballet, noting the barriers she encountered in her study of the art form and how she developed credibility and expertise. The perseverance she needed to become a teacher generated a resiliency that carried through to her students. In 2021, I conducted interviews with Sandra Fortune-Green and Lauri Fitz-Pegado, dancers who studied with Ms. Jones, and analyzed relationships between expertise and credibility, as well as defined characteristics that encompass a Black teaching style of classical ballet. Ms. Jones is described by her pupils as someone who taught with tremendously high expectations and a high standard of excellence. In my research, I uncover why one of the characteristics of Black ballet teachers is holding children to high expectations, historically and currently, and how this has been shaped by environments and interactions. Three questions motivate this inquiry: 1. What was the teaching style of Doris Jones? 2. How did she build credibility as a teacher? 3. How has her teaching shaped future generations of teachers?

Studying the significance of Black classical ballet teachers is challenging due to a lack of documentation. In addition, most ballet companies and schools adhere to Eurocentric norms and perpetuate systemic barriers. There is a damaging myth that Black people are not interested in studying ballet, even though there is a long history of Black schools and teachers in America.[1] Even teachers of color can uphold systems of Whiteness in their teaching of classical ballet.[2] Given the scarcity of material about Black ballet teachers, I examine the experiences of Black teachers in White dominant environments of primary, secondary, and higher education to draw correlations between teaching strategies and barriers encountered.

Across disciplines, Black professors have the lowest faculty progression, retention, and tenure rates.[3] Black professors, however, are more likely than other ethnicities to have a terminal degree.[4] The discrepancies in tenure and promotion of Black faculty can be attributed to the time-consuming expectations to mentor Black students and to serve on university committees for greater ethnic and racial representation.[5] At predominantly White institutions, Black faculty are often pigeonholed into teaching Black studies courses.[6] Scholarship that is qualitative and diversity-centered attracts less funding and is not published in highly respected journals which also contributes to the lower promotion and tenure rates for Black professors.[7]

In a study of sixteen professors of African descent, professors undertook measures to significantly adjust their communication style to prove credibility, approachability, and professionalism.[8] The assimilation was in response to students and colleagues at predominantly White institutions regularly questioning Black professor's credibility.[9] Research reveals a "credibility hierarchy" with White men ranked above Black men, who are above White women, who are above Black women.[10] Black female faculty also battle stereotypes of being "aggressive and less competent" or expected to behave like "the Mammy."[11]

As a result, Black female educators must fight harder than their counterparts to prove credibility. Social science researchers have shown that expertise is typically independent of content knowledge and is assigned to individuals by a constituency willing to attribute expertise to them.[12] In other words, people need "to have at least one reasonably large group of people—a constituency or niche—who consider that you are an expert."[13] Expertise varies by discipline, although there are some "gold standards" acquired through professional licensing or subjective criteria.[14] In ballet schools, teachers are often valued if they have performed with a prestigious White company: this establishes a ballet teacher's "expertise."

In spite of these obstacles, there is a long history of Black ballet teachers and educators in schools. Prior to the 1954 Brown v. Board of Education case that desegregated public schools, Black female teachers educated Black children to positively contribute to Black communities.[15] Their teaching style has been described by researchers as authoritative with high expectations of their students.[16] Class settings tended to be lively and learner-centered with high emotional involvement, call and response, symbolism, creative analogies, and participatory discussion. Studies show this approach was grounded in deep care for children with the aspiration that they succeed in their pursuits and contribute to communities.[17]

Social science research on the demographic mix-match between student and educator reveal White teachers are less likely to expect Black and Hispanic students to complete a college degree.[18] Additionally, educators hold significantly higher expectations for students of higher-income, higher-educated families than lower-income families or those with high school diplomas, which include disproportionately more Black and Hispanic students. In one study, teachers were asked about students' work ethics, their relations with classmates, skill levels, and perceived behavior.[19] Findings showed that White teachers rate Black students' scholastic aptitude lower than Asian students and White students. However, nonwhite teachers did not rate students of color lower than White teachers rate White students.

Cultural competency in teaching is defined as the ability to draw on a student's prior knowledge, which enriches student behavior and learning.[20] Cultural conflicts arise when teachers do not understand a student's behavior, body language, values, worldviews, home environment, or learning style.[21] One study revealed that Black children in particular resist learning when their language is overly corrected, and when their interests and culture are ignored.[22] A lack of competency contributes to fear, unnecessary criticism, overly harsh punishment, and microaggressions. In order to overcome dominant norms, educators must become knowledgeable of Black students' language, style of presentation, community values, traditions, history, and practices. Black teachers are more likely than their White counterparts to be effective cultural translators.[23] This review of literature provides the foundation as well as frameworks for analyzing the teaching of classical ballet. I am a Black classical ballet teacher early in my teaching career who is curious about the characteristics of Black teaching, cultural competency in teaching, and how pioneering teachers such as Doris Jones navigated immense challenges to constructing credibility.

Trailblazers: Doris Jones, Sandra Fortune-Green, and Lauri Fitz-Pegado

Doris Jones was born in Malden, Massachusetts, and her grandmother was the first Black woman to own a home in Malden, which she left to Jones' mother. Jones' parents subsequently purchased homes in Boston and Martha's Vineyard and supplemented their income with rent from boarders. Ms. Jones describes her parents, Walter and Mattie, as great social dancers. Her father, Walter, was a musician who played the piano and harmonica while dinner was being prepared. Walter taught Ms. Jones how to dance—schottische (a slow polka) and two step—and her mother encouraged her pursuit of the arts. Ms. Jones recalls, "Every Monday morning, she would keep me out of school and take me to the theatre–all the big bands, all the others that came on the key circuit or low circuit and they changed their shows every Monday, and we would go."[24] Jones recalls seeing icons like Josephine Baker, "Eubie" Blake, Ethel Waters, and Noble Sissle. Ms. Jones enrolled at the Practical Arts High School and, at age 14, studied tap with Johnny Price. She accompanied him to the school of Lulu Philbrook where she began teaching tap to Ms. Philbrook's students in exchange for ballet lessons. Starting classical ballet lessons at the age of 15 or 16 is very late for a dancer. When she was 8, her parents asked if she could train in ballet with Philbrook, and they were denied because of the color of her skin.

Jones started teaching her own pupils in Boston and put together a performance of seven students (three were family members) for the Delta sorority with handmade costumes by her mother. By the next September, Jones had thirty students, and she taught in her family home for $.50 per week per student. During summers, she taught at Camp Atwater in East Brookfield, Massachusetts, where she met Claire Haywood from Atlanta who was teaching visual arts. Haywood encouraged her to come to Washington, DC at the age of 25 to start a school of dance, but the path was not easy. Jones supplemented her income by running an elevator and teaching for DC Parks and Recreation. She conducted ballet classes in her basement and then rented a room at the YWCA for afternoon classes. Ms. Haywood started taking classes with Ms. Jones, eventually quitting her government job. The school then transitioned to a studio on U Street where it grew. Since there were no companies for their students, Jones and Haywood created Capitol Ballet, a semi-professional company, in 1961.

In an oral history, Jones describes the journey from renting space to owning their own studio at 1200 Delafield Place NW, where the school resides to this day.[25] When Dr. Martin Luther King was assassinated, uprisings in cities led to White people moving to the suburbs, which lowered housing costs, and made it possible for Jones to purchase a home. However, when the owners found out that Jones and Haywood were Black and had cash, the price went from two to three thousand dollars.

Jones credits a strong guild under the leadership of a White man, Robert Cantrell, as being important to the success of the school and company. Cantrell facilitated Capitol Ballet performances at the French and English Embassies, as well as the White House. Jones adds, "He's the one who made the contact with the Russians for us to take that little girl over in 1973 to be in the ballet competition."[26] The "girl" is Sandra Fortune-Green, the only American invited to the Second International Ballet Competition in Moscow in 1973.

Sandra Fortune-Green and Lauri Fitz-Pegado trained together at the Jones Haywood School of Ballet in the 1960s and early 1970s. Since 2006, Fortune-Green has served as Artistic Director of the Jones Haywood Dance School. Fitz-Pegado studied dance at Vassar College and the Dance Theatre of Harlem School. She worked for the U.S. Department of Commerce where she was Assistant Secretary and Director General of the US and Foreign Commercial Service. Fitz-Pegado is now a faculty member at Jones Haywood Dance School.

Fitz-Pegado and Fortune-Green describe Ms. Jones as a methodical teacher who insisted on excellence in technique and behavior, promptness, consistent attendance, proper etiquette, and grooming. Ms. Jones was encouraging and process-oriented with a keen ability to analyze the body and identify technical mistakes. Fitz-Pegado states, "You just knew that Ms. Jones was going to give a correction that was so insightful and that was so immediate. Whenever Ms. Jones was in the room there was the urge to pull up more, to stretch your knees more—I wanted to please her; I wanted her to be able to see I was making progress." Ms. Jones progressed her students' technique and artistry by choreographing pieces for them. They recall her choreography at all stages of their development and in all genres: ballet, pointe, tap, and modern.

The demand for excellence was overt and, by today's standards, blurred the line between teaching and emotional or verbal abuse. Fitz-Pegado states, "Things that were said to us that were rather insulting sometimes." This tough love approach contributed to dancers' resiliency, which Fitz-Pegado and Fortune-Green recognize as necessary for Black dancers in professional ballet. The by-product was a close sisterhood that formed amongst pupils. Students sought to dance well to please their teachers, and to avoid their wrath, especially Ms. Haywood's. This sisterhood enabled them to commensurate and handle the tough love. Fitz-Patrick says, "Some of it became funny because we were bonded in a way—we became family."

Though Jones had minimal formal training in ballet, and Haywood even less, they attracted acclaim as teachers. Fortune-Green and Fitz-Pegado describe how their credibility came from three sources: strategic partnerships, performances that showcased their school, and success of their alumni. Both Fitz-Pegado and Fortune-Green received Ford Foundation scholarships awarded by George Balanchine and administered through the School of American Ballet. The scholarships were renewable through annual selection and both women described working very hard to keep them. This partnership enabled them to attend the School of American Ballet Summer Courses in New York City, and Jones and Haywood received pedagogy training setting them apart from Bernice Hammond and Therrell Smith, who were also Black ballet teachers in the DC-area. George Balanchine, Arthur Mitchell, Kay Mazzo, and other New York City Ballet artists came down periodically to guest teach and select scholarship recipients. Fitz-Pegado and Fortune-Green describe the robust recruitment of dancers, especially boys, from the DC Public Schools and the exceptionally high standard all students were held to.

Performances by the Capitol Ballet further solidified the credibility and expertise of Jones and Haywood. The company was invited to perform at the inauguration of Richard Nixon, at Fisk University, and many other venues. They frequently sold out George Washington University's Lisner Auditorium. Their repertory included choreography by Ms. Jones, Louis Johnson, and Billy Wilson. Capitol Ballet was a huge factor in amplifying the beauty of Black dancers in ballet, and the excellence of Jones and Haywood as teachers. Their notable alumni include Chita Rivera, Hinton Battle, and Sylvester Campbell. Fitz-Pegado states, "They were not very humble about it." Fortune-Green chimes in, "They were braggadocios." This vital act of self-promotion is congruent with existing scholarship on Black professors establishing credibility in the educational setting.

Jones took the time to teach Fitz-Pegado and Fortune-Green how to teach. Around age 14, Fitz-Pegado began to teach, and Ms. Jones mentored her, observing her classes and carefully spelling out what she wanted her to do with the children. Both Fitz-Pegado and Fortune-Green grew up with a foundation in pedagogy imparted by Ms. Jones, and they recognize the significance of being a Black ballet teacher for Black children. Fortune-Green says, "We are better suited as teachers for our children. Because what we can say to them, we can say it in a way that a White teacher cannot say it. The kids are not offended. Parents are okay with it. I just think it makes you stronger as a Black child that wants to pursue ballet as a career." This speaks to the power of both representation and cultural competency in education. While there may be White teachers who teach Black students effectively, Fitz-Pegado says, "It is not true that you teach a White child and a Black child the same way."

Another distinguishing element of Black teachers in classical ballet is fostering students' resiliency. Fortune-Green considers this just as relevant today as it was in the 1930s and 1940s. When Fortune-Green attended the School of American Ballet, she was passed over for corrections by Muriel Stuart, yet her training with Jones equipped her to apply corrections that were given to others. She offers another example of Dionne Figgins, one of her students, who joined Dance Theatre of Harlem in the early 2000s. Figgins was initially hazed by DTH Artistic

Director, Arthur Mitchell, yet her resiliency was unshakable. Fortune-Green recalls that Mitchell said, "Those Jones Haywood girls are tough; you can't break them."

Discussion

The experiences and perceptions of Black classical ballet teachers are vital to creating a more racially diverse and culturally inclusive art form. The challenges faced by teachers in terms of establishing credibility and expertise have been greatly overlooked and under-researched. My training and professional performing career were well supported by teachers and mentors of all ethnicities, and I rarely thought of my skin color as a barrier to artistic growth and opportunities. Nevertheless, I encountered significant microaggressions and challenges to my credibility as a teacher.

For example, when I was asked to teach a class at The Jacqueline Kennedy Onassis School at American Ballet Theatre (ABT) in New York City as a substitute teacher, I was so excited. I observed the Level 2 teacher with the 9 and 10-year-old group for a week and took meticulous notes to ensure my class resembled the teacher's. We had a wonderful time together doing exactly what the children usually do in ballet class, and afterwards, a student came up to me and asked, "Are you a modern dancer?" It immediately hit me, "I didn't match her image of what a ballet teacher was supposed to look like."

Fast-forward five years, and I was directing a satellite campus of The Washington School of Ballet in a neighborhood of Washington, DC that is 95% African American. The majority of students and teachers at this campus are Black, since it is important that teachers reflect the identities of students. I filtered all parent complaints, and they were overwhelmingly from White parents about their child's experience with a Black teacher. When I listened attentively to the complaints, they all come down to one thing: the teaching style of the instructor.

This chapter reveals that Black teaching styles are rooted in excellence and high expectations for students. Black ballet teachers possess a cultural competency that allows them to effectively relate to Black children. Black ballet teachers must work hard to build credibility with their constituency—their immediate community and the larger dance world. Black ballet teachers believe in building character and resiliency so black children may be not only successful dancers in the profession, but successful in any future endeavor. At the end of the oral history interview, Jones was asked, "When you look over all these years, what do you see as your legacy?" She replied, "Gee, I don't know, has to do with children achieving. And I think about it–you're interested in me because of my teaching and dance. But I was just interested in making good citizens through the dance, through the discipline of the dance."[27]

Notes

1. Lauren Erin Brown, "As Long as they have Talent: Organizational Barriers to Black Ballet," *Dance Chronicle* 41, no. 3 (2019): 359–392. doi:10.1080/01472526.2018.1518076.
2. Crystal U. Davis and Jesse Phillips-Fein, "Tendus and Tenancy: Black Dancers and the White Landscape of Dance Education," in *The Palgrave Handbook of Race and the Arts in Education*, ed. Kraehe A., Gaztambide-Fernández R., Carpenter II B (London: Palgrave Macmillan, 2018), 571–584. doi:10.1007/978-3-319-65256-6_33.
3. Jonathan S. Abelson, Natalie Z. Wong, Matthew Symer, Gregory Eckenrode, Anthony Watkins, and Heather L. Yeo, "Racial and Ethnic Disparities in Promotion and Retention of Academic Surgeons," *The American Journal of Surgery* 216, no. 4 (2018): 678–82; Donnetrice 2018.
4. Devon Wilson, Donald Dantzler, Damian Evans, and Richard McGregory, "Do Racial Disparities Exist in the Labor Market for Educators?" *Journal of Economics, Race, and Policy* 3, no. 3 (2020): 195–204. doi:10.1007/s41996-020-00055-0.
5. Kimberly A. Griffin, "Voices of the 'Othermothers': Reconsidering Black Professors' Relationships with Black Students as a Form of Social Exchange," *The Journal of Negro Education* 82, no. 2 (2013): 169–183. doi:10.7709/jnegroeducation.82.2.0169; Lori Walkington, "How Far have we really Come? Black Women Faculty and Graduate Students' Experiences in Higher Education," *Humboldt Journal of Social Relations* 39 (2017): 51–65.
6. Nell Painter, "Black Studies, Black Professors, and the Struggles of Perception," in *A Companion to African-American Studies*, eds. Lewis Gordon and Jane Gordon (New Jersey: Blackwell Publishing Ltd, 2006).
7. Donnetrice C. Allison, "Free to be Me?: Black Professors, White Institutions," *Journal of Black Studies* 38, no. 4 (March 2008): 641–662.
8. Allison, "Free to be Me."
9. Allison, "Free to be Me;" Louis et al, "Do Racial Disparities Exist?"
10. Fang-Yi Flora Wei and Katherine Grace Hendrix, "Minority and Majority Faculty Members in a Historically Black College/University: Redefining Professors' Teacher Credibility and Classroom Management," *Qualitative Research Reports in Communication* 17, no. 1 (2016.): 102–11.
11. Walkington, "How far?"
12. Neil M. Agnew, Kenneth M. Ford, and Patrick J. Hayes, "Expertise in Context: Personally Constructed, Socially Selected, and Reality-Relevant?" *International Journal of Expert Systems* 7, no. 1 (1994): 65–88.

13 Agnew, Ford, and Hayes, "Expertise," 66.
14 Robert R. Hoffman, "How can Expertise be Defined? Implications of Research from Cognitive Psychology," in *Exploring Expertise Issues and Perspectives*, ed. Robin Williams, Wendy Faulkner and James Fleck, 81–100 (London: Palgrave Macmillan, 1998).
15 Abiola A. Farinde, Ayana Allen, and Chance W. Lewis. "Retaining Black Teachers: An Examination of Black Female Teachers' Intentions to Remain in K-12 Classrooms," *Equity & Excellence in Education* 49, no. 1 (2016): 115–127. doi:10.1080/10665684.2015.1120367.
16 Jacqueline Jordan Irvine, "Beyond Role Models: An Examination on Cultural Influences on the Pedagogical Perspectives of Black Teachers," *Peabody Journal of Education* 66, no. 4 (Summer 1989): 51–63.
17 Richard H. Milner, "Challenging Negative Perceptions of Black Teachers," *Educational Foundations* 26, nos. 1–2 (2012): 27.
18 Gershenson, Holt, and Papageorge 2016.
19 Patrick B. McGrady and John R. Reynolds, "Racial Mismatch in the Classroom: Beyond Black-white differences," *Sociology of Education* 86, no. 1 (January 2013): 17–3.
20 Lisa Delpit and Joanne Kilgour Dowdy, *The Skin That We Speak: Thoughts on Language and Culture in the Classroom* (New York: New Press, 2008); Irvine, "Beyond Role Models."
21 Irvine, "Beyond Role Models."
22 Delpit and Dowdy, *The Skin That We Speak*.
23 Irvine, "Beyond Role Models."
24 Doris Jones, "The History Makers: Doris Jones," interview by Larry Crowe, July 25, 2003. *The History Makers Digital Archive A2003.169.*
25 Jones, 2003.
26 Jones, 2003.
27 Jones, 2003.

12
ADJUSTING PEDAGOGIES FOR DEVELOPING ARTISTS

Age-appropriate Classes for Classical Ballet

Misa Oga

Classical ballet is often associated with words like "conservative," "exclusive," and "elitist." However, in my teaching of classical ballet, I emphasize the value of learning within an inclusive educational environment and the value of empowering students to lead fulfilling lives and careers. I believe ballet training is beneficial to every dancer in the class and should be enjoyed by all individuals regardless of age, race, and abilities. I frequently teach dancers varying in ages, from two-year-old toddlers to university students, from pre-professional dancers to adults. It is rewarding to teach students in every stage of life. Regardless of students' needs and different teaching approaches for each age, I aspire to cultivate an appreciation for ballet, as well as an environment that nurtures life-long skills. While honoring the integrity of classical ballet, I foster confidence and individuality through ballet training.

I agree with Alonzo King as he said, "Dance training can't be separate from life training. Everything that comes into our lives is training. The qualities we admire in great dancing are the same qualities we admire in human beings: honesty, courage, fearlessness, generosity, wisdom, depth, compassion, and humanity."[1] In my teaching practice, I aim to create a student-centered environment by bringing open and generous energy into the class, and offering students the space to approach their work with confidence and authority. As a young student

DOI: 10.4324/9781003283065-15

and aspiring dancer, I remember how my performance in class was significantly influenced by my teacher's energy and behavior. As I experienced many different teaching styles, I credit several mentors in my life who generously blessed me with their plethora of knowledge and energy in the classroom, allowing me to flourish as a dancer and as an individual. My goal is to provide this positive and nurturing classroom for my students. As a teacher, I aspire to model these admirable qualities inside and outside of the studio. In the next sections, I hope to provide several examples of how I apply my experiences and teaching practices for varying age groups.

Pre-school: Ages Two through Five

Because ballet classes can begin at a very young age, it is important that teachers for pre-school age children foster curiosity, excitement, and joy. Young children cannot learn from verbal instruction only; they learn from observing and imitating adults. As a teacher, I aim to show admirable qualities such as compassion and kindness, especially since this may be students' first experience away from their caregivers. I welcome each one personally when they walk into the studio, acknowledge dancers by their names, and express how wonderful it is to see them. Even simple things, such as teaching correct posture, can be encouraged by saying "You are very important. Stand tall and proud!"

I have found that young children respond best to repetition. Even at the young age of two, children can recognize familiar steps, and also recognize certain songs and melodies that are familiar to them. When I incorporate repetition into my choice of steps and music, children are enthusiastic and confident. Because young children are excited to participate in ballet class when they are actively engaged, I incorporate songs such as "Twinkle, Twinkle Little Star" and "Row, Row, Row your Boat." When introducing new steps into their vocabulary, I find it meaningful to approach the movement with a musical song or phrase that is already familiar. I aim for students to go home feeling accomplished, but also have something that they can remember and be reminded of during the week.

Another effective practice is to encourage singing in my classes. When dancers use their voices in ballet class, this can be empowering. Young children sing starting "around the age of 9 months,"[2] and most children enjoy using their voices. Children in my classes appreciate using their voices to learn the combinations, including the musical phrases and ballet terms. In many of the combinations, I teach dancers to sing the ballet vocabulary as we are learning and practicing the steps. This fosters repetition and consistency in music and movement, also allowing the dancers to remember new material. Instead of seeking mastery of material at this stage of development, I view my role as a teacher of pre-school age dancers as an educator who provides dancers with varied movement experiences.

Already at this age, it is valuable for students to be introduced to the idea of having consistent and clear limits to maintain safety and to learn acceptable behaviors. Certain skills, such as listening when the teacher is speaking, can be taught by explaining that they are kind when they are quiet and listening. Taking turns across the floor not only teaches patience but also fosters respect for their peers. Saying hello and goodbye to each individual in the class also can instill confidence and encourage positive relationships. Additionally, it is important that classes are short so that the younger dancers feel that they want to come back the next time. As a teacher, I aim to show enthusiasm for every effort and for every student.

Mid-childhood: Ages Six through Nine

When students enter the early years of school, they begin to understand the idea of cause and effect. It is especially important for dancers to feel that their efforts are translated into feeling successful physically, socially, and cognitively. At this age, students can remember and comprehend what their teachers and peers think of them. Also at this age, logical thinking emerges. It is crucial that instruction be logical and simple so dancers can feel confident and can comprehend what they are being asked to do. I aim to demonstrate movement clearly and precisely, as well as provide strategies for dancers to remember concepts and corrections.

As social relationships are important for students of this age, I introduce combinations in ballet class that foster social skills and cooperation. Combinations that require facing a partner, making a gesture to a partner, clapping when a dancer performs a movement, or simply running around a partner, engage students' attention. Additionally, handclapping exercises are enjoyable, as well as valuable. Traditionally, handclapping games, which are often learned and practiced on school playgrounds, have an educational component: not only does handclapping cultivate rhythmic understanding and complex coordination, but it also fosters social skills and cooperation. Moreover, movements crossing the midline, such as a typical clapping game of "patty cake," encourage bilateral integration skills, as well as neurological development of the right and left hemispheres of the brain.

I find it valuable for children to explore ways in which they can creatively produce movement. This is the beginning of training and motivating dancers to become future choreographers. In other words, I make time in a ballet class to encourage children to improvise to music. When improvising, children often perform repetitive movements which are typically simple twirling and bouncing movements.[3] I feel it is important to allow this improvisation and spontaneous dancing. As a teacher, I respond to their creations in ways that will encourage their confidence and their ability to create movement. While the steps may not be technically correct, it is meaningful and effective to watch and positively respond to the dancer's movement. As children grow older, it is common to observe dancers become more sensitive and self-conscious of their own movements. It is my goal to make improvisation an activity that generates positive feelings within the ballet class, since this will instill confidence and courage as dancers grow older.

Early Adolescence: Ages Ten through Fourteen

By early adolescence, some ballet students train with the goal of becoming a professional dancer. Regardless of their career paths, dancers in these levels associate training with a purpose, and teachers must be able to communicate transparently when describing goals for each student and for the class. At this age, dancers are now capable of sustaining attention and processing thoughts. Additionally, they are able to feel empowered and successful when they achieve their goals. I enjoy teaching these levels, as dancers understand the importance of a daily process. Some of these dancers are in the middle of their growth cycles, which can frustrate a student's sense of accomplishment. I find that focusing on the artistic aspects of dancing, meaning developing musicality and emphasizing movement qualities, contributes to students' finding joy in the training, and empowering these dancers.

At this age, I also find that students are searching for ways to become independent. Creating opportunities for students to feel that they have control enriches their development. I have found that giving students the responsibility of being prepared—such as sewing their own shoes and arriving to class with ample time to warm up—and expecting them to succeed as responsible dancers, can be very effective. It is common for dancers of this age to start comparing themselves to their peers. However, as a teacher, creating opportunities for students to feel accomplished and valued, is crucial to providing an inclusive environment. Other aspects that can be accomplished at this age include honest communication and honing a dedicated work ethic.

Additionally, I value verbal articulation in the classroom and encourage students to share their understandings of the material. Commenting on class material not only instills understanding and critical thinking, but also facilitates confidence and willingness to voice ideas in front of peers. Again, encouraging students to use their voices can be deeply empowering. Moreover, personal ideas and experiences enrich the learning of every individual in the classroom, as well as my own development as a teacher. I find that dancers also enjoy having conversations on current ballet topics that they see on social media, especially topics that impact companies and dancers around the world. As a teacher, I value and respect dancers' abilities to think critically and form their own opinions. I also find it is helpful to have conversations with students about not comparing themselves to their peers. Having a conversation about different strengths in the classroom helps in maintaining a positive learning environment.

In each ballet technique class, I set goals and expectations for my students, artistically and technically. By providing positive reinforcement as well as detailed corrections, I teach young dancers to focus on and prioritize their personal growth. I aim to teach dancers that their time and efforts are valuable, and to make every individual's progress their own priority. As a teacher, I make sure to reward effort and improvement. As dancers learn to focus on themselves and are disciplined in their work ethic, I often receive comments from parents that their academic work has progressed as well. I value the changes in cognitive abilities as well as their abilities to have meaningful conversations, and to think critically.

Maturing Artists: Ages 15+

As dancers reach high school, many students struggle with balancing academics, training demands, and social interactions with family and other relationships. As a mentor and a teacher, I teach dancers that a healthy balance is essential to their dance training and to their growth as a dancer. As mental and emotional health and wellbeing are crucial for ballet training and performance, I aim to help dancers pursue healthy lives. It is important for me to have an open door for my students so that I am available for their questions and concerns. Often, I find that by talking through their concerns, I can help students find the positives and, ultimately, empower them to succeed in many situations.

Within the ballet class, and in conversations with my students, I aim to provide insights about different career paths. Personally, as a young dancer, my teachers taught me that the end goal of the ballet training was to become a professional dancer. As a result, the only celebrated path I knew was becoming a "ballerina." In contrast, I hope to educate my students that there are many rewarding and valuable career paths. I personally know of many individuals who I have danced with, who have gone on to become teachers, doctors, physical therapists, psychologists, costume designers, lighting designers, and other successful individuals in their fields. Many will attribute their ballet training and experiences—especially the perseverance and critical thinking they engaged—as key to their success in any sector.

As an educator I have observed that certain personality types are drawn to particular activities and occupations, such as ballet. Additionally, ballet training can nurture distinct personalities and qualities. I was drawn to ballet because it required attention to detail and diligent, consistent effort. From a young age, I have always been detail-oriented and a perfectionist. In elementary school, I would retake tests if I did not get a perfect score and would spend hours on a single homework assignment. If I misspelled a word on a handwritten report, I would rewrite the entire paper and start over to make sure that every word was evenly spaced and legible. As I became older, I noticed that this trait enriched my training as a ballet student: I never lost focus or motivation in the art form that is considered "never perfect." I had an intense passion for dancing and performing. However, this strong desire to be successful also created anxieties and unhealthy habits. As I began teaching, my focus shifted, and I was happier. I found joy in teaching dancers and spending time in refining my everyday class structure and being thoughtful in my teaching and towards students. Even though I was still young and of dancing age, I chose to focus my energy and time on teaching.

My sister, Chisako Oga, is currently a soloist with Boston Ballet. Although we were raised similarly in our home as well as in our ballet training, we have very different personalities. Where I tend to overthink and spend hours analyzing, Chisako is straightforward and accomplishes tasks very easily. She is intelligent and a very hard worker. She is also a natural performer. Upon graduating from the San Francisco Ballet School, Chisako became a trainee and later joined the company. She then successfully rose through the ranks at Cincinnati Ballet and became a principal dancer at the young age of 21. She loves performing in Boston and finds joy in every opportunity that she is given. On top of her busy rehearsal and performance schedule, she is taking university courses to earn a degree in accounting. Just as Chisako and I have different personalities that have helped us find our pathways in ballet, it is important for me as a teacher to get to know my students and to cater their training to their needs and personalities. As many individuals have different learning types and tendencies, it is crucial to create a student-centered learning environment for the most effective learning.

Conclusion

Productive learning is fostered in a positive, mindful, and inclusive classroom. Through my studies and pedagogical research, I commit to presenting material in a reflective manner. I agree with dance scholar Jessica Zeller who eloquently articulates that "progressive ballet pedagogy via reflective practice can preserve—rather than distort or dilute—the classical tradition's emphasis on form and style."[4] Meanwhile, I also believe in establishing training goals for students, encouraging each dancer to reach their greatest potential. Through a reflective approach and by being transparent about my pedagogic choices, I empower individual students to achieve this great potential.

As the world evolves, ballet must also evolve. As a teacher and a mentor, I commit to lifelong learning. Teaching entails responsibilities to both broaden my knowledge base and to approach a class by focusing on students' needs. I aim to prepare dancers for their individual aspirations and careers. To accomplish these goals, it is essential to mindfully consider each student and to analyze every class. Additionally, I make time to research and understand different practices and ideas that can help guide individual students. Through my teaching and example, I hope students also cherish education and pursue ongoing learning. It is important to me that students feel confident, valued, and are thoughtful. As Alonzo King said, the qualities that we admire in individuals are the same qualities that we admire in dancing. Different personalities and strengths can be contributed to the growth of the whole class, and to the future of this beautiful art form.

Notes

1 Alonzo King, https://blog.linesballet.org/2016/09/12/lines-ballet-bfa-program-celebrates-its-10th-anniversary-speaking-with-faculty-and-alumni/
2 Diana Deutsch, "The Development of Music Perception and Cognition," *The Psychology of Music*, (Cambridge, MA: Academic Press, 1999), 215.
3 Gary E. McPherson, *The Child as Musician: A Handbook of Musical Development* (Oxford: Oxford University Press, 2015), 296.
4 Jessica Zeller, "Reflective Practice in the Ballet Class: Bringing Progressive Pedagogy to the Classical Tradition," *Journal of Dance Education* 17, no. 3 (2017): 99.

13
BALLET AS ARTISTIC, SCIENTIFIC, AND EXISTENTIAL INQUIRY

Incorporating Ballet's Broader History in a Syllabus and in the Studio

Jehbreal Muhammad Jackson

Now, that the veils of ballet's "purifying" practices are rending, we see beyond their gloss and fortified walls to excavate what remains of its lost legacies and erased voices. As we do so, we address the many ballet companies that continue to employ racializing costume designs and narratives in their performances, while they also reproduce uncontextualized and reductive fables as "tradition." In our pursuit of restoration, reformation, and healing, it is imperative that an empathetic balm permeate every crack of ballet's fractured infrastructure and pervade the form's culture, meaning ballet classes, dance history courses, choreographic contexts, and institutional philosophies.[1]

This chapter offers practical suggestions for amplifying ballet's non-European foundations. One lineage comes from the Islamic governance of Spain, or al-Andalus, from 711 CE- 1492 CE. Another is the diasporic Bukôngo tradition, that predates and parallels that of Islamic Iberia and enters Europe through early modern Spanish ports and stages.[2] I will draw our attention to the mathematic, scientific, and philosophical principles that appear to pervade Andalusi and Bukôngo compositional systems. I trace the entry of these systems, focusing primarily on the *Sarabande*, into the French courts.[3] This exploration is complicated by archives and racial depictions that are inseparable from the establishment of hegemonic ideologies that supported Europe's colonizing missions. The racial tropes crafted for one racialized group were applied to many others, which can

DOI: 10.4324/9781003283065-16

lead to conflated and confusing accounts.[4] The French ballets of the 1600s, in particular, reveal the joint development of colonization and the standard ballet divertissement tradition (performed as a procession of nations) that fantasized about the communities that were/would be colonized.[5] In an attempt to recuperate the integrity of the appropriated traditions, while dissecting the hegemonic coupling of court ballets and colonization, I investigate Islamic and Bukôngo cosmological artifacts in tandem with documents from early modern Europe.

This research focuses special attention on the *Sarabande* as, potentially, an example of African and Islamic art forms synthesizing not just in the imaginations of early modern Europeans, but in the dance form itself that reflects a deep commitment to an atomic and geometric understanding of the cosmos. This understanding does not emanate from "European" ideologies, but those of the Bukôngo religion, as depicted on the *N'kisi Sarabanda* cosmogram (Figure 13.1), and through the Islamic rational theology of Kalām Atomism enacted in the *shabaka* (Arabic: grid, net, web) designs of the Alhambra's "Hall of Two Sisters" *Murqanas* (stalactite) vaulting (Figure 13.3a-b), and Moorish gardens. This examination suggests an enduring presence of Afro-Islamic agency, spirituality, and intellect while also highlighting a

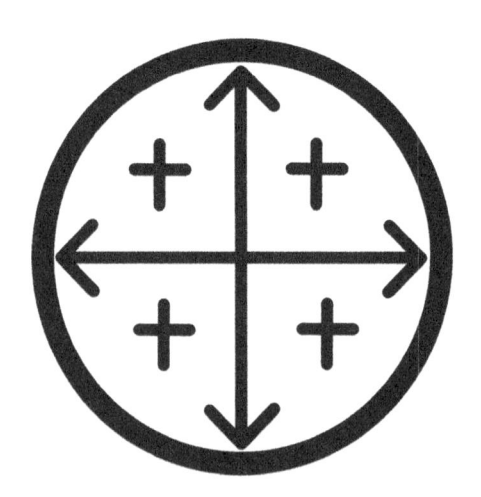

FIGURE 13.1 The *N'kisi Sarabanda* is a spiritual signature ("firma") of the *mpungo* (spiritual ancestor or natural force) *Sarabanda*. It likely influenced the *en croix* pattern of ballet technique.

tension between influence and impersonation that has persisted in the very DNA of classical ballet to this day.

The Bukôngo religion is an African Indigenous Religion (AIR) that employs a scientific cosmology, linking the spirit world to the natural world through scientific explanations. As Kiatezua Lubanzadio Luyaluka observes, it shares commonalities with many other AIRs and is believed to be one of the oldest and least altered spiritual practices on the continent that evolved out of Kemetic (ancient Egyptian) and Kushite cosmologies like the Memphite creation story depicted on the Shabaka/o Stone (710 BCE) (Figure 13.2).[6] The story includes the deity Atum, progenitor of the atom concept.

Kalām Atomism and Greek Atomism are also believed to be derived from the Kemetic deity Atum.[7] Graham Pont illuminates that the Greeks modeled their theories on those of Kemet, and Plato's concept of musical spheres and dancing celestial bodies applied to dance as well as music.[8] Andalusi Moors adopted, developed, and introduced these philosophies to Renaissance Europe. In their unique ways, the various arts of al-Andalus subdivided, fractalized, and mathematically rationalized their materials while balancing them with

FIGURE 13.2 The Shabaka/o Stone created in 710 BCE conglomerate stela. The star-like pattern is attributed to it later being used as a nether millstone.

FIGURE 13.3A Close-up reduction of eight-point star that anchors the *Murqanas* (stalactite) dome in the "Hall of Two Sisters" in the Alhambra palace built between 1238 and 1370 during the Nasrid Dynasty (the last dynasty of Islamic rule in Spain). It reflects the Kalām philosophy of an atomically interconnected universe. The "created world" is represented by the botanical vines, plant, and flower shapes (#'s 5 & 12) that weave throughout *shabaka* (grid) patterns, and the permanence, order, and exactitude of the creator are shown in the precision of the geometric patterning of points, lines, planes, and right angles (#'s 1–4, 6, 7 & 9). Design: Raheem Tutein

botanical images of nature to enact the existential principles that were being explored.[9] This unity provided a common language for Andalusi polymaths to transmit centuries of wisdom across fields, time, and space. During the unique cultural moment when Bukôngo met with Islam in early modern Spain, and prior, I suggest that these kindred cosmological compositions contributed to establishing the basis for Western modern artistic practices, including classical ballet. This is seen most vividly in the continual expansion and evolution of geometric explorations in the body, as ballet dancers become living and breathing mathematical/directional compasses.

FIGURE 13.3B Full view of three-dimensional *Murqanas* design in the "Hall of Two Sisters" in the Alhambra palace. (Wikimedia Commons)

Past

In the seventeenth century, the courts of Louis XIII and XIV absorbed and depicted Spanish art and culture by appropriating the *Sarabande*, taken from the Spanish theater's *Zarabanda*. French court ballets integrated this foreign dance into their own repertoires, exemplified by the 1626 ballet *Grand Bal de la Douairière de Billebahaut*, and Jean-Baptiste Lully and Moliére's *comédie* ballets of the 1660s. Spanish theater had absorbed the *Zarabanda* from the many Afro-Indigenous diasporic communities that were present and continually arriving in Seville during the transatlantic trade of the 1580s, including, but not limited to, Moors and their Morisco descendants, Congolese, Guinean, Indigenous American, and African American people.[10]

Scholars have long debated about the obscure foreign origins of the Spanish *Sarabande*.[11] This study aligns most closely with Mara Lioba Juan Carvajal whose comprehensive study synthesizes the various arguments by revealing influences from Africa, the Americas, and Islam. She argues that the diasporic zarabanda genre potentially has roots as far back as the tenth century meeting of Islam and Bukôngo traditions and subsequently took two parallel paths. One traveled northward into the Mediterranean. The other traveled south of the Sahara, through the Americas and returned to meet the first branch in Spain.[12] Despite these complexities, French ballets centralize the *Sarabande*, giving it climactic importance.

In the *Grand Bal*, the "Dances of Europe" section comes as the penultimate moment of the ballet, culminating a procession of various nations. The "Grenadines" are the dancers of the *Sarabande*, Granada being the last remaining center of the Islamic rule of Spain before the 1492 expulsion of the Moors and Jewish peoples (Figure 13.4).[13] In Lully's 1666 *Ballet de Muses*, the "Mascarade espagnole" is a series of *sarabandes* that depict the "true national character" of Spain and honor the marriage of Louis XIV to the Infanta Maria Teresa of Spain. According to Albert Cohen, Lully monopolized on the European fascination with foreign traditions, and gradually adopted popular Spanish techniques and compositional practices. Eventually, the *Sarabande* became more of a compositional tool than a depiction of national character.[14] Lully, a composer and choreographer, learned directly from Spanish performers who, very likely, worked with Afro-diasporic dance masters or informal Afro-descended teachers themselves. Nicholas R. Jones and Noémie Ndiaye illuminate how dance masters of African

FIGURE 13.4 Photo Credit: © RMN-Grand Palais / Art Resource, NY. Artist: Rabel, Daniel (1578–1637) Description: Dancers performing a sarabande, four figures. Album Rabel Daniel - Folio 46. A collection of drawings related to the *Ballet de la Douairière de Billebahaut* danced by Louis XIII in February 1626 in the hall of the Louvre. Ink and watercolor, 28.5 x 44 cm

descent were present in Spain in the early modern period and taught Spanish performers their dances as well as other popular practices.[15] Jones notes that non-African performers sought accuracy in their portrayals of African-descended characters for their Afro-diasporic audiences in Seville.[16]

Daniel Rabel's drawings of the "Grenadines" do not darken the skin of the dancers as Rabel does for dancers of other nations. This could indicate the absorption of this dance form into Spanish quotidian life apart from its association with Moors and Africans. It could also reflect the racial ambiguity of early modern Spaniards and/or the wide range of Moorish skin tones. The word "Moor" was used much like the word "Black" is in the twenty-first century to describe a person of certain or uncertain African descent, likely mixed with Arab, Syrian, or other lineage.[17] It was used in descriptive, prescriptive, and pejorative ways; sometimes as a blanket term for anyone of African descent, a title for religious affiliation, and other times conflated with or distinguished from other words like "Negro."[18]

The term is important to this research for several reasons. First, as hegemonically inflected historical documents use this word, it is important for me to be mindful of its complexities while also demonstrating its flexibility, reflective of these historical uses. Second, I hope the term elicits the broad spectrum of not only skin tones but also the ethnic lineages of the occupants of al-Andalus and early modernity. "Moorish" associations are not limited to the equally troubling "Berber" term or the "Imazighen" of North Africa, as they also include sub-Saharan populations and migratory mixing with Middle Eastern populations, mixing that extended as far as Indigenous American populations.[19] Third, along with fears of religious rebellion against the Catholic crown, the religion of the Islamic Moors became associated with blood lineages from Africa, which were increasingly coupled with darker skin complexions and were marginalized, dehumanized, demonized, and eventually exorcised. Nevertheless, Spain retained Moorish and Islamic philosophies, sciences, culture, and artistic practices. Rabel's drawings reflect the ethno-cultural erasure of the Moors that accompanied the growing anti-Moor sentiment, and deliberate "cleansing of blood" or "whitewashing" of Moorish culture. Like other aspects of Moorish/Andalusi culture, the *Zarabanda/Sarabande* was so loved by so many that it continued to be danced despite its connection to the Moors and Africans.

K. Meira Goldberg reveals the complex relationship of Spain to its Moorishness, noting that Spain was at once repulsed yet enamored. Goldberg looks at the simultaneous expulsion, amplification, and Black racialization of Islamic Moors by the Catholic regime which sought to erase the people, but kept their intellectual and cultural practices.[20] Barbara Fuchs reveals that the cultural world of the Moors was so deeply enmeshed and foundational to Spain that it was rendered indiscernible and inextricable from Spanish identity.[21] It took visitors from the surrounding European nations to note Spain's "Moorishness" and "Africanness." An example of this indiscernible/inextricable influence is the design and popularity of Moorish gardens, that share formal and cosmological features with the other Islamic arts. Fuchs, Yasser Tabbaa, and Christopher J. Pastore reveal that Italian Renaissance gardens are clearly fashioned after Islamic garden design, which utilize Islamic *shabaka* patterns (Figures 13.5).[22] Jennifer Nevile has argued that Italian Renaissance and French gardens, like Moorish gardens, reflected the pervasive preoccupation with cosmic order through proportion and geometry.[23] They also appear to have corresponded to the floor patterns of Baroque dances. In addition to illuminating how this correlation applies to foundational court spectacles like *Le Ballet Comique de la Reine* (1581), often cited as the first court ballet, Nevile demonstrates this correlation by mapping floor pattern choreographies from the sixteenth century *balletto, Dolce Amoroso Foco,* onto the garden pathways embedded in the garden compartment in *L'Ambrogiana,* powerfully revealing a clear correlation between the two. This correlation evokes earlier accounts of Moorish/Morisco performances in Moorish gardens and the importance of elevated vantage points to observe the garden's geometric patterns.[24] The adoption of the Moorish usage of geometries in space coincides with embodied geometries in the *Sarabanda,* whose European iterations depicted Moors, Africans, and various other ethnicities.

The Bukôngo religion and its diasporic iterations, including the Palo Monte Mayombe tradition that developed in Cuba, emerge as important precedents to the *Sarabande.* The *N'kisi Sarabanda* (Figure 13.1) is a reproduction of one found on the National African Burial Ground website. It exemplifies cosmograms, or spiritual signatures ("firmas") that are found throughout the Americas and that share a common religious ancestor, the Bukôngo religion, traced to the historical kingdom of Kongo. "Sarabanda" is an mpungo (a spirit of an ancestor or natural force) in the Cuban Kongo-based Palo Monte Mayombe religion derived from Bukôngo traditions, also associated with healing, metal, and equivalent to the Yoruba deity Ogun.

Judith Bettelheim argues that the Palo Monte Mayombe influence generates a "recognizable aesthetic structure and pictorial iconography" in the context of contemporary Cuban art,[25] and I extend these connections to note the global influence of Bukôngo practices. Grey Gundaker reveals alignments across the diasporic offspring of Bukôngo, as they share a common philosophical origin, and asserts that there is no fixed meaning of the Kongo cosmogram, or *dikenga*, because "a key premise of *dikenga* ideology is that nothing ever survives 'intact' because nothing ever survives in a fixed form. Period. Ever. Anywhere."[26] This fluidity allowed the *dikenga* to survive as well as confound Eurocentric oppression. Gundaker explains that it "stands to reason that people have used mnemonic signs to help them continually remake a recognizable world," legibly across the diaspora. In other words, during and after the trans-Atlantic slave trade, the *dikenga* served as "an enduring moral compass" and offered, "guidance for peaceful and violent times alike."[27]

For Bettelheim and Robert Farris Thompson, the *Sarabanda firma* "references the four moments of the sun," and is "the Kongo cosmogram most important to spiritual continuity and life itself."[28] Similarly, the African Burial Ground website states:

> Nkisi Sarabanda, symbolizing the signature of the spirit, is a representation of a bakongo cosmogram. This symbol portrays how the Congo-angolan people viewed the interaction between the spiritual and material world, or in other words between the living and the dead... Nkisis show the development of African American culture in how they are essentially African objects, but are constructed through American materials. This also reveals an aspect of the melting pot of African and American culture. Sarabanda just connotes "the highest spirit"... Communication appears to take place at the center of the cross, where the worlds intersect, and it was believed that spirits sat at the center of the sign. The arrows represent the four winds of the universe, and the symbol as a whole resembles the form of a spiral galaxy; this indicates their interest in astronomy and affinity towards nature.[29]

These symbols served as tools to access the spirit world, across time and geographical contexts, operating through nonverbal communication and resisting strictures of the transatlantic slave trade.[30] The diasporic Bukôngo traditions intermingled with peoples and cultures of the Americas and Islamic communities. These complex and connected lineages share a contact zone in early modern Spain and evidence of their influence on court dances can be found in the growing popularity of the *Sarabande* after its appearance on Spanish stages and subsequent transmission throughout the courts of Europe.

The French and Italian dancing manuals shift from prescribing parallel feet before 1600 to geometrically turned-out legs after 1600.[31] It is not a coincidence that Spanish playwright Lope de Vega's *Las ferias de Madrid* (1589) describes the *Zarabanda* as requiring "*zambo*" (or "sambo") feet. This refers to a "bandied" or "bowed legs" position, African/Indigenous ancestry, and a type of yellow monkey, a racialized depiction of African/Indigenous Americans.[32] The word "*compás*" (Spanish for "measure") is also used with "zambo." "Good measure," which alluded to well-balanced proportions, mathematical figures, and good taste/judgement, was an important rubric for art used across early modern Europe.[33]

Turning specifically to the formal qualities embodied while dancing in "good measure," Ester J. Terry clarifies connections between proportions and movements. The Italian term *misura* gains prominence simultaneously with the late sixteenth century *moresca*, danced by sub-Saharan Africans in the courts of Kongo (a regional home of the Bukôngo religion) for an emissary of Portugal. The Portuguese and Italian reporters, Duarte Lopes and Filippo Pigafetta, in their account titled "A Report on the Kingdome of the Congo" in English, "would have understood the implications of deploying *misura* in relation to courtly dances." Terry argues that this "turn of phrase…connects the Kongo moresca to European court decorum."[34] The phrase originally appears as "danzano a misura" in fifteenth century Italian dance treatises as a way to train nobles in "decorum and virtue, and the legitimate right to rule… These sources provide the earliest written mentions of the moresca in Italian regions and the first written philosophies on embodied movement in a European region."[35] De Vega evokes this tradition in his description of the *Zarabanda*. Dance was both intellectual and creative, used as a moral tool and exemplar of proper behavior, as were the *N'kisi Sarabanda* and *shabaka* designs. The geometrically rotated position of the legs, like the formal compass qualities of the *N'kisi Sarabanda* and *shabaka* designs, evoke the geometric patterns inscribed on and off the floor while performing standard movements of classical ballet (Figure 13.5).

Present/Future

This embodiment of geometries is a hallmark of 20th and 21st century ballet, and central to ballet pedagogies, from the first actions at the barre to the last combinations that move across the floor.

Drawing from my experiences as a ballet student, professional practitioner, and ballet teacher, I have grown to emphasize the ritualistic nature of ballet practice. More specifically, I draw attention to an alignment of mind, body, soul, sounds, and space as a microcosm for life. The discipline required to enact these geometries points to Andalusi and Bukôngo cultures, where art, science, religion, and philosophy worked in tandem to understand relationships between humans and cosmos. Linking concepts of balancing in ballet to the principles of opposing forces in life makes the practice of ballet immediate, spiritual, and relevant. By honoring these artistic, spiritual, and scientific roots of ballet technique, we, as educators, can eliminate the exclusionary and toxic pedagogies that are rampant in predominantly white institutions.

Practitioners, choreographers, directors, and funders must reassess the extra-European references in Lope de Vega, Daniel Rabel, and Jean-Baptiste Lully, as well as the European relationship to al-Andalus and sub-Saharan Africa. The Africanist and Islamic aesthetics were at once rejected and admired by Christian Europeans. These fraught relations and deliberate erasures reveal Europe's own struggle with its identity. Like *shabaka* patterns and the *N'kisi Sarabanda*, ballet's wisdom resides within its deep structures. The science enacted to execute its steps becomes embodied knowledge and spirituality, exploring ways to exist. We have many more pieces of episodic history to put together and questions to ask of them so that we don't subscribe to toxically curated histories. We can contextualize and correct them for the future.

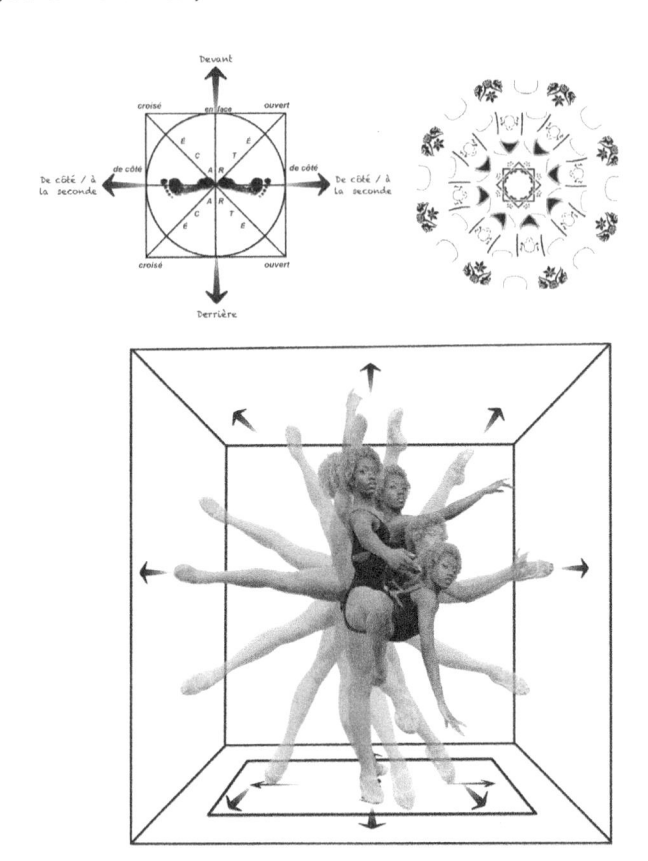

FIGURE 13.5 Upper left corner: Ballet's foundational "zambo" geometric leg rotation within the personal square of eight-point cardinal (*en croix*) and ordinal directions reflecting the eight-pointed Islamic atomic star of creation, a staple of Islamic art. Drawn by Raheem Tutein. Adapted from Jeffrey Scott Longstaff, "Organizations of Chaos in an Infinitely Deflecting Body Space." Below: Ballet dancer, Marja' Miller, in profile with geometrically degreed leg heights and botanical upper half. At the center of the floor is a diagram of the floor patterns (also seen in upper left corner). The three-dimensional ballet vocabulary, like the *Murqanas* dome, is extrapolated from the two dimensional eight-point star and enacts the same geometric, scientific, and cosmological principles as those in the *N'kisi Sarabanda* and the *Alhambra*. Design: Raheem Tutein, derived from Jeffrey Scott Longstaff. "Organizations of Chaos in an Infinitely Deflecting Body Space". *A Conference on Liminality and Performance.* Brunel University Twickenham; 27–30 April 2000.

Notes

1 See Theresa Ruth Howard's *Memoirs of Blacks in Ballet* https://mobballet.org and Phil Chan's *Final Bow for Yellowface* https://www.yellowface.org. For an example of racialized characters see "La Bayadère" (2013), *Bolshoi Ballet* at 26 minutes: https://www.youtube.com/watch?v=vM3E_tURxAM&t=1560s
2 The Chaconne, the Canary, and the Moresca are other court dances that have non-European origins/influence. I urge scholars to follow these leads with special attention to Basque, Indian, Persian, Syrian, Chinese, and Indigenous American influences.
3 Special thanks to Kaba Kamene, Khari Joyner, K. Meira Goldberg, Seth Stewart Williams, Seth Kimmel, Paul A. Scolieri, and Cornel West for their guidance with this research.
4 Noémie Ndiaye, "'Come Aloft, Jack-little-ape!': Race and Dance in *The Spanish Gypsie*," *English Literary Renaissance* 51, no. 1 (2021): 121–151.
5 Noémie Ndiaye, "Rewriting the *Grand Siècle*: Blackface in Early Modern France and the Historiography of Race," *Literature Compass* 18, no. 10 (2021).
6 Special thanks to Solange Ashby for assistance with this research. Kiatezua Lubanzadio Luyaluka, "African Indigenous Religion and Its Ancient Model Reflections of Kongo Hierarchical Monotheism." *Journal of Black Studies* 48, no. 2 (2017): 165–89.
7 A. I. Sabra, "The Simple Ontology of Kalām Atomism: An Outline," *Early Science and Medicine* 14, no. 1/3 (2009): 68–78; Yasser Tabbaa, "The Muqarnas Dome: Its Origin and Meaning." *Muqarnas* 3 (1985): 61–74; Ivan van Sertima, "The Egyptian Precursor to Greek and 'Arab' Science," *The Golden Age of the Moor* (New Jersey: Journal of African Civilizations, 1992), 397–405; George G.M. James, *Stolen Legacy* (1954; reis., Summit, NJ: Start Publishing, 2013); Kamene Kaba Hiawatha, *Shabaka's Stone: An African Theory on the Origin and Continuing Development of the Cosmic Universe* (Seattle: Amazon Digital Services LLC, 2021).
8 Graham Pont, "Plato's Philosophy of Dance," in *Dance, Spectacle and the Body Politick, 1250–1750*, ed. Jennifer Nevile (Indiana: Indiana University Press, 2008), 267–278.
9 Dwight F. Reynolds, "Music Theory and Performance Practices," *The Musical Heritage of Al-Andalus* (London: Routledge, 2020), 127–142; Yasser Tabbaa, *The Transformation of Islamic Art During the Sunni Revival* (Seattle: University of Washington Press, 2001); Gülru Necipoğlu, *Topkapi Scroll: Geometry and Ornament in Islamic Architecture* (California: Getty Center for the History of Art and the Humanities, 1995), 95.
10 Nicholas R. Jones, "Black Skin Acts: Feasting on Blackness, Staging Linguistic Blackface," *Staging Habla De Negros: Radical Performances of the African Diaspora in Early Modern Spain* (University Park: Penn State University Press, 2019).
11 Most recently, K. Meira Goldberg illuminated the dance's encoded Blackness in how it was described and listed with other dances associated with the African Diaspora in early modern Spanish sources. Nicholas R. Jones traced its origins to Afro-Cuba, via the Bukôngo religion. Across Europe as

in France, the Sarabande was associated with Spain, and Spain itself was reductively seen as an Africanized, miscegenated, and "Orientalized" other. Spain had many anti-Moor/Morisco treatises that associated the Zarabanda with the Moors/Moriscos. Dwight F. Reynolds explains the 1612 Expulsión jusificada de los moriscos espa.oles [The Justified Expulsion of the Spanish Moriscos], "was published under the name of Pedro Aznar Embiz y Cardona, though historians attribute it to an Augustinian monk named Jerónimo Aznar Embiz y Cardona. This vehemently anti-Morisco disquisition characterizes the Moriscos as being overly fond of gatherings and festivities that featured raucous entertainments, story-telling, dancing, singing, promenades amidst *gardens and fountains*, and 'bestial' activities accompanied by all manner of clamor and outcry, and claims that they often went 'screaming' through the streets. A rich array of musical instruments accompanied their singing and their dances, such as the *sarabanda* and the *zambra* including adufes [Ar. al-daff, tambourine], *sonajas* [finger cymbals or castanets], *gaitas* [double-reed instrument], *atabales* [Ar. al-tabl, drum], *añafir* [Ar. al-nafir, trumpet], *axabebas*, [Ar. al-shabbaba, flute] *albogues* [Ar. būq, small reed instrument], *laúdes* [Ar. al-'ud, lute], guitars and *rabeles* [Ar. rabāb, fiddle]." "Music of the Moriscos (16th-17th c.)," *The Musical Heritage of Al-Andalus* (London: Routledge, 2020), 231. Emphasis mine. See Robert Stevenson, "The First Dated Mention of the Sarabande," *Journal of the American Musicological Society* 5, no. 1 (1952): 29–31; Daniel Devoto, "Encore Sur 'La' Sarabande," *Revue de Musicologie* 50, no. 129 (1964): 175–207; Ralph P. Locke, "Songs and Dance-Types," *Music and the Exotic from the Renaissance to Mozart* (Cambridge University Press, 2015), 101–136; K. Meira Goldberg, "Nonsense of the Body," *Sonidos Negros* 101-136; Jones, "Black Skin Acts," 53–55.
12 Mara Lioba Juan Carvajal, La zarabanda: pluralidad y controversia de un género musical (Mexico D.F., Plaza y Valdés, 2007), 130–133, 224.
13 *Grand Bal de la Douairière de Billebahaut*,https://gallica.bnf.fr/ark:/12148/bpt6k55234766/f14.item.
14 Albert Cohen, "Spanish National Character in the Court Ballets of J. B. Lully," *Revista de Musicología* 16, no. 5 (1993): 2977–2987.
15 Noémie Ndiaye, "Black Moves: Race, Dance, and Power," *Scripts of Blackness: Early Modern Performance Culture and the Making of Race*, edited by Geraldine Heng and Ayanna Thompson (Philadelphia: University of Pennsylvania Press, 2022), 187–234; Jones, "Black Skin Acts."
16 Jones, "Black Skin Acts," 61.
17 Dana Marniche, addendum to "The African Heritage and Ethnohistory of the Moors: Background to the Emergence of Early Berber and Arab Peoples, From Prehistory to the Islamic Times," (first published 1991 in the *Journal of African Civilizations* 11). Dwight F. Reynolds, "The Qiyan of al-Andalus," in *Concubines and Courtesans: Women and Slavery in Islamic History,* eds. Matthew S. Gordon, and Kathryn A. Hain (New York: Oxford University Press, 2017), 100–118; Cristina de la Puente, "The Ethnic Origins of Female Slaves in al-Andalus," in *Concubines and Courtesans: Women and Slavery in Islamic History,* eds. Matthew S. Gordon, and Kathryn A. Hain (New York: Oxford University Press, 2017); "Moor,

n.2." *OED Online*, Oxford University Press, December 2022, www.oed.com/view/Entry/121965.
18 Noémie Ndiaye, "Performative Blackness in Early Modern Europe," in *Scripts of Blackness: Early Modern Performance Culture and the Making of Race*, eds. Geraldine Heng and Ayanna Thompson (Philadelphia: University of Pennsylvania Press, 2022), 12–14.
19 Ivan van Sertima. *They Came Before Columbus* (New York: Random House, 1976).
20 K. Meira Goldberg, *Sonidos Negros: On the Blackness of Flamenco* (New York: Oxford University Press, 2019).
21 Barbara Fuchs, *Exotic Nation: Maurophilia and the Construction of Early Modern Spain* (Philadelphia: University of Pennsylvania Press, 2011).
22 Yasser Tabbaa, "The Medieval Islamic Garden: Typology and Hydraulics," *The Production of Meaning in Islamic Architecture and Ornament* (Edinburgh, 2021); Barbara Fuchs, *Exotic Nation: Maurophilia and the Construction of Early Modern Spain* (Philadelphia: University of Pennsylvania Press, 2011), 148–149; Christopher J. Pastore, *Expanding antiquity: Andrea Navagero and villa culture in the cinquecento Veneto* (dissertation) University of Pennsylvania, 2003: 132–284.
23 Nevile argues that the gardens of the Italian Renaissance possibly provide floor patterns for the Renaissance court dances that move from Italy to France and that shift from geometrical to curvilinear designs: "Throughout the fifteenth to seventeenth centuries these arts shared similar design principles: order and proportion, geometrical forms and figures, and symmetry. In garden design and architecture human skill and knowledge transformed the matter of nature into an artificial human order, but this was still an order that reflected the numerical order of the cosmos" (296). "The primacy of geometric designs gave way to "curvilinear patterns, 'S'-shaped curves, arabesques, arcs, and embroidery-like scroll patterns both in the choreographies and the gardens" (307). Both the geometric and botanical paradigms reflect preexisting elements in Islamic art. The gardens themselves materialize the depicted images in Islamic architecture and visual art as well as the philosophies and cosmologies enacted in the *N'kisi Sarabanda*. For striking similarities and their formal constructions, see Nevile's analysis of the villa *L'Ambrogiana* by Giusto Utens (1599) and court ballet spatial design (300–308). Jennifer Nevile, "Order, Proportion, and Geometric Forms: The Cosmic Structure of Dance, Grand Gardens, and Architecture during the Renaissance," *Dance, Spectacle and the Body Politick, 1250–1750* (Indiana: Indiana University Press, 2008), 295–311.
24 See endnote xv. Tabbaa, "The Medieval Islamic Garden," 387.
25 Judith Bettelheim, "Palo Monte Mayombe and Its Influence on Cuban Contemporary Art," *African Arts* 34, no. 2 (2001): 37.
26 Grey Gundaker, "The Kongo Cosmogram in Historical Archaeology and the Moral Compass of Dave the Potter". *Historical Archaeology*, 2011, Vol. 45, no. 2. (2011): 175.
27 Gundaker, "The Kongo Cosmogram," 175.
28 Bettelheim, "Palo Monte Mayombe," 46–48.
29 "Nkisi Sarabanda," *African Burial Ground*, nps.gov.

30 Luyaluka, "African Indigenous Religion," 166; Wyatt MacGaffey, "Dialogues of the Deaf: Europeans on the Atlantic Coast of Africa," *Implicit Understandings: Observing, Reporting and Reflecting on the Encounters Between Europeans and Other Peoples in the Early Modern Era* (Cambridge, UK: Cambridge University Press, 1994), 254–255.
31 Edmund Fairfax, *The Technique of Eighteenth-Century Ballet* (forthcoming). https://eighteenthcenturyballet.com/turnout/
32 "sambo, n.1," *OED Online*, Oxford University Press, December 2022, www.oed.com/view/Entry/170350. My study relies more specifically on the OED definition, etymology, and particular "bandied" and "bowed" description of "zambo" legs. Early modern descriptions of the Zarabanda's characteristic hip movements are most easily facilitated with the femurs and feet rotated outwards, not inwards. Moving the hips when the knees are inwardly rotated and pressing together is particularly difficult to do anatomically. The outward rotation of the legs and feet would also link more closely to the mathematical/geometric compass characteristics evoked by de Vega with his use of the word "compás," which was defined in Sebastián de Covarrubias's Tesoro de la lengua castellana o española (1611) as a tool "used by geometers and all craftsmen; also architects like farmers and carpenters." To this day it is a tool used to draw circles, "right angles," "the square," "the line," and "all kinds of figures." Covarrubias links the tool to dance stating "… it has two legs: one points to the center; the other turning around it forms the circle" (229), functioning as the legs and feet do in ballet which also draw and embody lines, circles, and angles. In a first position stance, the knees are also together while the legs face outward. Upon bending the knees a "bowed" effect occurs. I also point to the OED as it gives the diasporic use of this word in France, the Americas, and Spain that reveals its potency across transnational colonial contexts.
33 Esther J. Terry, "Choreographies of Trans-Atlantic Primitivity: Sub-Saharan Isolation in Black Dance Historiography," in *Early Modern Black Diaspora Studies*, eds. C.L. Smith et al. (New York: Palgrave Macmillan, 2018).
34 Terry, "Choreographies," 75.
35 Terry, "Choreographies," 75.

14
DIVE IN

Keesha Beckford

I'll just jump in, I think to myself. I sit on the ledge of the pool with the other three-year-olds as our kind instructor schools us on water safety and what we are going to do in swim class. Our parents watch from the bleacher seats above. *Isn't the pool just a big bathtub?* The shimmering turquoise water looks fun and inviting. *I want to experience it for myself, not sit around listening to some guy prattle on. I came to swim, not to be lectured.* I spring into the pool. It's not as easy or joyous as I hoped, and I feel myself sinking. What will happen to me? I feel the instructor lifting me, sputtering and bewildered to the surface. I have done something wrong. I feel slightly ashamed but also strangely proud of myself for being a badass.

***

"When I heard her say, 'They don't know what I can do, mom!' we had to schedule a meeting with you." Amari's mom tells me over a Zoom conference. "We want to make sure this is the right place for our daughter. We know the training is excellent. Diversity less so."[1]

As the lone Black ballet faculty member, I hate having to play defense for these questions from Black parents. We offer fantastic training, and my peers are all compassionate, nurturing teachers whose teaching I believe in 175%. On the other hand, only a smattering of Black students attend the upper levels of the school, and if there were a Black Academy Faculty Union I could hold it when me, myself, and I went to the toilet. Put simply, the optics are bad. "I understand," I answer. "I want it to be. I hope it will be. Amari has enormous potential. We are not holding her back; we work extremely slowly and conservatively here. I have every confidence that if she sticks with us, she will reach her goals."

"Amari wants to be a ballet dancer; she wants to be in the Pre-Professional Division," her father answered. "That's her dream."

"I love hearing that." I smiled. "And I want to help her get there. Amari has natural facility. She has turnout, as in good rotation in the hip joint, and beautiful extension. She can really get her legs up! But she must work more mindfully. Sometimes I give her a correction and it almost appears that she is not listening. I know she hears me, but I don't see that she is applying what I am saying. Sometimes I feel that she is ignoring me."

Obviously concerned, the mom's brows furrow; the dad sits silently. "Amari is a good kid and a hard worker. She'd never ignore you."

"Oh no no no, of course she's a good kid. That's just it. I don't think she is doing this to spite me." I put my hands in prayer position as a way of showing my sincerity and my belief in Amari. "She is working extremely hard, but unfortunately not in a way that benefits her. I think that some of her other teachers emphasized flat, 180°-turn out and high extensions as the endgame, without teaching proper alignment and muscular engagement."

"This is my fault." The mom covers her face with her hands. "We have moved so much, and she has had so many different teachers. She must be getting so much conflicting information."

I hated that these poor parents felt they had failed their daughter even though they had tried to give her the best they possibly could. She had studied at good studios in Washington D.C. and Columbus, Ohio. "Oh, please don't blame yourselves. There are so many different schools, and even more philosophies of how to build a dancer. It's impossible to know what's right without expert advice, and even experts have differing viewpoints."

"We'll talk to Amari about working hard in class." The dad says. "I think she is working hard but focusing on what she knew before."

"I think so," I reply. "Please let her know that I am not trying to hold her back. No one wants her to succeed in ballet more than I do."

"Well, maybe not no one." Her mom smiles. "But I'll bet you're in the top five."

"I'll take it." I said. "If you wouldn't mind, please talk to Amari about really, really taking in the feedback I give her, and to ask questions if she doesn't understand."

The parents nodded.

"Oh, and also, we started a committee to support BIPOC students. We hope you'll join us."

"Thank you. We'll try to come." said both parents at the same time.

"Thank *you*!" I chirp. "Bye! Have a great rest of your day!"

We sit smiling awkwardly and saying four more sets of goodbyes before I abruptly press "End Meeting" and they disappear from my view. It was true. I am rooting for Amari's success with all I have. She is talented. While I was never bendy and would only be flat turned out if someone took off my legs at the hip joint and put them back together with reconstructive surgery and a sacrifice to the Gods of Hip Rotation, I saw myself in Amari. All Amari wanted was to dive into ballet. She didn't want to bother with the rules, the cautionary tales, the dangers, the detail. She wanted to get in the waters and make magic.

I wondered what Amari craved as a young Black dancer in 2022. She appeared uninterested in wearing brown tights and shoes or her hair in a pouf, two monumental shifts in ballet aesthetics that so generously and graciously allow Black dancers to finally acknowledge our natural hair and god-given skin tones. Some organizations were content to deliver these paltry concessions, wipe their hands, and congratulate themselves on a job well done. Amari continued to wear pink tights and pink ballet slippers. Every now and then she wore her hair in a braided style, but most of the time her hair appeared to be blown out, put into two French braids and fashioned into a bun. Perhaps she sought to avoid further othering herself, even though there were other girls of color in her class who wore flesh-toned tights. Perhaps the trappings of inclusivity mattered less than feeling truly valued.

As a young girl, I too wanted to be appreciated for the fact that in every class I took I showed my burning passion and energy to dance. Feedback felt like someone holding me back. As constructive as feedback was meant to be, it felt like the exact opposite—being torn down and diminished. I was listening, and I was trying, but stubbornly and misguidedly, I wanted to do it my way. I wanted to take class and feel strong and beautiful. To be told otherwise hurt.

I wanted to throw myself into exercises and choreography. I have always been a mover, someone who dances with full-out passion all the time. I'm also a jumper and turner, although less so as I approach the age where AARP rolls out the ol' red carpet. But back then I had absolutely zero grasp of how to take class with a sense of mindful detail. I loved class and I tried to do my best, but I had the body awareness of a tomato and did not learn any form of muscular engagement at all. I saw that other dancers, a number of close friends, seemed to have everything come naturally. They had banana feet, turnout, and I remember standing behind a girl at the barre whose leg just floated up in *à la seconde*. My leg never floated anywhere no matter how hard I tried.

Little did I know that years later I would feel hurt by the idea that my body maybe wasn't wrong, but that it definitely needed a lot of work. Many of these things were issues common to Black bodies. If I don't work very carefully, I can build very bulky muscles; without monitoring my food intake, I grow stocky. I have what teachers called a curvy spine, with a high muscular butt that to the unskilled eye (or those who used white bodies as their measuring stick) looks like I am in an anterior tilt or pelvic arch, even when my spine is in its optimal alignment. My feet lack any real arch to speak of and my insteps are at best straight, far from the banana feet which can be super weak but are the stuff of dreams and fetishization. These feet can make dancers seem like the second coming even if they dance with all the aplomb of mashed potatoes from a box. For better or worse, when I was young no one informed me about my limitations. My teachers instructed me to pull in my stomach and tuck my tailbone over and over again, and tried to help me better articulate my feet. It wasn't until I went on pointe when a friend clued me in that another classmate had gossiped, "Keesha's a good dancer, except for her feet on pointe." The walls of my ignorance about my lack of facility came tumbling down. The floodgates of self-doubt had been opened. Still, I took classes religiously, thinking I was simply doing my best with what I had. My natural ability to jump and turn plus my dynamic movement carried me through. I am lucky that as a child I never connected my shortcomings to any racialized notions of an ideal ballet body, nor did I take corrections as a means of singling out the lone Black girl in the class. I am careful to make sure that my students never feel that particular sting. It is of the utmost importance that students don't experience feedback as microaggressions and feel their teacher's nurturing hand in their corrections.

Pilates and a few teachers I met in my twenties changed my life. How had I never understood this before? I remember hearing turnout came from the hips but no one talked about deep rotators. All I heard was pull your stomach in without any discussion of how the spine must lengthen to drop the tailbone and how the pelvis must remain vertical for the abs to have any effect on alignment at all. Why didn't more people take the time to help me figure this out much, much earlier? Did they not know? Or had they tried to tell me, and I just didn't get it?

My teachers loved me, encouraged me, and imparted their knowledge the best way they could. For this, I am grateful. Who knows, maybe if they had been more honest about my structural limitations and stronger with their corrections I would have given up. Or maybe, in the spirit of "I'll show them!" I would have worked my literal ass off to implement their corrections and I would have had a completely different career. I'll blame some holes in my training on the predominant pedagogical style of the 1970s and 80s. The consensus I get from talking to friends my age is that our teachers did not deliver instruction with today's level of detail. They offered imagery, but little anatomy. Teachers were not racking their brains trying to find out the best way to explain things that simply didn't click. They offered a correction, or they shrugged their shoulders and continued with class. Many of us had little grasp of what we were doing, as we were imitating instead of understanding. Those with natural gifts stood on a pedestal.

It is vital for me to be the teacher I myself needed as a young Black girl who wanted to dance more than breathe. I take assiduous care to help students understand their unique mechanics, what they need to do to correct imbalances, strengthen their turnout, stabilize their shoulder girdle for efficient and lovely port de bras, or train their feet. After workshopping a correction, I continually ask students what they feel so that they can become more aware of the sensations of improved placement, instead of solely relying on the mirror to reflect what they are supposed to look like.

I teach all my students how to take class. They must understand that corrections—so long as these corrections are delivered with care and respect— show that the teacher sees potential and seeks to stimulate growth. When a dancer receives a correction, they must acknowledge what was said, try to apply the feedback, and work to remain consistently mindful of this correction so that it becomes part of their approach. The student must be encouraged to ask a question if they don't understand a correction. At the same time, a teacher must remember that some corrections, no matter how many different ways they are said, will not find fertile ground at the time of delivery. Haranguing a student to implement a correction they are unready to receive is an exercise in futility and frustration, leading to unhappiness for everyone.

My thoughts often turn to the Hippocratic Oath, "First, do no harm." What does this mean for dance teachers? It's messy. As a teacher you never know what kind of student is going to walk into your studio, but you do know that the student walking out should have their body, mind, and spirit enriched, rather than diminished, by your teaching. While you as a teacher are but one person, you must carefully calibrate expectations for each student, realizing that while students must do their best, everyone's best is different. Furthermore, knowing that different students respond differently to different messaging, I am always in search of discovering a student's often individualized kernel of technical enlightenment. This level of self-imposed pressure can make teaching draining—not being able to help a student with a given concept can feel like personal and professional failure. I remind myself that I am neither a doctor nor a magician. Sometimes I've done all I possibly could have.

But I'm continually hopeful. As draining as it might be to keep searching for the right way to reach a student, going through the process of advancing and retreating as far as feedback is concerned, it's worse than the regret of feeling you didn't do enough. We talk about brutal honesty as dance teachers. But what about compassionate truth? Don't all students deserve that courtesy, especially those who see themselves as dancers at a young age? I wish there was some way to let talented dance students, especially talented students of color, know that they are seen, loved, and valued, while at the same time explaining the intense effort they will need to exert to achieve their dreams.

There is no way for me to know what it would be like if I could go back in time and teach my younger self. Instead, I take extra special care with all the little Keeshas who come into my studio burning to dance, unaware of the tools they lack, but simply dying to immerse themselves in everything dance. I advocate for these dancers with administration, check in with their parents, and most of all, I make sure that that dancer grasps that it's their responsibility to put in the work and the time to progress. I hope my students of color know that I will always point out areas for growth, and I will always be their cheerleader. I don't know where their training will take them, but I'm on a mission to ensure that they are equipped to swim in the waters of dance as far and as fast as they choose.

Note

1 Names and places have been changed to protect privacy. These are conversations that took place with the author.

PART 3
Futurities

15
A WILLINGNESS TO SHED | CRAFTING ALTERNATE REALMS & POSSIBILITIES IN MOVEMENT

FUTUREFORMS

Sidra Bell

We are the collection of many hands

The process of making dances is one of continuous arrival and a tearing away of structures to allow for the emergence of ideas that collide and intersect in unpredictable ways. Friction and counter-positionality are necessary elements to bear ideas that burst into emotional states. A hybridity of perspectives is born from the collision of bodies and their abstraction of meaning as we know it through verbal understandings. Multitasking. The mind and body are limbic. Traditional ballet is composed to demonstrate effortlessness and as a representation of behavioral mores and class. As a choreographer, I work in broken languages, drawing together ideas from my human movement story. Disparate experiences in formal dance training, academic pursuits, and an upbringing in an expansive family of artists correlate with the development of new language, portals towards generation, and design.

As artists we are the collection of many hands, voices, and stories. Legacies in jazz, theater, and visual arts, family bonds, and building community are crucial to my journey. Nothing is my own. Information passes through me to be voiced again and reassembled. As a director, I frame what exists and translate forms for expanded integration into various communities. Repetition begets a rigorous drive towards unknown facets of form and, ultimately, reconfiguration. The lexicon of ballet has been a device in my work to tread between off-axis verticality and the rootedness of traditions I studied at Dance Theatre of Harlem and The Ailey School. The narrow paths of execution, rituals, and devotion that classical ballet requires attracted me as a young dancer to exhaustive studio training while attending degree programs in liberal arts throughout my education. I absorbed the language of ideas and methods of synthesizing concepts to rip them apart. I followed a traditional course of study that was a delineated path to professional life at both academies. Guided by artists from seminal traditions in ballet and modern forms, the daily structure and discipline appealed to me.

As an introspective child, I gravitated toward modes of deeper expression beyond the verbal. My parents, composers, directors, and pianists advocated for me to be in environments that specifically emphasized inclusion and circular learning approaches, including Montessori and all-female schools. These groundbreaking academies focused on the technique of the body and analysis rather than the performative aspects of competitive dance. I was encouraged to love learning as a means, not an end. I was encouraged to build stamina for play. I ascribe to a practice of infinite research.

A process that gives creative authority to multiple voices in the process

As I have moved through the various steppingstones of a career as a choreographer, I have developed a process that gives creative authority to the dancers in the room. Working with breakdancers, actors, ballet dancers, and intergenerational communities allowed me to consider a space that is plastic and willful. An environment has evolved, giving the power of choice to the artists. I am fascinated by shape and the delineation of space in the body. I am animated by the space between forms, the journey through constructed environments, and the indications the body can create that are unseen. Exquisite and ephemeral planes. I enjoy the parameters and limitations of the physical form as a source for endlessness in the making of images and the manipulation of energetic presences onstage.

My work often feels de-compositional

I tend to look at the compositional structure as a dispersal of forms that play together in space, often in discordance, with some cues, games, and outlines that form the liveness of a moment. My work often feels

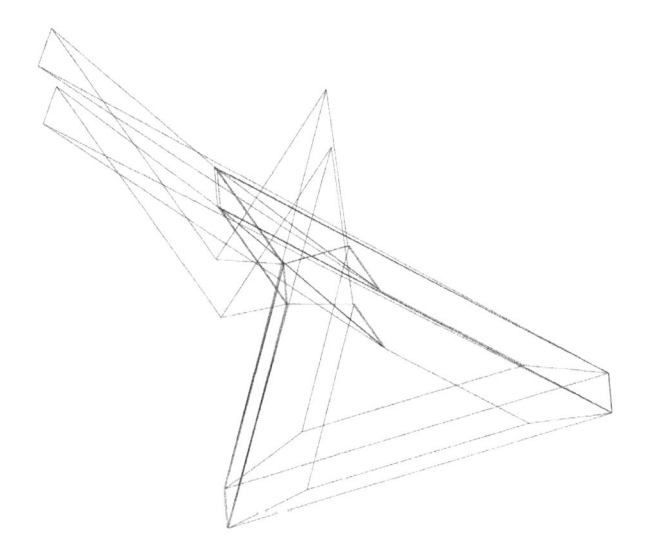

FIGURE 15.1 Image by Sidra Bell

de-compositional, shedding its direct use of formal, classical ideas from seminal techniques. I see movement as a series of events in the body and space. I use duration as a mechanism to disarm and relax my collaborators. Looking into the process as a viewer may stir feelings of chaos or disorder, forcing the eye to find something to fixate on and frame. Non-linearity causes the tension we need to abstract representational ideas. The organization of my dance has multiple meanings and entry points. My direction of the dance is in the structural weaving and the stacking modes. I leave the mental work to the voyeur allowing them to knit together the schematic and to stay unattached to knowing within control systems I present.

Dancers and choreographers must be adept to survive the changing ecology and collapsing structures

The demographic I serve most as a maker and mentor are creatives at the earliest stages of navigating university dogma into the transitional realities of working professional lives as performers, choreographers, and educators. There is no blueprint or stable version of success in today's contemporary performance landscape. I often ask my mentees to redefine their vision of success on their terms which still seems to be an unorthodox way of approaching higher education in the field. I ask them to reform their conception of a sustainable creative life rather than focusing on career ends. The realities of our time, including the movement towards a shared economy and declining funding for the arts, prevent young artists from approaching the form with a standard and singular mindset around working structures and tiered role-playing in the studio practice. Dancers and choreographers must be adept to survive the changing contemporary ecology. Shape shifting, self-presenting, and creating new systems have been essential to building a sustainable fabric to develop my craft.

We must work between the codes of various institutional frameworks, unspoken expectations, and behavioral skins to craft individual pathways. Playing in the discomfort and radicality of changing languages is improvisation. Working with our agency within collective mind hives. Contemporary artists toe a line between building a career and fostering ongoing curiosity. How can these pursuits merge into a life journey that has no end to exploration? The composition of an idea happens over a series of experiences and can contain unpredictability and risk. Allowing for presence, multiplicity of cognizance, and astuteness to events in real time can also translate to how you approach the formality of a technical process. Centering the slow and the meditative, taking in more to cultivate craft over product.

As a dance maker, I am a translator of the worlds I visit. Shedding skins and codes of conduct as I encounter challenging artistic terrain. Utilizing the language and physical history of my storied body, I meet my collaborators somewhere in between where the terms of engagement must be mutually agreed upon. Mirroring, building sentences of movement, playing games, scoring, reiterating, skill building (teaching each other generously), sharing, failing, journaling, archiving states, dissolving into nothingness. Starting to try again.

Dance seems to be a conduit and medium between forms of visual art, poetry, sculpture, sound, theater, and jazz interplay

My improvisational practice has been a combination of praxes I have encountered in my travels, observing prominent teachers and my nomadic curiosity about the possibilities of the body. The math and modalities of William Forsythe, the ferocity of Ulysses Dove, the quiet complexity of Kevin Wynn,[1] the deep-seated, hollow postures of Graham, the interior seeing of somatic techniques, the redistribution of the body's weight from earthbound physical work, and the exquisite detail of ballet through the toes and fingertips all fascinate me. The body as a source is enough. Stories that predate our existence inform the energetics of NOW. The future is now. In an improvised space, the unspoken community agreement is to bring each artist's well of knowledge to the table and to allow for something shared to emerge from the combination of sustained effort and observation. In culmination. The process starts nebulously, and I ask the movers in the space to peer into their bodies, imagining it from the inside. The objectives are simplified to allow for entry into the community without intimidation or a hierarchical notion of form. This allows for continuous arrival from divergent perspectives in a circular practice. Uncovering form collectively.

How do we shape experience from the inside or reproduce the shapes we see in nature, architecture, hear in sound waves, or feel in heat maps? Dance seems to be a conduit and medium between forms of visual art, poetry, sculpture, sound, theater, and jazz interplay. A slippery tissue, a fragile network. Generating movement from physiological and anatomical possibilities is the research of bringing shape to fruition. Developing mechanisms to achieve heaviness, lightness, flight, deep folds, and extrusions. Giving shape to social structures and relationships, working from the abstract to meaning, and then disrupting it all over again.

Upending social structures that inhibit creative possibilities.

In creating work for ballet dancers, my approach has been to instill a process that is unilateral where all dancers are shaping movement from my body. Building community is essential in spaces that work with a tiered structure. How can we all engage in the game of creating a dance? We are all participating in the act. I do not preempt the process within any research before a creative residency. I use my body's knowledge and impulses to create movement in the moment, allowing liveness to slip into the dancers' bodies, moving further away from the academy space. Upending social structures that inhibit creative possibilities. Each dancer's interpretation, enactment, and embodiment of what they see or hear in the prompting is part of the visual landscape and the world of ideas being created in collaboration with my guidance.

The dance critic Lisa Jo Sagolla writes, "[Bell]'s work evokes a freakish, punk aesthetic, with garishly made-up performers doing ugly repetitive movements to relentless rhythms and disturbing buzzing noises."[2] The critical sentiments have prompted me to shift my choreographic process and ask the questions: What is ugly? What is disturbing? What is freakish? What systems in our field create the languages and limit our expectations of human bodies? There is often implicit bias in dance criticism and writing about our bodies' expressions. I design and play with elements and identities in my work. They dialogue with and against each other creating rifts that feel discordant. Perhaps I disturb lyricism and break formal adherences germane to Western constructs of "beautiful bodies" in traditional performance, offering a wider spectrum of representation. Maybe not wide enough. Images feel familiar as they are rendered from cultural tropes and patterns, yet something is off-center, out of pocket, loose, and extreme. Maybe too extreme for digestion.

So, when we improvise

We respond to the intuition of our bodies, reacting to the ease or discomfort of a pathway. We either choose to go forward and work inside of the edges of friction within a pattern or move away and closer to habit. Improvisation is a generative act that lets the mind recourse through various opportunities and suggestions. We craft material from the process of resourcing and gathering information. In that way, the process is hyper-analytical and technical. There are rules that get established over time.

It is an uncomfortable process as we chart unknown factors. It helps to have other brains in the room. Let us have multiple brains operating all at once. Making muscles all together, building them up, and taking chances in intervals. Repeat those patterns that are unfamiliar until they start to multitask and dialogue within us. It is us in practice. It is possible to develop muscle memory and take in all the idiosyncratic detail of what felt spontaneous. It is like remembering a wild sunset.

Prompting you to:

> Settle into your bones
> Fill your chest
> Imagine your belly button attached by a silver string to your spine

Spread the skin along the surfaces of your feet
Open the walls of your heart
Stand in a slippery ether
View your body at a distance
Listen (in between)
Fall into
Dark, Deep Webbing
And then...
Let's make a circle to unravel
Picking up on the brilliant moments along the way as we spiral
Feel the sentience of each escaping moment
And then describe it repeatedly
Narrow your lens, cultivate its changing lifespan, keep it live
Keep the text so whatever you devised is there
And you're making a web
This is liberation in a way
Set up your own stories
And perhaps
Falling into a pool, getting pulled up
Don't be too narrow - feel completion
I always thought of this as the tongue of a serpent
Like my head is the tongue of the serpent
It's discreet and doesn't need to be bigger
You need to have a sense of what's going on
If it's real for you, then it's legible for us
Slow down
And now...
Let's figure out what the mechanism is
Flex your arms a little bit more
So, we get the geometry of the body
You don't need to come to any final decision.
Give yourself some possibilities
I always think of the limbs as being like fences (to break through)
So, if we think of...
The structure of limited actions gives us range
Then we are playing with range or limitation
A phrase is born
So...
Structure is important in that way

FIGURE 15.2 Image by Sidra Bell

I feel…
Like we are floating now.
In a wave pool or something with newts or in a dark cave
Dwell in this constructed universe and center play
Straddle worlds to undo patterns.
And then…
Become didactic. Stop. Repeat. Stop. Capture.

Notes

1 "The Kevin Wynn Collection," https://www.youtube.com/watch?v=CtKEQPyEPP4
2 Lisa Jo Sagolla, "Gallim Dance and Sidra Bell Dance New York," *Backstage.com,* July 31, 2019, https://www.backstage.com/magazine/article/gallim-dance-sidra-bell-dance-new-york-62872/.

16
HONORING THE LEGACY OF ANTIRACIST BALLET TEACHING & LEADERSHIP AS MODELED BY BLACK AND BROWN-OWNED, BLACK AND BROWN-LED, AND BLACK AND BROWN-SERVING DANCE ORGANIZATIONS

Iyun Ashani Harrison

I relocated to New York City from Jamaica in the mid-1990s to study at The Juilliard School. At that time, many Black and Brown ballet students aspired to study and work with groundbreaking, predominantly Black and Brown dance companies such as Dance Theatre of Harlem (DTH), Alvin Ailey American Dance Theater (AAADT), Ballet Hispanico, and Complexions Contemporary Ballet. Over the past twenty-five years, I have observed a shift where gifted Black and Brown ballet students have become less enthusiastic about dancing with these organizations, opting instead for white ballet companies such as American Ballet Theatre (ABT) and New York City Ballet (NYCB). Black and Brown ballet dancers not only desire to join white ballet companies but also anticipate becoming principal dancers, following the examples of Lauren Anderson,[1] Misty Copeland,[2] Taylor Stanley,[3] Angelica Generosa,[4] and Chyrstyn Fentroy.[5]

The possibility of Black and Brown dancers gaining access to white ballet organizations started in the mid-twentieth century. Prior, primarily white-passing dancers of color were more frequently granted access. Arthur Mitchell would become the first identifiably Black man to become a full-time dancer with a major American ballet company,

DOI: 10.4324/9781003283065-20

NYCB, in 1956. During this period, some Black and Brown ballet dancers with financial means and talent would migrate to Europe to pursue ballet careers.[6] Others worked with racially inclusive companies such as American Negro Ballet, founded in 1937; ABT's Negro Unit, founded in 1940; Capitol Ballet, founded in 1961; Oakland Ballet, founded in 1965; DTH, founded in 1969, among others. Other Black and Brown dancers switched movement genres, dancing with modern dance organizations such as AAADT, founded in 1959, or Philadanco!, founded in 1970.

The generational shift among Black and Brown ballet dancers and their expectation to break white-constructed color barriers is, in some ways, a positive development signaling progress in crucial diversity, equity, and inclusion initiatives. Unfortunately, some Black and Brown ballet dancers and white practitioners view training and careers in white institutions as legitimizing. Black and Brown dancers who ascribe to this line of thinking endure white-constructed educational and professional hurdles, such as assimilating to rigid Eurocentric aesthetics and enduring microaggressions and racialized criticisms to achieve validation. Due to the psychologically damaging effects of whiteness in many learning environments, I posit that Black and Brown dancers are better served without traversing predominantly white ballet organizations. Progressive and inclusive educational models already exist in Black and Brown institutions. They allow students of color to learn in healthful, self-affirming, and holistic environments that celebrate their cultures and physical attributes. These institutions produce world-class professional dancers and decenter whiteness as a normative standard by removing culturally specific Eurocentric dogmatic standards.

Positionality and Possibilities

Like many Black and Brown ballet dancers, I received foundational training from educators of color who demonstrated ballet teaching excellence. The son of Jamaican actors and businesspersons Christine Ann Bell and Arthur Stafford "Ashani" Harrison, I began formal training at the Jamaica School of Dance, studying the Royal Academy of Dancing children's syllabus with Kathy Gibbon. I supplemented my studies in a Vaganova-based curriculum privately with Norma Spence and later trained at the Danza Contemporánea de Cuba. Significantly, my education was grounded in the socio-political, postcolonial philosophies of 1970s Jamaica, where whiteness was decentered. By age seventeen, my Caribbean training had prepared me for admittance to The Juilliard School, after which I danced with Ailey II, DTH, and Ballet Hispanico. I am an advocate, educator, choreographer, and founder of Ballet Ashani, working primarily in the ballet idiom.

What might it mean to decenter whiteness in ballet? The development of ballet technique, choreography, and the ballet canon have their origins in whiteness. Revisionist scholars can expand the narrative, adding, restating, and amplifying the histories, work, and contributions of artists of color. For instance, scholar Brenda Dixon Gottschild amplifies the hybridity of American neoclassicism by revealing its European and Africanist movement aesthetics.[7] Still, ballet's schema is tied to European, white ethnic dance. I propose repositioning ballet technique as distinct from its exclusionary practices by actively resisting the propagation of white aesthetic values. Notably, this approach to ballet teaching already exists in the African diaspora and provides a more holistic pedagogical model.

My purpose is three-fold: first, to highlight Black and Brown ballet teachers already practicing progressive pedagogies which provide blueprints for challenging ballet's racial crisis; second, to intervene in the devaluation of Black and Brown ballet artists, leaders, and institutions and instead elevate and support their work to progress the American ballet industry; and third, to bring attention to the challenges faced by identifiably Black ballerinas, particularly dark-skinned, Black women who are least represented on American ballet stages.

It is not my intention to deepen the emotional and psychological traumas of colorism within Black communities nor diminish the racism encountered by white-passing dancers working in white institutions. Nonetheless, it would be an oversight to ignore that fair-skinned women of color have integrated more easily into the white *corps de ballet* and more often reached the principal rank than their dark-skinned counterparts. This bias is apparent from as early as the 1940s with leading ballerinas such as Alicia Alonso (Latina) and Sono Osato (Asian American) of ABT, Maria Tallchief (Osage Nation) of NYCB, and Janet Collins and Raven Wilkinson (African American) of the Metropolitan Opera Ballet and Ballet Russe de Monte Carlo, respectively.

My goal is to decenter white ballet organizations and amplify Black and Brown institutions practicing progressive teaching and organizational practices. Ballet schools in Brazil, Cuba, Colombia, Dominican

Republic, Haiti, South Africa, and Venezuela, and historically Black and Brown institutions in the United States, produce excellent Black and Brown ballet professionals. And I believe the industry should emulate their antiracist teaching practices. In the following sections, I provide four examples modeled by the Maria Olenewa State School of Dance – Rio De Janeiro, Brazil, Arthur Mitchell's Dance Theatre of Harlem, The Ailey School, and Baltimore School of the Arts.

Escola Estadual de Dança Maria Olenewa

I was introduced to the remarkable Brazilian ballet training system through its alumni who danced with DTH while I was a company member. DTH employed several exceptional Black and Brown Brazilian ballerinas, including Bethania Gomes, a former principal dancer. Before DTH, Gomes trained at Escola Estadual de Dança Maria Olenewa (EDMO) in Rio de Janeiro, Brazil, and later joined the Municipal Theater of Rio de Janeiro. Founded in 1927 by Russian ballerina Maria Olenewa, EDMO is a state-funded, public educational institution that aspires to "train excellent dancers who can work in different dance companies in Brazil and abroad with bodies capable of dancing in different languages and styles."[8] A distinguishing factor in their pedagogy is a commitment to cultivating artists who are "sensitive to social and artistic issues, capable of…transforming the society in which they are inserted."[9]

The school has prepared Black and Brown children to study and perform with the world's most prestigious companies for nearly a century. In 1967, before founding DTH, Arthur Mitchell was appointed by the United States Information Agency to form the National Ballet Company of Brazil.[10] During his Brazilian residency, Mitchell developed a relationship with EDMO and gained visibility within the national ballet community. In the following decades, these connections led to the recruitment of Brazilian ballerinas who joined DTH: Simone Cardoso (soloist), Cristiane Cristo (soloist), Rejane Duarte (corps de ballet), Bethania Gomes (principal), and Ingrid Silva.

The school's strengths reside in several factors: free tuition, entry by audition, and a defined, scaffolded ballet curriculum.[11] Because space in the school is limited and tuition is free, students feel a sense of pride for being admitted. There is a culture of healthy competition, with many dancers thriving in the learning environment and aspiring to join the municipal theater. The ballet hosts masterclasses, auditions, and competitions, ensuring students are well-informed and connected to the international ballet industry. Faculty are former professional ballet dancers or educators trained in pedagogy, including Brazilian faculty of African descent, such as former company dancer Mercedes Baptista and ballet educator Dona Consuelo.[12]

Though EDMO and the broader Brazilian ballet training system can be celebrated for tremendous success in developing Black and Brown dancers, it is critical to state that Brazil contends with explicit attempts to whitewash African descendants by encouraging racial mixing to construct a new national and racial identity.[13] These attitudes result in colorism and separatist actions, euphemistically disguised as social class bias, which evades the convergence of class and race where Brazilians of African descent represent half of the nation's population and live disproportionately in poverty.[14] The remnants of these socioeconomic and racialized constructs also plague the school and company.[15]

For instance, although the municipal theater employed its first Black ballerina, Mercedes Baptista, in 1948, there have been few identifiably Black women hired by the company, and none have ascended to the rank of principal dancer.[16] Dancers and school leaders report a culture of microaggressions toward darker-skinned women. They share stories of being treated as exceptions to their race and more blatant acts, such as racialized casting.[17] Though Black and Brown ballet dancers are encouraged within the school, these hiring practices suggest there is no place for them in the municipal theater. As a result, many Brazilian dancers of African descent relocate to Africa, Europe, and North America to pursue ballet careers.[18]

Dance Theatre of Harlem

I first saw DTH on Jamaican public television, watching the company's performance of Agnes de Mille's *Fall River Legend*. As an undergraduate at Juilliard, I studied at DTH's summer intensives and attended company performances. I was inspired by the company's divergence from Eurocentric ballet sensibilities in body type and repertory. In tandem with the dancers' tremendous technical and artistic abilities, DTH created a unique space where I could envisage myself as a neoclassicist. It represented an antiracist ballet, far less encumbered by white aesthetics than any company I had seen.

Later, when I danced with DTH, I witnessed excellence in ballet achievement throughout the company's ranks based on inclusive ideals. DTH featured dancers of differing body shapes, sizes, heights, physical ability, technical virtuosity, artistry, and stylistic range. Mitchell employed women who did not conform to the stereotypical ballerina line: hyper-extended knees, one-hundred-and-eighty-degree turnout, and highly arched feet. He privileged dancers with dynamic movement qualities, speed, artistry, stage presence, and individuality. Critically, DTH presented a vast array of Black and Brown racial characteristics, such as hair texture and skin color, featuring many darker-skinned ballerinas. Though Arthur Mitchell was criticized for colorism, no other ballet company depicted such a spectrum of Black and Brown dancers during his leadership. Despite being a protégé of NYCB, Mitchell created a powerful and democratic counterpoint to George Balanchine's ballerina.

Notably, DTH curated an ensemble of Black and Brown performers from the United States, Africa, Canada, The Caribbean, Central and South America, and Europe. This created an organizational culture where Black identities were nuanced and inclusive, affirming the plurality of Black experiences. This sense of inclusive Blackness extended to the company's Black-themed repertoire, which included adaptations of European classics like *Creole Giselle*, African diaspora choreographies such as *South African Suite*, choreographed by Mitchell, Augustus Van Heerden, and Laveen Naidu, and neoclassical-African American vernacular hybrid dances such as Robert Garland's *New Bach*.

The Ailey School

The Ailey School is the official training institution of AAADT and was founded in 1969 by Alvin Ailey and Pearl Lang. In 1984 Denise Jefferson was named director, and over a twenty-five-year period, led the organization in an integrative curriculum that emphasized training in ballet, modern, and African diaspora techniques.[19] Though categorized as a modern dance institution, the school prepares students for Ailey's choreography. Ailey's work is a hybridized dance style centered on Africanist movement aesthetics and Black narratives and relies heavily on ballet aesthetics and vocabularies. As such, ballet is an integral curricular focus.

The Ailey School serves three types of students particularly well. The first group is athletic dancers with the capacity for an extreme range of motion, who are trained in techniques of the African diaspora and American modern dance. The school provides remedial ballet training for these students to develop and clarify foundational ballet skills. The second group is ballet-trained dancers interested in modern dance: the school introduces them to modern and techniques of the African diaspora. The school acts as a connecter for the third group, international students, providing U.S. entry visas.

Tracy Inman and Melanie Person have been codirectors of the school since 2010: Inman heads the Professional Division and Person, The Ailey/Fordham BFA, and ballet program. Person, an alumna of the School of American Ballet and former principal dancer with DTH, explains how she hopes to build on Jefferson's leadership:

> Denise Jefferson passed on her desire to have a diverse pool of teachers – racially and experientially. This diversity is true not only of the ballet faculty but across the techniques and various levels of the junior and professional division programs.
>
> The school focuses on providing students with technical dance training and an understanding of artistry. I am interested in teachers who can create a healthy learning environment where these elements are realized. Anyone can learn dance techniques, although each student's degree of mastery may differ. I am interested in dance education that serves the whole person.
>
> My vision is that the school's ballet training helps students gain proficiency in the technique, facilitating their entry into a contemporary ballet, modern company, Broadway, or wherever. Ballet is a methodology, a tool—not an end goal.[20]

The success of the school's alumni affirms the institution's effectiveness in ballet teaching: students have joined DTH, Alonzo King LINES Ballet, Complexions Contemporary Ballet, Ballet Hispanico, and Collage Dance Collective.

Baltimore School for the Arts

I became familiar with the high standard of ballet training at the Baltimore School for the Arts (BSA) while studying at Juilliard and observing peers Michael Snipe Jr. and Jermaine Spivey. I learned more later while recruiting prospective college students there. Founded in 1979, BSA is a public performing arts high school in Baltimore, MD's inner city. The admission-by-audition program consistently ranks as a top public arts school, created with the intention of providing "pre-professional arts training to Baltimore's children."[21] Moreover, 62.3% of Baltimore's residents identify as Black or African American, making it a Black-serving institution.[22]

TWIGS (To Work In Gaining Skills) is a critical curricular offering of the school. A free after-school program, TWIGS enrolls Baltimore City children between second to eighth grade and serves up to 700 students a year: "each year, roughly fifty percent of the incoming [first-year] class at B.S.A. have been trained through TWIGS."[23] Together, BSA and TWIGS provide gifted students opportunities to train in ballet and modern dance between the crucial ages of 7 and 18.[24] Building on a solid ballet training tradition established by the noted African American ballet dancer Sylvester Campbell, the current faculty includes former dancers of the Shanghai Ballet and Bolshoi Ballet Academy.[25] Michael Snipe Jr., an alumnus of BSA, danced on Broadway and with professional companies. He reflects on his time at BSA:

> It had a knack for recognizing, unlocking, and nurturing students' potential. I had never heard of ballet before high school, and by sophomore year I performed works by Balanchine, Ron Cunningham, Hinton Battle, and Lisa de Ribere! My teachers would provide me with free extra classes at other schools, and BSA paid for field trips when my family couldn't afford them. The professionalism, rigor, and discipline prepared me to survive and thrive professionally. As a teacher and psychotherapist working with performers, I often revisit the relational values I learned there.[26]

The school's success as a Black-serving ballet organization is illustrated by the number of Black alumni who have performed with ballet companies, including Lenai Alexis Wilkerson (Cincinnati Ballet), Darius Barnes (NYCB), Nardia Boodoo (Washington Ballet), Bahiyah Sayyed Gaines (Ballett Frankfurt), Kiyon Gaines (Pacific Northwest Ballet), Jermel Johnson (Philadelphia Ballet), and Jermaine Spivey (Cullberg Ballet).

Conclusion

Black and Brown-owned, Black and Brown-led, and Black and Brown-serving dance organizations have long practiced democratic ballet teaching and art-making that decenter whiteness. The points below identify throughlines of their antiracist teaching praxes, which include:

- Faculty and creative and administrative staff are well-qualified Black and Brown professionals who do *not* exhibit internalized racist attitudes.
- A shared understanding that ballet training is not superior to other genres and serves students in numerous ways beyond the studio.
- Visual uniformity is rejected as an aesthetic priority, and students include different races and body types. Teaching spaces are adorned with images that depict diverse groups, and educators cite racially pluralistic examples when discussing ballet achievement.
- Organizations value the discipline of ballet training while encouraging student individuality and self-exploration.
- Educators have inclusive body aesthetics and liberal ideas of what constitutes "good physical ability."
- Educators do not ascribe physical characteristics to race. They do not generalize about Black and Brown dancers' feet, buttocks, lumbar spine, thighs, body proportion, skin, or hair. Ascribing physical characteristics to race is unscientific and expresses racist attitudes.
- Organizations assume that Black and Brown students will be successful, regardless of their race, culture, ethnicity, or nationality, if they display the requisite coordination, range of motion, rhythm, performance qualities, intelligence, and work ethic.
- Educators do not assume negative stereotypes about students based on socioeconomic background.
- Educators do not ascribe intellectual, behavioral, or temperament characteristics to race.
- Organizations understand that students of different races and ethnicities have unique needs. This consideration extends to ballet practices, such as applying stage makeup or creating a ballet bun hairstyle. For instance, students with dark-brown and black skin tones may be challenged to locate and apply stage makeup to highlight their bone structure. Similarly, it may be difficult for

some Black students with natural or short hair to achieve a bun. Black ballet teachers often break from aesthetic norms to honor students' features and create inclusive environments.
- Scholarships are liberally provided to talented students from poor, working, lower-income, and middle-class socioeconomic backgrounds.
- Black and Brown-serving institutions provide foundational training opportunities for talented older children and young adults who may not have had access.
- Black and Brown faculty and creative and administrative staff understand the technical aspects of performance production, such as lighting and costuming. For instance, if there is a challenge seeing a dark-skinned student on stage, they break from aesthetic convention, making necessary lighting adjustments. Similarly, with costuming, they understand that 'skin tone' does not mean pink or beige and adjust costumes to match students' skin.
- Black and Brown faculty and creative and administrative staff develop culturally relevant teaching and artistic practices and programming which engage Black and Brown students and audiences. For instance, choreographers sometimes create new work that integrates racially and culturally legible themes for their communities. Ballet students may learn existing ballet variations; however, an equal focus on culturally pluralistic choreography decentralizes whiteness.
- Black and Brown-serving institutions create institutional networks connecting students and external partners, facilitating continued education and personal and professional opportunities.

Each of these throughlines advances the third aspiration of this chapter: to train, employ, cast, and promote dark-skinned ballerinas because ballet suffers from their absence. Suppose we recall Lauren Anderson's radical retelling of iconic ballet roles such as Aurora in *Sleeping Beauty* and Odette in *Swan Lake* while a principal dancer with the Houston Ballet in the 1990s. Her interpretations drew from Black cultural experiences and breathed new life into European story ballets, making them legible to audiences. Similarly, dark-skinned ballerinas such as Precious Adams (English National Ballet), Katlyn Addison (Ballet West), Aesha Ash, India Bradley, and Andrea Long (NYCB), Michaela DePrince (Boston Ballet), Ebony Haswell, Paunika Jones and Akua Noni Parker (DTH), and Ashley Murphy (Washington

Ballet) demonstrate elegance, passion, individuality, intelligence, and dynamism with their brilliant technique, artistry and stage presence. It is time to refute the lies that dark-skinned ballerinas are scarce, underprepared, or disruptive to the uniformity of the *corps de ballet*. If dark-skinned men can populate the corps of world-renowned ballets, so can dark-skinned women. We must confront this contradiction by addressing the blatantly racist and sexist exclusion of dark-skinned ballerinas.

One of the crucial outcomes of the protests in response to George Floyd's murder by police, and the significant social media pressure that followed, was the acknowledgment that Black and Brown people required more than performative support. The events of 2020 forced leaders and organizations to move past tokenizing hiring practices to implement meaningful change. Some ballet organizations' immediate response was to implement old D.E.I. initiatives.[27] This approach keeps whiteness and white institutions at the conversation's center rather than focusing on the equitable distribution of resources that would impact Black and Brown ballet artists and institutions in the long term.

When DTH went on a nine-year hiatus due to financial collapse in 2004, it had a roster of forty unionized dancers, a junior company, and a thriving school.[28] Upon its return, it reemerged as an ununionized ensemble of sixteen dancers, and the school reduced its scope. How would DTH change if it had resources akin to its white New York City-based counterparts? With its $6.7 million annual budget, could DTH attain similar levels of excellence if it were funded like ABT ($46,000,000), or NYCB ($83,000,000)?[29] If we equitably fund enduring beacons of Black and Brown ballet excellence with their democratic aesthetics, would we see qualitative and quantitative growth in the ballet industry? Furthermore, how would the industry shift if smaller and new Black and Brown companies received financial support? Not to be understated, a critical aspect of supporting these organizations is encouraging young Black and Brown talent to reinvest in them. White ballet companies reap the benefits of recruiting the best and brightest Black and Brown artists, draining Black and Brown organizations of their most distinguished artists. Perhaps the pathway toward achieving an antiracist ballet industry is *not* through integrating white organizations but by reinvesting in historically significant Black and Brown ballet institutions and budding Black and Brown artists.

Notes

1 "Lauren Anderson," *Houston Ballet*, https://www.houstonballet.org/about/ece/teaching-artists/lauren-anderson/.
2 "Misty Copeland," *American Ballet Theatre*, https://www.abt.org/people/misty-copeland/
3 "Taylor Stanley," *New York City Ballet*, https://www.nycballet.com/discover/meet-our-dancers/principal-dancers/taylor-stanley/.
4 "Angelica Generosa," *Pacific Northwest Ballet*, https://www.pnb.org/artists/angelica-generosa/.
5 "Fentroy," *Boston Ballet*, https://www.bostonballet.org/Home/Global/Profiles/Artists/Principal-Dancers/Chyrstyn-Mariah-Fentroy.aspx.
6 For example, Sylvester Campbell danced with the Dutch National Ballet from 1960 to 1972; Raven Wilkinson danced with the Dutch National Ballet from 1967 to 1974 (and was encouraged by Sylvester Campbell to audition for the company); Christopher Boatwright danced with the Stuttgart Ballet from 1974 to 1982; Paul Russell danced with the Scottish National Ballet from 1977 to 1981. For more information, see Ken Sandler, "The Black Ballet Barrier," *The Washington Post*, February 27, 1983. https://www.washingtonpost.com/archive/lifestyle/style/1983/02/27/the-black-ballet-barrier/
7 Brenda Dixon Gottschild, "Stripping the Emperor: George Balanchine and the Americanization of Ballet," *Digging the Africanist Presence in American Performance* (Westport, CT: Praeger, 1998), 59–80.
8 *Maria Olenewa State Dance School*, Translated by Google, http://theatromunicipal.rj.gov.br/eedmo/.
9 *Maria Olenewa State Dance School, Translated by Google*, http://theatromunicipal.rj.gov.br/eedmo/.
10 Jennifer Dunning, "Arthur Mitchell," *New York Times*, September 19, 2018, https://www.nytimes.com/2018/09/19/obituaries/arthur-mitchell-dead.html
11 Bethania Gomes and Rejane Duarte, interview by author, July 2022.
12 "The stories of Mercedes Baptista, Consuelo Rios, Bethania Gomes, and Ingrid Silva," *Negra Voz*, podcast audio, February 10, 2020. https://podcasts.apple.com/us/podcast/as-hist%C3%B3rias-de-mercedes-baptista-consuelo-rios/id1478566960?i=1000465275786.
13 Sarah Lempp, "'Whitening' and Whitewashing: Postcolonial Brazil is not an Egalitarian Rainbow Nation," *The Postcolonialist*, March 4, 2014. http://postcolonialist.com/culture/whitening-whitewashing-postcolonial-brazil-means-egalitarian-rainbow-nation/.
14 Howard Winant, *The World Is a Ghetto: Race & Democracy Since World War II* (New York: Basic Books, 2002).
15 "Stories," *Negra Voz*, 2020.
16 "Stories," *Negra Voz*, 2020.
17 Bethania Gomes and Rejane Duarte, interview by author, July 2022.
18 "Stories," *Negra Voz*, 2020.
19 "History," *The Ailey School*, https://www.alvinailey.org/school/philosophy/history.

20 Melanie Person, email sent to author, November 29, 2022.
21 "About," *Baltimore School for the Arts,*https://www.bsfa.org/about.
22 "Baltimore City," *Census,* https://www.census.gov/quickfacts/baltimorecitymaryland.
23 "TWIGS," *Baltimore School for the Arts,* https://www.bsfa.org/twigs
24 "Dance Curriculum" *Baltimore School for the Arts,* https://www.bsfa.org/arts/dance/dance-curriculum.
25 "Dance," *Baltimore School for the Arts,*https://www.bsfa.org/arts/dance.
26 Michael Snipe Jr, email sent to author, December 2022
27 Theresa Ruth Howard, Panelist for Antiracism in the Arts, Old Dominion University, October 18, 2022.
28 Djassi DaCosta Johnson, "Our History" *Dance Theatre of Harlem,*https://www.dancetheatreofharlem.org/our-history/.
29 "Dance Theatre of Harlem 2020 Total Revenue" *ProPublica,* https://projects.propublica.org/nonprofits/organizations/132642091; "2021 Impact Report," *American Ballet Theatre,* https://www.abt.org/wp-content/themes/abt/uploads/2021ImpactReport/docs/ABT-2021-Impact-Report.pdf; "NYCB 2020 Total Revenue," https://projects.propublica.org/nonprofits/organizations/132947386

17
BALLET'S EVER-PRESENT PRESENCE

Thomas F. DeFrantz

The cultural pull of ballet as a realm of influence accelerates. More and more, young people think of ballet as the way that dance moves them from an interest to a practice, or from an awesome spectacle to something they simply must do by any means necessary. Ballet becomes foundational to any training that allows for a career in dance; ballet takes over the narrative of what it means to engage in dance. Even as some dance programs in higher education move away from requiring ballet for dance students— and these programs are few and far between—ballet continues its stranglehold on the idea of dance as an art in the United States. How has this happened? How is it that ballet becomes a stand-in for the idea of dance as an art form, inevitably worthy of public attention?

Cultural Capital

Ballet takes up a vast amount of real estate in a general cultural imaginary concerning dance. A cultural imaginary might be an aspect of culture and its value, or *capital*, that define the way that people understand a relationship of a thing's value to its form. Why is ballet so well-regarded in general? The form holds high cultural capital across many different communities in locations all around the planet.

Cultural capital has been effectively theorized by French sociologist Pierre Bourdieu in his 1979 volume, *Distinction*.[1] Bourdieu was concerned with how taste manifests, especially in relation to social class and social identity. People make distinctions concerning locations, practices, objects, and the human communities with which they are willing to be affiliated. These distinctions emerge in relationship to social exchanges but also in terms of economic exchange. In many ways, cultural capital determines the amount of economic and social value that an object or a practice might be able to hold. Ballet is thought to be a "high value" physical expression and, as such, something that should be maintained by institutions that can control its quality and presentation to the general public. Ballet holds high cultural capital, creating an ongoing impression of specialized quality, profound physical discipline, and unerring capacity to demonstrate aspects of grace, beauty, and fragility. In the United States, ballet aligns with other expressive forms that stand in as high-value remnants of a quasi-European past: opera, classical music, and fine art. Cultural capital surrounds these forms and imbues them with a sense of importance to the general public.

Cultural capital compels municipalities to invest in these forms, with the idea that an affiliation with these art forms will demonstrate refinement and sophisticated taste. Thus, museums, concert halls, and opera stages that welcome ballet have been built in many cities across the United States. This specialized real estate contributes to the sense of value that surrounds ballet, as the general public believes that the specialness of these buildings is inherent to the specialness of ballet as art.

Of course, cultural capital is at once illusory and entirely real. There might not be much endemic to ballet that would ensure it to become the foundational dance form for professional and amateur training in dance. And yet, through time and repetition, ballet has become the primary cultural marker for dance in the context of the United States. This lines up with Bourdieu's theorization that cultural capital and taste cohere through embodied practices, and that the attention paid by a mainstream of participants enlarges through time to encourage more and more people to contribute to the value accredited to a form. That value may be economic or imaginary, but it has real effects in the world.

Colonial Roots of Ballet

Ballet in the United States rose as a fantasy space of theatrical dance deployed to create a connection to colonial manners, understood by many to be refined and honed by time. And it is true that ballet had enjoyed hundreds of years of uninterrupted development by 1929 when Dorothy Alexander created the group that later became the first professional organization for its practice in the United States, the Atlanta Ballet. As ballet continued to develop in the United States, it allowed artists to claim physical affinity with European creative practices. The event of ballet took on an aspect of "civilizing" the harshness of American social life. Ballet's reliance on simple classical music, usually performed live, contributed to a sensation of antique simplicity, unfettered by the capitalist concerns of modern life.

Practitioners of ballet honed its pedagogical ability to train some dancers toward a certain excellence in its contours. And ballet assuredly colonized professional dance in the United States, setting an exclusive standard of dance activity that became the *lingua franca* for professional dance artistry, even alongside the emergence of modern dance. Remarkably, ballet and modern dance each resisted aspects of African American musicality and physical gesture in their formation. Where ballet called for "lightness" and "grace," qualities of motion that are often irrelevant to excellence in African American artistry, modern dance progenitor Isadora Duncan wrote in 1927 of her desire to create an idiom that would resist the "inane coquetry of the ballet or the sensual convulsion of the Negro."[2]

The racialized nature of colonial encounters becomes essential here. The *colonial* might be a structural logic of conquer, one that assumes that the organizational methods of the colonizer are to become the ultimate considerations for the colonized, the disavowed, and the impoverished. As Black Americans were continually forced into impossible circumstances of a school-to-prison pipeline and racialized discrediting in every part of public life for generations, an urgency to prove capacity in the processes of the colonizers took deep root in our social psyches. Ballet stands in for a certain kind of powerful whiteness here, an aesthetic remedy for the many injuries that Black Americans and other marginalized people of color have endured.

Ballet emerged in contradistinction to the African American dances that stressed communal gathering and the sharing of passionate joy among participants. And ballet developed as a container of special import to measure white cultural achievement. For many dancers of color, to prove excellence in ballet is to resist colonial and racist asymmetries that would deny our presence in "sophisticated" modes of creativity. The contradiction here becomes obvious: ballet becomes a test for an elusive humanity, a humanity often denied to people of color in the United States. At the same time, ballet as a form offers no interest in structures of life that surround Black people in everyday circumstances. In this way, ballet operates as a colonial agent of assimilation for all who engage it, whether to prove a certain humanity or to imagine an illusory class mobility toward a perceived European sophistication that is less available to many in the United States.

Ballet on the global stage operates in a distinctive manner according to where it is practiced. Bourdieu's formation of culture as a phenomenon of locality can remind us that place matters. While ballet movements might seem similar from one studio to the next, the social structures that produce life in Taiwan, for example, are distinctive from those in South Africa. How young people come to practice ballet in these places, or Vietnam, or the Philippines, will be particular in relation to social life in these locations, as well as in neighborhoods in Oakland, CA, Atlanta, GA, or Manchester, VT. Thus, there is no singular way to consider how ballet operates among large anonymous populations; there can only be ways to consider how ballet continues to operate for particular people in particular locales.

How Language Matters

But what do we mean when we say ballet? Do we mean some sort of classical technique, as in Vaganova or Cecchetti? Or do we mean the basic movements structured in a classroom format, with some sense of barre-work, plié, tendu, développé, and grand battement? Is this about stretching in several directions simultaneously, even as part of the body is held still? Does it draw more students into the studio when we say "ballet" because we think we know what that might be?

It matters how we use language in relation to dance practices. When we place dance forms into a context of "classical art," we tend to elevate them to a place of prominence that distinguishes them from everyday activities. This might be fine if we followed this practice for any dance genre offered as a formal practice in a college classroom. But the logic of cultural capital predicts that some forms of classicism will be considered more important than others. Too often, when we label dances to be "social" or "vernacular," we imply that these are forms that require little expertise. We imply that these forms do not value aesthetic excellence; that these forms of dance exist along simplistic lines of pleasure in their execution. Labeling ballet as a "classical" art, we participate in a hierarchical rendering that separates it from other dance forms. And in moving towards ballet as a primary form of dance, rather than forms of dance concerned with participatory joy, or the caring for rhythm, Americans were able to preemptively reduce the Africanist impact on an emergent classicism. Classical dance became ballet in the United States, reducing everything else to a secondary category of importance.

Ballet Training

Ballet training in the United States began with a catch-as-catch-can format for years, continuing until the emigration of a significant number of Russian artists, many of whom had been affiliated with the Ballets Russes. Most famously among these, George Balanchine established the School of American Ballet (SAB) in 1934. Balanchine developed a training model quickly, which became a respected standard of progressive, professional achievement. Balanchine's choreography for film, Broadway, and the ballet stage fascinated audiences, and scores of dancers sought his training methods. Balanchine's preferred fast movements, downward-directed energy made evident by a deep plié, and a presentational approach to exercises that always open the dancer toward the audience became standard for American ballet dancers. SAB fed the New York City Ballet, and in time dancers from that company dispersed to direct other major organizations across the country, including Miami City Ballet, Philadelphia Ballet, Pacific Northwest Ballet, and the celebrated Dance Theatre of Harlem. By now, Balanchine and SAB's influence extend deep into how ballet is practiced around the planet.

Balanchine himself may have been interested in an anti-colonial ballet world, one that has still not emerged even generations after his death. Significantly, scholars, including myself, have pointed out that

Balanchine sought to establish his school and company as an entirely integrated assembly of white and Black artists working together. That anti-colonial gesture was squashed by the racist presumptions of financial backers who excluded people of color from Balanchine's studio and company and professional ballet training across the United States for decades.

Balanchine training became quite particular as one mode among several. Cecchetti, Vaganova, the Royal Academy of Dance syllabus, and more recently, the National Training Curriculum disseminated by the American Ballet Theatre each seek to stabilize teaching methods and outcomes to gather ballet practice towards a characteristic style. The proliferation of approaches means that most students and faculty likely combine elements of these methods, as narrow training in a singular style does not predict the versatility most professional artists covet. In some ways, the 21stcentury availability of a variety of approaches to training returns most young dancers who are unable to study at SAB or ABT itself to the catch-as-catch-can format of a century ago.

Is Ballet Inevitable?

The question of ballet's seeming inevitability connects to a very American desire to control territory, configured here as an art practice in dance. Ballet had been the leading form of theatrical dance respected in Europe for hundreds of years; some Americans wanted to prove their ability to participate in its time-proven practices. Even today, as dancers ask inevitable questions about the necessity of ballet as an aspect of training, the useful nature of its method continues to support its ubiquity. Ballet stands in as a gathering notion, a standard to work from, and a practice by which to measure other forms. Of course, it need not have been ballet that became the primary form of dance in the United States. What if it had been tap dance? What if an American-made dance practice that allows for the exploration of rhythm and musicality had become the "most basic" bit of dancing that young people engaged in, moving towards dance as an activity? We can only speculate toward another parallel universe where ballet was placed adjacent to other forms rather than as the leading, most important, and singular component of interest in dance.

Ballet offers an escape from everyday structures of life for any who engage in its practices. And ballet's highly stylized, theatrical manifestations appeal to people who need fantastical imagery, unusual stories, and unexpected explorations of turning, leaping, and balance. Ballet becomes a way to recognize dance as a specialized movement, a theatrical method for social exchange that can be shared among large numbers of people regardless of their level of participation across time. Ballet thus performs a crucial physical task, allowing multitudes access to its simplest terms in movements that are decidedly different from other gestures and motions found in everyday life.

What Ballet Demands

As a physical practice, ballet offers ways to be in motion through an elongated body, one that engages muscles isometrically along a center axis. The basic stance of ballet reaches up and away from the floor, emphasizing a stretching of limbs and feet. In ballet practice, the body is treated as a stretchable object that reaches simultaneously in opposite directions, curving as needed in the back so that the shoulders can be positioned variously in relation to the limbs. Ballet techniques are designed to produce a general effect of lightness with energy directed upward towards the rear walls of the halls of performance where the dancing happens.

Ballet is generally practiced in a studio or on a stage; it matters that ballet is a form that tends to require a specialized environment for its terms to be recognized. As dance, it does not belong to "the people" wherever we might be, and its aesthetic impact is built upon an exclusionary logic that predicts special access for some—those willing to go into the theater and remain stilled while the performance unfolds. While cheers and "bravos" may follow a dynamic array of turns and jumps in a ballet performance, ballet generally does not call for sustained participation from its witnessing audience. Ballet calls for a rarefied physicality, entirely affected and distinctive from everyday movement, and usually performed in specialized shoes for women and men. Its audience is to remain generally still and quiet as the dance happens, evaluating its successes and achievements. In this, ballet sets up terms of engagement that require judgment from its audience in a manner, not unlike its original practice in the 15th and 16th century courts of Europe.

This essential scrutiny of the performer is built into ballet as a practice. This need to assess the form and achievement of the performer forces ballet into an asymmetry of roles for the dancer and audience.

This power dynamic invites the audience to scrutinize the artist in a manner not unlike the role of a sovereign or wealthy patron regarding the peasantry, encouraging a disavowal or exotification of the dancer. Ballet proceeds from a judgmental relationship with the audience, choreographer, and teacher that can easily extend into an unhealthy self-assessment for the dancer, often built upon watching oneself dance in the mirror.

As we consider the terms of racialized pedagogies and the scrutiny of bodies, it can become obvious that tendencies toward racism, misogyny, and body-troping are built into ballet as a practice. Crafting anti-racist pedagogies here might go against the very foundations of ballet training, even as these new practices are surely essential to understanding any sort of future for the form.

Limitations of Ballet as a Profession

Ballet as a profession contends with serious limitations. Ballet offers minimal material rewards for all the effort that goes into its practice. There are very few jobs for professional ballet artists, and many of these positions are part-time or part-year. The profession is ridden with injury and an extremely short career timeline. While the attention afforded to ballet dancers comes amid the seemingly-glamorous physical surround and attractive costumes of the stages and studios where it is performed, it is not an easy profession to endure. Competition for roles and an opportunity to be featured plagues social interactions among groups of dancers. Structural racism and homophobia restrict access to the stage for queers of color, queers, and people of color in general. The working environments for ballet dancers are as rife with the unfair asymmetries of gender, class, and age as in any other US-based profession. And audiences and critics bring high expectations into the room with them, raising the stakes of performance beyond any sense of normalcy. It bears repeating that in the United States, ballet is always configured as special, outside of everyday concerns, and a demonstration of the fantastical.

These aspects also make ballet attractive to those who enjoy risk and the ephemeral nature of gesture. Ballet cannot be effectively "captured" even when it is filmed; the experience of being in the live presence of skillful ballet artists far exceeds the capacity of film technology. The limitations of the form attract some to it, and dancers enjoy the unlikely reliance on impermanence that is foundational to its execution. But even as many people are drawn to try ballet or engage it in order to practice the stretching and balancing that it requires, very few—a minuscule number—are allowed to perform in professional circumstances. This limitation by number forces the form into a horrible routine of elimination, one that rewards those most like their predecessors. In this manner, dancers tend to replace those who came before them, reproducing the racism, misogyny, and homophobia of the recent past.

Futuring Ballet

Ballet will have to continue to open its practice to the thousands of children and young adults who are drawn towards its contours. The parents and guardians of these young dancers will continue to support ballet practice as best they can to respond to the desire that flows from the audience toward the people moving onstage. And ballet will inevitably change in response to these expanding publics who want to dance and want to dance ballet.

To imagine open space for ballet as a training and performance practice, we will need to expand our sense of how ballet can feel. The challenge here is enormous: general publics tend to think they know what ballet looks like, what sorts of gestures and movements define it, and who should do it. As ballet expands towards unexpected vistas, it will need to be able to look different than it has. It will need to understand its histories differently, according to the routes of affiliation that have determined people's presence in the form. And it will need to be taught differently, allowing people to enter its particularity with a clear-eyed determination that might be matched by a reward of affirmation and encouragement.

The shift in perspective that will allow publics to accept a variety of body types and physical approaches to ballet takes time to coalesce. For example, we find many examples of Black excellence in ballet over the past fifty years in the context of the United States.[3] Inevitably, these dancers bring a particular physical address to the craft, even as an ongoing narrative of inappropriateness or lack of skill still surrounds Black presence in the form. White supremacy is baked into ballet training in a way that moves people of color, trans, gender-fluid, and disabled dancers out of the mainstream formations. This is surely the challenge of rethinking how we teach and share our practices of ballet.

The Dance Remains Present

By now, we know that **the dance will not be denied**. People will dance, and dance will shape consciousness and pleasure, and group dynamics. Ballet is a dance form that people practice for many reasons, and it will not simply disappear because we begin to realize that its practices have been harmful to many.

Ballet has gained an unavoidable place of high-value cultural capital. This explains why so many dancers feel it easier to claim a relationship to ballet than not. As ballet stands in for dance, it has become commonplace to compare any form of dance with ballet in order to characterize how dancing materializes. Ballet stands in for disciplined, specialized dancing that demonstrates "grace," "lightness," "fragility," "elegance," and "strength." Its form socializes girls and femmes to move with strength and delicacy at once, in gestures that have been culturally recognized as belonging to white femininity. Dancing ballet, we feel this affiliation of ballet with a white feminine in the context of the United States, even as we might believe that ballet training should be available to anyone who wants to dance at any age: as a method of socializing through movement that has a patina of classicism and historical gravity.

The contradictions of the form and its politicized histories surround its practice. And still, we dance, and we dance ballet. We wonder at the stretchings of the limbs and extremities and the counter-balances and lifts that predict something other-worldly. We marvel, at times, at the smooth movements that glide and turn with a flowing tautness, one that does not refer to the rhythms of the earth or the body as so many other dance forms do. We imagine, differently and among each other, what it would be like to float and fly for a moment in the leaps of ballet that seem essential to its recognition. And we wonder how it could be if we all could engage this form that has so much to offer to our sense of fantasy and physical discipline.

Notes

1 Pierre Bourdieu, *Distinction: A Social Critique of the Judgement of Taste* (Cambridge, MA: Harvard University Press, 1987).
2 Isadora Duncan, *My Life* (Garden City, NY: Garden City Publishing, 1927), 339–343.

3 Thomas F. DeFrantz, "Ballet," in *Encyclopedia of African American History and Culture* (Detroit, MI: Gale, 2016), 183, and "The Race of Contemporary Ballet: Interpellations of Africanist Aesthetics" in *The Oxford Handbook of Contemporary Ballet*, eds. Katherina Farrugia-Kriel and Jull Nunes Jensen (New York: Oxford University Press, 2021), 562–580.

18

TWELVE STEPS TO BALLET'S CULTURAL RECOVERY

A Guide to Creating an Antiracist Organizational Culture

Theresa Ruth Howard

In June 2015, MoBBallet (Memoirs of Blacks in Ballet) was launched in Miami during a breakout session at the Dance/USA conference. The platform grew out of my article *The Misty-rious Case of the Vanishing Ballerina of Color: Where Have They all Gone* published on my blog, mybodymyimage.com. It took to task the narrative of the mythology of Misty Copeland being the one and only Black Ballerina, and the erasure of the many legacies of Blacks in Ballet. Copeland catalyzed awareness of the lack of diversity in the field, especially the lack of Black professional dancers in predominantly white companies, and in 2016 MoBBallet's first official act was collaborating with International Association of Blacks in Dance (IABD)[1] to organize and facilitate the first-ever meeting of ballet artistic directors at the conference was held in Denver, Colorado. This was where the roots of DEI (Diversity Equity Inclusion) work in ballet were planted.

Joan Myers Brown, founder of Philadanco! and IABD, asked if I would help Denise Saunders Thompson organize a ballet audition specifically for women of color. Fifteen directors confirmed their attendance, and, anticipating that none of these directors would willingly sign up for a discussion about race and Blackness in ballet, or the lack thereof, I suggested that we have a "meet and greet" and lock the doors! We then engaged in a conversation about Black dancers.

Prior to this event, white ballet leaders had never openly discussed the lack of diversity in the field or acknowledged the scarcity of Black or African diasporic professional dancers. In addition, the impact of systemic racism had never been interrogated as a root cause for these exclusions. Although taken aback, the unsuspecting 15 directors were apprehensive but receptive to the conversation. Most committed to continuing the conversation which developed into a movement to address Inclusion, Diversity, Equity, Anti-Racism and Cultural Competence (IDEA & CC) in ballet.

In 2022, these dialogic learning spaces have not only become normative, but they are also now a requirement of effective leadership in ballet. As my work in the field developed, my platform expanded. Carving out this space was neither simple nor planned, but rather instinctual and organic. I ground my vision and leadership in my experiences as a professional and an educator. These experiences are stitched together like a Faith Ringgold quilt, connecting my observations and theories with insights from dialogues with directors, dancers, and other stakeholders in the field.[2]

In 2017 I was invited to deliver my first keynote address at the Dutch National Ballet's biannual Positioning Ballet conference in Amsterdam to an audience of forty international companies and press. The speech, "We are not Unicorns" tapped into the human experience of being Black and othered in the predominantly white world of ballet and set in motion a series of provocations for artistic directors. When I accepted the second invitation for another keynote at Positioning Ballet, I penned what I consider my thesis, titled "Deconstructing the Culture of Ballet and its Leadership." In the conclusion, I drew motivation from the 12-step program used by Alcoholics Anonymous.[3] Many of the conversations I had been having felt like therapeutic rehabilitation sessions, so I took the 12 steps, and amended them specifically to reforming ballet.

When I presented these steps on the first day of the conference, they were a hit, especially Step 1: "Admit that ballet has a problem!" Portions of my speech follow, since they are the blueprint for my approach:

> *At a certain point, I realized that the lack of diversity in ballet was only a symptom of a culturally systemic problem and if I wanted to make sustainable change, I would need to study the historical roots of the culture of ballet and its leadership. I began*

to see diversity as a tool akin to the barium sulfate dye you take before a CT scan to create contrast. The issues surrounding the lack of diversity in ballet help to illuminate some of the breakdowns and systemic problems in the culture of ballet and dance. In this way, in my work as a consultant and diversity strategist, I found it necessary to address the very culture of ballet.

This led me to look more deeply at the connections between culture at large and that of ballet where they aligned. Culture is defined as a system of patterns around hierarchies, religion, beliefs, and values. It is the collective behavioral programming of a group of people that is considered the tradition and is passed on generation to generation, often going unchallenged. [4]

The process of socialization is an organic necessary by-product of cohabitation.

Shared codes of conduct allow us to set agreed upon or accepted rules of interaction. We are all born into a multiplicity of cultures—some are fixed like our nationality, race, ethnicity, others are adopted through relationships, education, sexual orientation, or where we live and work. Sometimes they fit together easily.

Sometimes they contradict. This amalgam of cultures is the foundation of our social identities, our core sense of self. That's why cultures are so deeply and profoundly personal, they tell us who we are, and where we fit into the world.

Each subculture is a tiny bubble that exists within a larger bubble of ethnicity and race and the even larger bubble of nationalistic culture. The construction of race created the ultimate tribalism in the form of racism as a by-product of white supremacy. The cultural bubble of whiteness has been globally adopted and, with it, the oppression of non-white peoples. We are firmly in the midst of a global culture shift. As the tectonic plates of the larger cultural bubble shift, the smaller internal cultures within are destabilized.

What was once accepted as a norm is no longer tenable. We have seen this in the Catholic Church with the culture of pedophilia and the entertainment industry with the culture of sexual predation, and we have also seen it in dance, specifically ballet. What they all have in common is that these abusive behaviors were held as open secrets [that] many in the respective industries were aware of and made excuses and adjustments for. All three industries have subsequently found themselves under scrutiny due to the abuses of power manifesting in sexual and *psychological abuse.* It was the #MeToo movement that empowered victims to lift their heads and their voices, resulting in the ousting of many priests, Hollywood heavy hitters and New York City Ballet's now former Artistic Director Peter Martins. Along with sexual and physical abuses, Martins has long been accused of being racially discriminatory.

I started to connect the dots between the similarities the three divergent fields shared. All three have hierarchical power structures with collective behavioral programming, and all center around a philosophy, person, or lifestyle that is glorified and idolized. To participate, these cultures require one to subscribe to their beliefs and practices, not to question, and ignore open secrets. One's loyalty and dedication are measured in supplication and silence. It is no coincidence the word "culture" begins with cult.

When cultures restrict, at the narrowest part they become unhealthy, toxic, even abusive. For the Catholic Church, in service to God, they are blind to godless deeds done by godly men. In Hollywood, where influential men are like gods, for fame and fortune, the community turns a blind eye to predacious, abusive behavior. A sort of virtuous blindness develops.

My theory about how ballet gets to this place is partly rooted in a culture where the natural erosion of physical, mental, and psychological boundaries is inherent and seen as necessary in our field. The construction of the culture begins when young dancers enter the training pipeline and extends through their professional career. I theorize that the beliefs that ballet has about itself relative to tradition, legacy and the aesthetics of classicism are the roots of the cultural structure.

Afterwards, I revised and unpacked the concepts and presented "Theresa Ruth Howard's 12 Steps to Ballet's Cultural Recovery:"

Steps 1 through 5 identify and name current issues in the art form and its cultural norms, specifically training, treatment of professional artists, repertory, technical expectations, and productions. Steps 6 through 12 offer solutions and best practices.

The 12 Steps amplify, at their core, the practice of reflection, individually and organizationally taking stock of one's actions and the making of amends which requires a level of humility. With any type of recovery, the first step is the most crucial, and without it we cannot begin the journey.

Step 1. Admit that ballet has a problem and that our culture has become unmanageable.
This was the one that resonated most deeply during my keynote. Once we have established that there is a problem, we can begin the process of unrooting it. This is impossible to do fieldwide if we cannot name the problem(s) and collectively agree upon them.

"Classical" spaces still hold an aroma of royal courts, where being at court is the highest honor. This is the source of the elitism and exclusivity in ballet, and her elder sister opera, that sets it above, or in a hierarchical relation, to other cultures and art forms. People in these settings start to believe they are beholden to, or can be sacrificed for, the art. Since we no longer serve monarchies, that loyalty has been transferred to the art itself. Ballet associates its longevity with its adherence to heritage and tradition (gatekeeping), especially regarding "standards." Gatekeepers take their duties so seriously they have rendered the forms a phantom of their originally innovative and avant-garde selves. As the forms became codified, efforts in preservation became calcification.

Due to this elitism and superiority of classical forms, they do not tolerate questioning. Since they have endured, they operate with the mentality of, "If the methods have produced dancers for centuries, why change or question?" This is why Step 1 is so crucial. We see a culture of sexual predation built into the structure of the Paris Opera in the 1860s, requiring economically and physically impoverished teenaged ballerinas to acquire *abonnés* (wealthy patrons) to support their salaries. Historically, ballet has cast the ballerina as both whore and saint, and her physical body has been under the jurisdiction of men. Her role in ballet's stories equate her with a voiceless animal or apparition. The cultures of romantic and classical ballets center women, placing her on a pedestal from which she cannot descend, removing her voice, agency, and power.

Steps 2 and 3. Examine errors associated with institutional racism and white privilege, and make amends; Have the courage to examine implicit biases and address them.
These steps ask us to confront the reality of institutional racism, and to investigate our personal identities, as well as the role socialization plays in our implicit and explicit biases. Only by becoming aware of systemic racism and its mechanisms can we, as a society, begin to identify where they exist, and how they present in the form. I use the metaphor of a large bubble for society at large, and smaller bubbles of subcultures within society, which include ballet. As a smaller bubble

within a larger society, ballet reflects societal values and norms, which include white supremacy. This is made visible in who ballet is for, its aesthetics and facilities, and definitions of grace, refinement, and elegance. Examining archetypes of the ballerina and cavalier makes these relationships vividly clear and connects with Step 4.

Step 4. Analyze and interrogate "heritage," "traditions," and "artistic standards and aesthetics" that support exclusion or create barriers to participation (racial, ethnic, economic). Address them.

Step 5. Admit that we do not have the answers and commit to trying to find them.

This step speaks to the hubris of those who have occupied the apex of the hierarchy for such a long time that they forget that their actions (and lack of action) have a direct effect on the base.

Steps 6 through 12 are action oriented:

- **Empower** informal leaders and allyship by yielding space
- **Commit** to creating a system of checks and balances
- **Commit** to transparency
- **Commit** to creating a healthier culture
- **Exercise** accountability
- **Gather** as a community for learning

These are designed to assign people in organizations with clear directions that change the internal and external cultures of ballet. These actions disable the autopilot manner in which people normally behave. Once we start identifying and questioning, a daunting reality becomes clear. Ballet has been following a template for so long that its participants have internalized the codes of the culture. Merely considering these reflective steps can seem like heresy, an assault on the art, a personal insult. This takes us back to the importance of understanding the components of cultures and how institutional racism is embedded within them.

You can place a hammer in a person's hand, but only the person decides if they want to wield it, and how often, and what they build or break. Organizationally, the burden of responsibility lies in the triad of power (the board, executive and artistic directors). However, with an "individualized" approach to anti-racism, which makes each employee responsible for combating racism within their respective sphere of influence, change can happen throughout an organization.

Step 6. Begin to empower informal leaders by developing effective, non-hierarchical communication within our organizations.

When we apply Step 6 and deputize the subtle but crucial influence of informal leaders, tapping into peer-to-peer trust, we infuse the organization with a shared sense of responsibility and accountability. This not only increases impact, but also makes new practices normative.

This is key to embedding behavioral and procedural practices into the fabric of an organization and its sustainability. Often one or two people in an organization are committed to IDEA work formally formally (HR, diversity representative or executive director) or informally (community engagement director, school director, etc.). They are the source from which the most effort springs. Subsequently *the work* becomes synonymous with them. It is regarded as their personal project or crusade, as opposed to an organizational core value and responsibility. They shoulder the burden for advancing the work, and should they leave the organization, the work leaves the building with them. The work stalls, leaving everyone looking around and thinking, "Who's going to do it now?" This does not foster buy-in or ownership.

An organization's cultural transformation is a heavy haul, but many hands make for light work. If we understand cultural transformation as a shared responsibility, a.k.a. "all hands on deck," efforts are spread evenly. No one can rest on their laurels with the expectation that someone else "has it." This is a sure-fire recipe for the work to wither and die. In contrast, shared responsibility from top to bottom of an organization, overpowers the compartmentalization, segregation, or relegation of the work to one or two key individuals.

Step 7. Practice allyship by yielding the space and the platform to those who are unrepresented, in body and/or voice.

This step asks ballet to recognize its "apogee" position in dance hierarchies. This requires a forfeiture of superiority by acknowledging that ballet is an ethnic, social dance sublimated to the proscenium stage. Vacating this throne frees space at the top and assists in leveling the proverbial playing field. This means that ballet must stop considering itself the authority, in order to learn from other forms and styles that have divergent cultures and ways of being. It means releasing beliefs like, "If you can master ballet, you can dance anything." Every dance form contains its own priorities and values.

Allyship can be enacted in relation to dance communities and individuals. In order to invite people into a space, space has to be intentionally made for them.

Organizationally, allyship requires addressing deficits and inequities, then actively using one's power and privilege to combat them. Allyship demands relinquishing your own benefits or status. Ballet is accustomed to being centered, and has been rapacious in its demands for deference and sacrifice. Toxic behavior by artistic directors, artistic staff, choreographers, and stagers is too often overlooked, condoned, and justified, especially if the abuser is respected for their artistic contributions. Allyship necessitates a decentering which is antithetical to balletic norms that depend on worship and allegiance. Cultural reform hinges on breaking these norms.

Steps 8 & 9. Commit to creating a system of checks and balances at all levels of our organizations; Commit to transparency both within our organizations and in the community at large.

These address specific accountability measures needed to support and sustain the reform. Many of the problematic elements of ballet's culture are sustained because of a lack of oversight, checks and balances, and accountability. You cannot have accountability without transparency. Since the administrative side of ballet organizations follows a traditional business structure where checks and balances are quite normal. This is especially true for the executive directors who must report to the board. The measures, metrics, and behavioral norms for administrative roles are more concrete and fit neatly into the "compliance scope" of human resources.

The artistic side of ballet organizations is far more elusive, from the unorthodox dress code, the tactility of the form, the verbal evaluation and assessment of the body, to the subjectivity of performance evaluation. Accountability is viewed as something that might encroach on the art. Most boards operate with a "hands off the art" mentality which harkens back to "Everything in service to the art." This a grave failing because the artistic director sets the culture of the organization. Often boards only begin to scrutinize the culture of a ballet company when a scandal erupts.[5]

Transparency is a key factor in building trust, and when organizations endeavor to build relationships with marginalized communities, they must assume that trust needs to be earned.

Historically, white people have an abysmal track record with doing right by, and keeping their word with, people of color. For Indigenous peoples and African Americans, white people's trust has been broken time after time, resulting in our dehumanization, genocide, burning, pillaging, murder, rape, abuse, and denial of basic freedoms and civil rights. Trust is not deserved; skepticism should be expected and the challenge of earning what was broken should be welcomed. It will take a level of commitment and endurance not yet reached by white people. Transparency is about honesty and authenticity in intention and motivation.

The transparency exercised within the organization should be the training ground for the way an organization should interact with and engage with the community (See Step 11). If you are inviting the community in, you have to unlock the gates and fling them open. The caveat is that you can no longer pay lip service to your core values: you have to show up, and when you do not, you should *expect* to be held accountable. Today, with the ubiquity of social media, the community is no longer voiceless; they can and will rise up, call out, and cancel.

Step 10. Commit to creating a healthier culture based on our core values, with a diversified power structure.

Step 10 moves us closer to the idea of embodiment and cannot be arrived at without a great deal of work. In order to create a healthier culture based on the organization's core values, we have to first evaluate how those values were generated. Were they drafted by the Triad of Power and passed down as a disconnected construct to be lived out by the employees? Or were they collaboratively designed? Are they actual, aspirational, or a combination? This delineation is vital because a strategy must be put into place to actualize the aspirational. Most importantly, the basic tenets of IDEA should be present within these values. To do so, you must fully understand where institutional racism lives and presents in you, the art, and the organization.

Steps 11 & 12. Demonstrate accountability for upholding the new vision and cultural philosophy of ballet; Gather as a community for education in support of the work.

In the early years of IDEA, the work was siloed. Today, gatherings like the IABD ballet audition, Positioning Ballet, the 2017–2020 Equity Project: Increasing the Presence of Blacks in Ballet, and Dance/USA Affinity Groups have become normalized.[6] Having one another as resources and thought partners has dramatically shifted the field and created common IDEA practices for organizations and the field. Peer to peer learning has been transformative to the field.

In January of 2022, I launched the Cultural Competence and Equity Coalition (C²EC), a membership-based organization that supports the embodiment of Inclusion, Diversity, Equity, Anti-Racism and Cultural Competence (IDEA & CC). I have curated a team of experts and developed a Curriculum of Change that addresses the needs of the field, from pipeline to performance, boardroom to box office, and beyond. Members work collaboratively to become antiracist and embed foundational tenets of IDEA & CC into organizations and the field. Most critically, C²EC provides accountability, which has been missing in our field. By encouraging members to exercise transparency, not only within the coalition, but also with employees, stakeholders, patrons and the public, C²EC is turning words into actions.

It is through MoBBallet and C²EC that I have consistently reiterated these principles:

1. Your motivations dictate your methodology.
2. Organizations are not constructs, logos, or brands, but **people**.
3. You cannot diversify if you are afraid of the people you are seeking to include.
4. Proximity promotes familiarity, and familiarity can eradicate fear.

The closing of my 2019 keynote "Deconstructing the Anatomy of Culture and Leadership in Ballet" feels apropos here:

> *I have faith in ballet because the people, the spirits that are drawn to it are those who innately tap into the most primal universal form of human communication.*

We are dancers, adroit at shifting our weight and finding our center. When the era of the impresario culture faded, ballet found a new center and thrived. When ballet crossed the ocean, lost its tutu, and was jazzed up, it found its center and continued to thrive. We, as lovers of ballet, must have more faith in its resilience; it is stronger than all of us combined. If we as a community stand by our vision, wanting ballet to thrive and remain relevant, and not our ground, that of an antiquated cultural system of gatekeeping, then we will move the form forward and show how the world should be. With that I say, *Let's take it from the top—5, 6, 7, 8, on the 1, let's get to work.*

Notes

1 The International Association of Blacks in Dance was founded by Joan Myers Brown in 1988 when the first International Conference of Black Dance Companies convened as a direct result of a grant from The Pew Charitable Trusts. Eighty professionals attended in Philadelphia, PA. For more information, see: https://www.iabdassociation.org/page/AboutUs
2 For an example of a Faith Ringgold quilt, see "Street Story Quilt" (1985) *Metropolitan Museum of Art*, https://www.metmuseum.org/art/collection/search/485416
3 The 12-Step Program was created to treat alcohol addiction and was developed by Alcoholics Anonymous in the 1930s. For more information on the 12 steps, see *Alcoholics Anonymous: The Story of how more than one hundred Men have Recovered from Alcoholism*, published in 1939.
4 Geert Hofstede defines culture as "the collective programming of the mind which distinguishes the members of one category of people from another." Hofstede, "National cultures and corporate cultures," in *Communication Between Cultures*, eds. L.A. Samovar and R.E. Porter (Belmont, CA: Wadsworth, 1984), 51.
5 Robin Pogrebin and Michael Cooper, "Vulgar Texts and Dancer Turmoil Force City Ballet to Look in the Mirror," *New York Times*, October 3, 2018, https://www.nytimes.com/2018/10/03/arts/dance/new-york-city-ballet-metoo.html.
6 "Dance/USA Affinity Groups," https://www.danceusa.org/councildescriptions

19
CREATING NEW SPACES IN BALLET REPERTOIRE

Today's Generation of Black Choreographers

Brandye Lee

On June 14, 2022, the curtain rose on *Reframing the Narrative* at the John F. Kennedy Center for the Performing Arts in Washington, DC. The weeklong experience, curated by Denise Saunders Thompson and Theresa Ruth Howard, featured performances by Dance Theatre of Harlem (DTH), Ballethnic Dance Company, and Collage Dance Collective, professional ballet companies that promote Black dancers. The latter two are outgrowths of the former, as their artistic directors are former DTH dancers: Nena Gilreath and Waverly Lucas founded Ballethnic in 1990 in Atlanta, Georgia and Kevin Thomas established Collage in 2009 in Memphis, Tennessee. *Reframing* featured each company's existing work by Black ballet choreographers and a new Donald Byrd ballet performed by an ensemble of professional Black dancers from various companies, including the English National Ballet, Les Ballets de Monte-Carlo, and The Joffrey Ballet. Byrd's work beautifully revealed his cast's beauty, capability, and sheer talent through contemporary vocabulary, intricate footwork and .imaginative partnering that grounded the dancers in the present but reached assuredly into the future.

While the *Reframing* performances presented a strong display in terms of the varied repertory and number of Black artists who danced on the Kennedy Center Opera House stage, the concept of Black ballet dancers collaborating with Black choreographers is not new. In fact, as a student at the historic Jones Haywood School of Ballet, I grew up watching DTH dancers like Charmaine Hunter, Lorraine Graves, Virginia Johnson, Christina Johnson, Judy Tyrus, Ronald Perry, Augustus Van Heerden, Lowell Smith, and Tyrone Brooks perform works by choreographers such as Billy Wilson, Arthur Mitchell, Geoffrey Holder, Alonzo King, and Alvin Ailey on the very same stage. Appropriately, a roll call of over 600 Black ballet dancers, projected on the Opera House curtain, preceded the *Reframing* program.[1] At the end of this illustrious list, "We are not unicorns" flashed on the screen. Indeed, one can say the same about Black ballet choreographers.

Historically, many Black choreographers have created work mostly for Black ballet companies or organizations they have established: Alonzo King at LINES Ballet, Robert Garland, and Arthur Mitchell, at Dance Theatre of Harlem, Donald Byrd at Donald Byrd/The Group and Spectrum Dance Theater, Waverly Lucas at Ballethnic, Dwight Rhoden at Complexions Contemporary Ballet, Kevin Thomas at Collage, and Doris Jones at Capitol Ballet. What has been far rarer in ballet's history are Black choreographers who create new work for predominantly white companies.

In her curtain speech, Howard called *Reframing* a ballet "blackout," alluding to the Black companies, artistic directors, dancers, conductors, choir members, curators, and even audience members who participated in the event, the first of its kind to take place at the Kennedy Center. The significance of this experience was not lost on the audience, one that has long loved and supported the brilliant Black ballet tradition, and there was applause for Howard's statement. In witnessing *Reframing*, I found this moment particularly poignant, as it emerged from the converging COVID-19 pandemic and Black Lives Matter movement, which together forced a reckoning with race in American society. A correlating micro-response in ballet has led to an examination of the art form's exclusionary culture and practices. Throughout the pandemic, Black dancers and their allies rallied to shed light on how white supremacist values are deeply embedded in ballet.

Equal attention was brought to how few Black dancers have been allowed to train and advance through the training pipeline to the *corps de ballet* of professional, predominantly white companies. Even fewer have been named principal dancers. Skillfully employing social media when much of the Western world stood at a standstill, dance activists like Nardia Boodoo, Chloé Lopes Gomes, Theresa Ruth Howard, and

Nicholas Rose drove home the point that maintaining the status quo was no longer acceptable.[2] They argued that creating a hospitable environment for Black dancers necessitates not only new opportunities for many more Black dancers, but also demands that Black people break through the glass ceilings of every rank in ballet companies. From company leadership to administration to the choreographers who are commissioned for new work, Blacks remain underrepresented. Howard asked the audience, "What does reframing the narrative mean for you?"

My answer to this query lies in a new generation of Black ballet choreographers who are boldly going where few have been invited in the past, and they are intentionally pushing the needle on ballet's troublesome diversity problem. As they enter the studios of predominantly white companies, choreographers like Christopher Rudd, whose *Touché* for American Ballet Theatre had its premiere in the fall of 2020, are conscious of change and reconciliation. Rudd believes "that many of the world's problems are caused by people being desensitized to the oppression of others and to the humanity of others."[3] Rudd has created work that he says is a combination of "art and activism" that represents a "march towards Black equality."[4] Much-needed artistic voices like his are slowly beginning to dismantle the whiteness of big-budget ballet companies.

I sought out five luminescent figures who recently created works in predominantly white spaces: Kyle Abraham, Sidra Bell, Amy Hall Garner, Darrell Grand Moultrie, and Claudia Schreier. Over an hour-long Zoom interview, I asked each choreographer a range of questions, not limited to: "How did your upbringing influence your trajectory to become a choreographer?;" "How do you think your modality of creating can be liberating or affirming for artists?;" "What makes your work refreshing for ballet audiences?;" "What does it mean for you to be seen in traditionally white spaces?"

While there were common threads coursing through the interviews, there were clear departure points as well. This chapter shares their truths to support a case for including more, not fewer, Black choreographic voices in ballet. This group of artists is by no means a monolithic group. By welcoming these creators into the fold, artistic directors at large-budget companies are signaling a necessary shift, one that not only supports but also enriches the evolution of the art form.

Sidra Bell is the founder and artistic director of Sidra Bell Dance New York. A well-regarded lecturer at the University of the Arts in Philadelphia, Bell holds a degree in history from Yale University and an MFA in choreography from Purchase College Conservatory of Dance. She made history as the first African American female choreographer at New York City Ballet. For Bell, human connection is paramount in her process, and she balances formal and informal elements of technique:

> A lot of my work is just about holding hands with the people in the space—maybe literally or not—but I'm sharing a process. I'm sharing an experience and it was really challenging, in a good way, training in very formal ballet structural environments. I always loved the language and the form on the body and studying that. For me, it was a science. But I never really loved performing. Reflecting back, the performative aspects of being in a dance space and having to politic through that environment was challenging; I was just so shy. So, I really loved being in class and studying. I've gone on and I've learned to overcome some of that shyness through language and connecting with people. Making dances is just about connecting with the people in the room, and I think I can bring some of that formal knowledge.
>
> I'm doing a residency here in Saratoga, NY where I'm just on my own moving and playing with my instrument again in a way that I haven't in many years because I've been directing more. But play has always been essential when I'm working with people. There's a lot of permission in my practice and process, and I think that's where the tension between formal and informal happens.

Kyle Abraham, a 2018 Princess Grace Statue Award recipient, 2016 Doris Duke Award recipient, and 2013 MacArthur fellow, is the artistic director for A.I.M., whose mission is "to create a body of dance-based work that is galvanized by Black culture and history."[5] Abraham has created works for the New York City Ballet and The Royal Ballet. Despite his decorated success, Abraham shares the nagging doubt that has followed him throughout his career:[6]

> I've sat in on some of these [diversity and inclusion] discussions that a lot of organizations are having to try to hear us more. Whether it's sticking or it's performative, I have no idea and we

won't know for several years to come. What people with a certain type of privilege are not really aware of, is that even when [Black choreographers] have the opportunity, we still have the burden of insecurity that they may not have. There's a lot of pressure on us that they won't have. Sure, I'm the first, but because I'm the first there's pressure in so many ways. There's pressure from Black people, because what if the work's not Black enough or what if it's just not good? I have to think about those things and consider them where my white counterparts wouldn't. I'm sure women have that same experience, if not all the more if you're a woman of color... You have to think about not only the gender divide, but you also think about race. And/or, if you think about transgender representation and the lack thereof, do we also feel like we're only in these spaces because they needed one of us, and it's not because we actually were talented? And we will never know.

Where if a white male gets asked to do something—granted there's a history of nepotism in a lot of cases—it's highly possible that they're going to get into that space not thinking anything other than they were qualified. As BIPOC artists, we will never know if we got the job because we were the best person for the job. That's a big hardship that I experience always, even still, with most commissions.

Claudia Schreier has won numerous awards, including the Princess Grace Award for Choreography and the Virginia B. Toulmin Fellowship for Women Choreographers at the Center for Ballet and the Arts at NYU. She has created works for Boston Ballet, Miami City Ballet, Dance Theatre of Harlem, and American Ballet Theatre Studio Company, and she is the choreographer-in-residence at Atlanta Ballet. Insisting on a baseline of respect, Schreier defies expectations by putting gender on the back burner when entering the studio. While Abraham concedes that gender and race can marginalize some Black women, Schreier's experience illuminates another possibility:

> I realized that, for the longest time, I was trying to get people to like me rather than respect me. I think this is sometimes a hallmark of women in leadership roles, where they don't feel empowered to do the job that they're setting out to do. It's not characteristic of being a woman; it's characteristic of being made hyperaware that

you're a woman. Fortunately, I never walked into the room thinking, "I'm a female choreographer," which I think is one of the reasons I've made it as far as I have—I didn't feel like I shouldn't be doing what I'm doing. But, to the extent that it did make its way into my process, I think I would walk in without setting expectations right away. And it changes how people approach your work right off the bat. I'm very soft spoken. My voice does not travel very far, especially with one or two KN95 masks on. So, I've learned how to project even more in the time of COVID. But to speak clearly and communicate effectively is paramount, and to let the dancers know that you respect them as much as they should respect you is so important.

What I used to do is walk in and say, "Hi guys, really excited to meet you," and then I'd just jump into the work. There was just this wasted opportunity to have that sense of human connection, which makes everything else that follows easier. So now, I walk in, and I tell them a little bit about myself, what I know about them, how thrilled I am to be there, a bit about the music, a bit about what the plan is, and bring them into the process a bit. And then, what's important for me is to address right off the bat: I will challenge you. I will push you very hard.

Darrell Grand Moultrie has choreographed new works for Dance Theatre of Harlem, American Ballet Theatre, Milwaukee Ballet, Cincinnati Ballet, Sacramento Ballet, Tulsa Ballet, BalletX, Oregon Ballet Theatre, and his alma mater, The Juilliard School. Moultrie, a 2007 Princess Grace Award for Choreography winner, speaks about Black music inspiring him to liberate dancers inside their bodies and choices:

> At a party, Black people have to dance. There's a rhythm that we have, so as we hear something, we may bop a certain way or use our shoulders. And we use our spine, we use our pelvis, we use the full body. It's great when you get that ballet dancer who can use their body along with the technique, because as we know, ballet training can be rigid. And, for dancers of all races, ballet can stiffen the spine. We have to find a point where dancers have the acceptance to release but also fall back to their technique. For me, it's our music that does this: hip-hop, jazz, Latin jazz, gospel. There's something about it that just speaks to your soul and

forces you to move. So, it's finding that and bringing it to every studio I go into. It's a comfort, so culturally, that's what I can bring: to encourage the dancers to stop being afraid to make a choice, and just be free with themselves.

A repeated racial aggression Moultrie experiences is being expected to choreograph works rooted in Black pain and struggle:

> I know and appreciate the pain we've gone through, and when I do want to do a piece about those types of topics I will. But I always make sure you see another side of us.
>
> And you see the side of us that's just laced with talent. The root of it is talent, not my ancestors' struggles.

Amy Hall Garner is a graduate of The Juilliard School and a freelance choreographer. She has created works for ABT Studio Company, Collage Dance Collective, BalletX, Dance Theatre of Harlem, Miami City Ballet, Carolina Ballet, and Joffrey Ballet School. Garner shares Moultrie's instincts on intentionally choosing joy:

> When I'm in the studio, I want to create something that's joyful, that uplifts, and that makes people leave better than how they came in the theater. That's where my work is rooted. It should also be a high level of excellence, and that's where I'm coming into my process at day one. I always try to choose joy. It's not always easy, but I try to make the dancers and the audience feel better after they've experienced or seen a piece of my work.

Garner also speaks on the transformative experience of being a role model for younger Black dance artists:

> I'm aware that when I step into a room and there are other Black dancers there, that I have a responsibility to uplift them in those spaces. Empowering them is a responsibility that I take seriously. I'm comfortable enough with myself now to stand in the space and demand artistic accountability from anyone who is in the studio. Being a woman of color, I'm thankful for the opportunity and I stand in it with respect.

While a new generation of Black ballet choreographers continues to navigate the joy and challenges of their pursuits, they are not in uncharted waters. These five choreographers stand on the shoulders of Black choreographers who came before them, like John Alleyne, Ulysses Dove, and Keith Lee. At *Reframing the Narrative*, veteran choreographer Donald Byrd stood as a creative pillar by utilizing the full range of his cast members' deft technique and nuanced artistry. His work was aptly titled "From Other Suns," an apparent reference to Isabel Wilkerson's volume about the Great Migration. This movement of over six million African American people from the South to points West and North occurred between the 1910s and 1970s. Watching this rousing work, I was reminded of how the Black American experience informs and is informed by our movement. It is in our DNA. From the Middle Passage to the Great Migration, from the Civil Rights Movement to the Black Lives Matter movement, we have been organizing and re-establishing ourselves in expert and myriad ways, through time and space. In a final image in Byrd's commission, the beautiful Black dancers twisted, turned, and maneuvered through space and soft beams of light, with deference and connection to their counterparts. One by one, they exited the stage. Past is now prologue, and Byrd's work seemingly beckons the next generation of Black ballet choreographers to step into the light.

Notes

1 "MoBBallet Roll Call," *Memoirs of Blacks in Ballet*, https://mobballet.org/index.php/impact/
2 Mary Scott Manning, "The Black Ballet Celeb Talking on Racism in Dance," *The Washingtonian*, June 21, 2021, https://www.washingtonian.com/2021/06/21/nardia-boodoo-washington-ballet-racism-dance/; "Racism in Ballet," *BBC News*, January 3, 2021; Siobhan Burke, "She's Been a Force for Change," *New York Times*, August 6, 2020, https://www.nytimes.com/2020/08/06/arts/dance/theresa-ruth-howard.html; Michael Crabb, "After Being Called Out, the National Ballet of Canada Increases its Diversity Efforts," *Dance* Magazine, June 24, 2020.
3 "Witness" by Christopher Rudd, *Works & Process*, June 15, 2021, https://www.youtube.com/watch?v=744ftK8ll58.
4 Christopher Rudd, June 15, 2021.
5 "About the Company," *A.I.M. by Kyle Abraham*, https://aimbykyleabraham.org/about.
6 "Artistic Director," *A.I.M. by Kyle Abraham*, https://aimbykyleabraham.org/artistic-director

20
BALLET'S FUTURITIES

Insights from Choreographers, Educators, and Scholars

Iyun Ashani Harrison

In December of 2022, Iyun Ashani Harrison organized a series of Zoom conversations, in groups and one-on-one, as schedules permitted. Choreographers, educators, and scholars were chosen based on their investment in ballet and in pedagogy, and their abilities to speak to and shape ballet's futurities. Because exclusion in ballet disproportionally affects people of African descent and Brown-skinned artists, the interviewees are primarily individuals who identify as Black or mixed race, who can amplify issues affecting their communities. They were selected to represent a range of Black experiences and avoid a monolithic perspective. The transcripts have been edited in collaboration with the interviewees and excerpts are shared here. Rather than suture the one-on-one interviews to pre-existing conversations, *The Break* is an interlude that features a singular voice, and signals an Africanist aesthetic, wherein the break is an amplification of a rhythm.

Choreographers

Since self-definition is an important aspect of equity work, Iyun asked each speaker to self-identify with the title of their choosing: Jennifer Archibald is a Movement Director/ Choreographer; Alonzo King is the Artistic Director of Alonzo King LINES Ballet; Claudia Schreier is a Choreographer/Producer.

Iyun: Jennifer, do you encounter difficulties making ballets that interrogate socio-historical issues? If so, what conditions and actions might ballet companies foster to present socially engaged choreographies?

Jennifer Archibald: If I don't have a diverse company in front of me, then that's going to affect how I develop a story and who I'm going to cast. I'm a choreographer who does everything on the spot, and I want to be able to read off the energies of the people who are in the room. Sometimes company directors may not know how to support a work that's about a Black experience: it can feel like someone is checking off a box while curating a bill. It's necessary that everybody within the organization is involved in the process. Does the organization understand what is needed to build and market a work rooted in Black experiences? I've been in numerous experiences where I look out into the audience and it's not diverse. I think sometimes having one Black choreographer on the bill isn't going to change that experience, so how do we get an audience that's more diverse in terms of age, gender, and cultural backgrounds? This is not a feat that one Black choreographer on the bill can achieve. I think the entire organization has to be much more aware of how they can tap into making audiences more diverse.

Iyun: Alonzo, when you are commissioned to make a work, what qualities do you look for in dancers?

Alonzo King: If the goal of your work is to help change the world, it means that we have to first change ourselves. Anything that we recognize as harmful, whether it be systems, or individual behaviors, we have to examine our own lives to see if it exists within us. If we look at examples of people who've changed the world—Mahatma Gandhi, Dr. Martin Luther King, Jr., they were immersed in self-reform. Gandhi chose a life of poverty to align with the masses of India. He was a barrister from a well to do family. He stepped down from his comfortable lifestyle and embraced poverty. If we are able to change ourselves first, we can then have an effect on the lives of thousands of others. The work from the start is seeing the idealized vision and beginning the process of removing anything blocking its radiance and clarity.

Claudia Schreier: A lot of what Alonzo just said resonates. When I was reflecting on the question, "What does it mean to be a Black female choreographer?" I realized my response has changed since 2020. I'm confident that if we were to have this conversation next year and the year after, my responses would change again. Determining what I want to do with my chosen art form six months to six years down the line is ever-changing, particularly in the context of impacting equity.

What was deemed acceptable when I grew up, in terms of body type, color of tights, hair, has all shifted significantly over the course of the last 10 years. If we aren't cognizant of the ways in which our backgrounds and training could be hindering others' experiences in the studio, then we risk doing a disservice to future dancers and leaders.

Alonzo: When I step into the dance space, whether outdoors or in walled rooms, the goal is to open the heart and teach the science. All work uses the same tools: reason, will and feeling. The obsession with the artist is statement, what is being said. The ultimate goal is to be led by intuition. We all may appear diverse, but we are the same. Yogananda tells us that the one thing that we humans have in common is that we want to avoid pain and suffering and find a joy that never goes stale. Science now tells us that nothing is truly solid. All things arise from the same source, and individuality or difference is in frequency or rate of vibration.

The plagues of the world are unabashed materialism, wars, religious sectarianism, racism, misogyny and ecological destruction. But what are we here to do? We are here to discover who and what we truly are, and, while in that search, to help as many people as we can.

Young America had a very insecure relationship with what was called at the time, The European classical arts. So many American-born ballet dancers Russianized their names for legitimacy. Mainstream dance history claims that ballet began with Catherine de Medici. This falsehood cuts off western classical dance from its lineage and its African, Persian, and Indian contributors.

Just as Flamenco can be traced back to India, so the contributions to western classical dance can be traced back to Arabic contributions. The term arabesque, the Pavane, pas de basque, all point to influence. Many great universities dotted the Muslim world and influenced the later universities of Paris, Oxford and other European centers. The University of Cairo boasted 12,000 students from all parts of the world, so great was the Arab fame for knowledge in mathematics, physics, chemistry, medicine, pharmacy and the use of anesthetics. The introduction of the so-called Arabic numerals, brought from India, was a great stimulation to the European mind. In algebra and spherical trigonometry, the Arabs made great strides; they built astronomical observatories and produced some of the best astrologers of the time.

While the monastery schools in Europe were teaching the flatness of the earth, the Arabs were using globes to teach geography. Arabic translations of Aristotle and other Greeks were the introduction of Europe, in the 15th century, to the genius of Grecian thought and literature. Thus, it was that the Arabs played a great constructive part in the onward march of progress. How could dance be omitted from this? Greeks looking to India, Persia, Africa.

Western Classical Dance is a science of movement that produces specific results and can be manipulated in countless variations and manifestations. Its source is nature and science. The celestial discoveries of Copernicus and Ptolemy, physics and the gravitational pull, they all inform ballet. It is a science not a style.

Every culture has a Cinderella story. Every culture has a Sleeping Beauty story. What are fairytales? They are metaphysical truths put into story form. When fairy tales talk about the magic wand, what is that? It's the spine. It is the will. In every culture, the spine is what creates things. It's the willpower. When people say people are spineless, it means they have no will. The magic wand is the straight up and down. Spine is intuition, which is the fairy godmother. The dark forest is the symbol of ignorance. The ignorance that we have to slice through with the sword of wisdom. At the end of many fairytales, after a victorious struggle, it says, "And they went to their father's kingdom and lived happily ever after." That's symbology for the return to Spirit.

Jennifer: When I'm commissioned to make a ballet, I feel like I'm choreographing and teaching at the same time. I'm creating work, but I'm also highly aware of everyone's experience within the room, from a cultural perspective and how they feel physically and mentally. I think it's important to make sure that the learning experience, meaning the physical experience of the rehearsal process, is very authentic and that everyone has a truthful experience when receiving and exchanging information with each other. I don't think that necessarily has to do with me being Black. And it doesn't necessarily mean that it has to do with the topic itself. It doesn't matter what I'm choreographing; I make sure that each artist is experiencing a personal connection during the process.

For example, you asked me about the Richmond Ballet commission *Guess Who's Coming to Dinner* (2022). As part of that process, we had to discuss the relationship of the Lovings [Richard and Mildred, of court case Loving v. Virginia]. We had to discuss what it was like to have an interracial relationship in the 1960s. And then I had to make sure the dancers in the studio understood what my experience was, in terms of how I connect with an interracial relationship, and then also pull out life experiences from every artist in the room, so that they can engage, reflect, and learn. That's why I used the word teach.

Alonzo: There has to be the recognition that we have to be generous in our time on Earth. We have to accomplish what we want to and become who we want to before we close our eyes to the planet. That's the real work. It's about self-reform. It's a symbol of transformation.

Jennifer: To echo what Alonzo says about self-reform, I think about how important it is for that transformation to be happening for everyone: the choreographer, dancers, and entire administration. Sometimes I see different departments in these organizations stick to their own job and not realize that there's so much more that could be experienced with the artists in the building. We can all learn from each other—and transform and reform—and come to understand the real, true objective of what this art can truly be.

Alonzo: Ignorance will always be the big problem. We make the mistake of defining ourselves as bodies instead of the blissful immortal soul residing in these temporary houses. A fatal education system is based on the banking model, which looks at people as winners and losers. The way we look at and treat human beings is hugely important in evolutionary cycles. How can anybody be a nobody—it doesn't make sense. Mainstream history claims we have come from an inferior past and are presently at the highest point in civilization; disregarding the reality that the golden ages of earlier civilizations were far superior to us. There is nothing new under the sun.

Claudia: Everything that I create comes from somewhere: an emotional place, an artwork that I've seen, a conversation that I've had, a piece of music that I was inspired by, or perhaps it's a social issue that I feel compelled to speak to. Or some combination of all of those things. With *Passage* [for Dance Theatre of Harlem, DTH] it came from a prompt. DTH engaged in a partnership with the Virginia Arts Festival and American Evolution to commission a ballet commemorating the 400th anniversary of the arrival of the first enslaved African to North American shores. Composer Jessie Montgomery and I were selected to realize it. Jessie and I share similar backgrounds, as she is also biracial, classically trained, and a native New Yorker.

For both of us, it started from a place of, "How much do we actually want to say here? What right do we have, first of all, to say anything? And how much of our own experiences and reflections should we impart on this as opposed to making it an abstract journey?"

We're both very proud of where it landed, but what Jennifer's talking about in terms of marketing and the messaging and how that can impact how a ballet is perceived really resonates. There was always a bit of hesitation toward what the audience was being told to expect to experience. We were also aware of how our identities as Black female artists were all wrapped up in this: my own personal journey of identifying as a Black woman and all its complications.

I think it's tricky to be put in a situation where you are almost assigned your comfort level with your identity before you've had a chance to actually decide that for yourself. We were talking at the outset about the significance of the racial makeup of companies we work with, but regardless of who you're working with, I think when the commission comes from the outside versus being an internal, self-initiated topic, the journey to get to the final product is very different. It can be illuminating and wonderful, but also challenging and taxing in its own ways.

Jennifer: In the grand scope of things, having everybody be self-reformed is more likely when a choreographer is the director of a company and school. When I'm making a commissioned ballet, I'm in the studio teaching the movement and then there are times I also inform administrative staff how the ballet can be sold. It can sometimes feel that I am put on a platter. I've been asked to make appearances in meetings and speak to board members and I'm not sure if all choreographers are asked to do this. Those moments stir you away from creating work because I'm choreographing for hours and I'm working in depth about a concept and trying to tap into a spiritual, authentic transmission between me and the dancers, and then you have to go talk about how to sell the concept. These are new responsibilities that I didn't know I had to take on. I didn't know that this is what I had to learn to do because I imagine many white choreographers are not taking on all these roles.

When I was asked to do a commission on the topic of the 1921 Tulsa Race Massacre, I had a choice to say "yes" or "no." To go back to what Claudia was saying, it's not that I'm not interested in the topic, but I just didn't come up with it myself. As a result, what you're creating shifts, and that shift opens a box of different expectations and responsibilities.

My ability to story-tell is what I thrive on. But the stories that I'm specifically sharing and diving into, are not always my ideas. Directors and producers pitch ideas all the time… I struggle with concepts that are being pitched versus dream works that I've always wanted to create. I am committed to creating stories that I think the world needs to see and learn from. These stories are not always necessarily rooted in Black experiences.

Claudia: It's important not to pressure artists to create work that establishes some false dichotomy about whether or not they're Black, whether or not they're female-identifying. Something that I've been grappling with when asked to speak to the Black experience, whether it's in conversation or in creating new work, is that there are deep-seated complexities: it's an experience that has been and continues to be shaped by its relationship with the white experience: oppression, and 400-plus years of horrendous atrocities.

The Black experience is not a monolith. As someone with Jamaican heritage, I have been reflecting on this a lot. The Jamaican experience, historically, is quite different from the African-American experience, though there's a lot of overlap. I do know that my ancestors fled into the mountains to escape the shores, which is why my family is from Clarendon. It's an entirely different experience from a lot of the people who identify as Black and have roots in the American South, for example. But this shared displacement of the diaspora is rooted in the actions of others. So, what does it mean to reclaim a Black identity and to reclaim my sense of Blackness without it being constantly brought back to this darkness and this heaviness that can never be undone?

Iyun: Jennifer, how are you attending to Blackness, vulnerability, and power in your work?

Jennifer: I'm very cautious. I do a lot of research before I go into a building to choreograph, to make sure that I can handle anything that gets thrown at me. When you're working in an environment where everyone is not making a conscious effort to be self-reformed, to use Alonzo's term, you have to be very specific. You are aware of how you're walking through the space, and it's taxing. Similar to what Claudia just shared. It shifted after 2020, and now we have a lot of people in the industry who are commissioning ballets to highlight issues or different conversations that stem from the Black Lives Matter movement. There are institutions that are receiving grants to present works about these topics. I don't always want to be hired to create a story about being Black. There's more pressure, which comes with more exposure, but I think it also comes with how the world is changing. I think it also comes with the types of audiences we are now creating for. I just try to make sure that I walk into a room and create the best work that I can do and that I am truthful to what I want to do.

The Break: Robert Garland

Iyun: Robert, would you tell me about your background with DTH?

Robert: My time at DTH began after graduating from Juilliard and dancing with Ballet Hispanico. When I was a principal dancer, I asked Mr. Mitchell if I could choreograph. He gave me my artistic and administrative skills. Mr. Mitchell gave me a huge job of choreographing three works for Sesame Street and the Children's Television Workshop, when they featured the company. One was "A Home in the Sky,"[1] and another was about counting.[2] The funny thing is that it was in 1990 and the dancers wore brown tights and brown shoes, and now people are pretending as though it's a new concept. Mr. Mitchell also put me in charge of The Kennedy Center Residency Program that so many professional dancers came out of: Devon Louis in Paul Taylor,[3] Alisha Rena Peek,[4] who is in Alvin Ailey, and Jazz Khai Bynum[5] at Ballet West.

Iyun: In your opinion, why's DTH culturally significant?

Robert: You can't talk about standard bearers, in many different fields, without talking about DTH. So many people passed through DTH. DTH was timely in a sense, because the post-Civil Rights period was about having access to areas Black people did not have access to before, like voting and ballet. The idea that politics and the arts are close is not surprising because they're similar. It's about access, whether it was becoming mayor of a city, like David Dinkins, or dancing the *Firebird*. DTH is about corralling the artistic, social, and educational and turning them into an amazing powerhouse of possibility. Like, I think our white colleagues still cannot imagine a world where a Trinidadian choreographer, Geoffrey Holder, can hold intellectual and artistic weight with a Georgian, George Balanchine!

Iyun: So, what're your plans for DTH?

Robert: Two things: 1. elevating and corralling all the disparate, beautiful, intellectual, and artistic energies that DTH has produced, and 2. uplifting all Black voices.

One of my jobs is creating pathways of communication where we can do things in a more organized fashion. I received a grant from Bloomberg who gave us money for a special project. My first project was DTH TV, a web-based television series where we interview artists and give children something to aspire to, outside of mainstream ballet. When I started working with Bloomberg, they said, "Robert, you're putting the cart before the horse because you have to figure out how to reconnect to your alumni, before starting another fabulous thing." And our development director, Ebonie Pittman, suggested that we create a LinkedIn for DTH alumni. So, in June 2023, we're going to have a private alumni platform, where you can search people and post job descriptions. Many of our alumni run schools, so maybe we could start a training program or syllabus for engaging children of color.

We also need to extend DTH's campus, so it's bigger than four dance studios because we hope to be at the forefront of conversations about diversity, equity, and inclusion. It was Mr. Mitchell's dream to have a campus that has more studios, meeting areas, a dorm, black box theater, and a broadcast studio, where people could have in-person and virtual conversations.

Iyun: From a leadership lens, how do you envision the future of dance?

Robert: There's so much that the African diaspora gives the American environment. Sometimes we're way ahead of the rest of the world. There are some aspects of Black culture that are very different from white culture. And sometimes, what's happened is that we take cues from white culture. One of those cues that bother me is how we talk about women leadership in dance. There's this huge discussion and I think, wait a minute, what about Joan Myers Brown, Cleo Parker Robinson, Debbie Blunden-Diggs, Judith Jamison, and Virginia Johnson? Black people's relationship to women is different from the larger culture.

I was recently in an advisory board meeting for Misty Copeland's foundation, which is doing some educational work in the Bronx. They asked us to tell them one decision we made that blew our minds and I said, "The decision to hire Tai Jimenez as DTH's school director." She is remarkable and has radical ideas about taking the DTH school to the next level. She's interested in creating a dance competition because she feels that's how dancers are found now. So, can we make a competition that is grounded and humane? The current competition environment is poisoned with the same issues as the ballet environment.

My desire for my people is that we celebrate our older institutions, like DTH, that were built to handle racial issues: I believe the NAACP and National Urban League will have a renaissance, for instance. In my generation, there were Black newspapers or radio stations in every city we visited. When DTH was going to Chicago, Black people heard and read about it. Now, that's completely gone. There's so little Black journalism. That's going to be the crux of my work, finding communicative pathways. When I just think about the diaspora, I think about Jamaica, Haiti, Dominican Republic, Cuba, and Brazil. I think about places where there are ballet schools, and it hurts my soul that we're disconnected. So, that's my work: I'm determined to reconnect Black people.

Scholars

Iyun: Clare, how might ballet create a more inclusive space for dancers of different races, genders, and sexualities?

Dr. Clare Croft (University of Michigan): So many ways. It's about representation, the stories told (and not told). It's about demographic questions: casting and who's in the room. And then institutional structures, too.

We white women hold a lot of space in ballet. I grew up in ballet; it was the dance practice that made me, the form of dancing most in my DNA from the time I was a toddler. (Although I think that surprises a lot of people today who know me as a middle-aged queer white woman.)

There has been too much policing of the doorways. I can't help but think back to how revelatory it was when someone said to me—in high school when I finally admitted I hated pointe work—"Well, you really like jumping, why don't you just take men's class instead?" Now young people have pushed even the most conservative in the ballet world to change, how gendered language is used, for instance.

I'll admit though, I really pause around what that might mean for dancers who are Black dancers, Latinx, Asian American. I want to be careful: some things changing doesn't mean all things are changing.

Iyun: That's so true! I'm inspired by what Peter Boal has accomplished at Pacific Northwest Ballet (PNB) with two female-presenting dancers who perform en pointe and identify with male or non-binary pronouns, Ashton Edwards and Zsilas Michael Hughes. It's intriguing to see this gender-representation in a recognized company, particularly because PNB has historically acted as a gatekeeper representing primarily white cisgendered folks. It appears the field has made some progress.

Clare: I think that's true, though less true for people identified female at birth. But I'm so excited for those for whom it is true. I feel like that's what we're talking about: what ballet spaces allow people to show up how they want. Growing up in ballet I learned the old mantra: "Leave your life at the door." That excluded a lot of possibilities, though sometimes, as a young person, that's also freeing.

The notion of what should be left at the door reminds me of how Thomas DeFrantz and others define whiteness as a system of exclusionary tactics. I think a lot of us have been watching those exclusions be challenged, at least a bit. In my classroom at the University of Michigan, my students, especially my Asian American students, have been so excited by the activism of dancers through Final Bow for Yellow Face.

Dr. Thomas F. "Tommy" DeFrantz (Northwestern University): Clare raises such an important point around the particularity of the practice of ballet and this idea that Alvin Ailey says the dance is for everyone. For Ailey, the dance must be capacious enough to be available to everyone at the same time. Not all dances are available to everyone because that's just not how life and experience work. I think there's something around the particularity of ballet that we're tussling with here. We're curious about the gatekeeping and quite pointedly critical of gatekeeping that replicates racist, misogynist, and homophobic structures.

We're also wondering together, what's special about ballet? Why are we spending time talking about ballet? And I feel like that was a specter in Clare's comments: the way that ballet takes so much space in our cultural imaginary, forces us to pay attention to it. Part of what we seem to be doing in our anti-racist, queer affirming, proto-feminist thinking is to recast its possibilities or its particularities. But then sometimes we snapback and say, "well what is special about ballet?" Are we looking for some other form of dance that is more available to more of us that maybe doesn't even have to be called ballet? And if we could do that, then what would we build?

So, I just think that in asking these questions, we raise many interwoven, interlocked, and embedded other questions around glamor or sensuality or grace. Can dark-skinned Black people, or what we call black-Black people, be graceful? These questions are real questions in the world. Is it ballet's responsibility to answer them? Maybe, maybe not.

Maybe we're talking about the possibility of expression in public spaces. Queer people, Black people, Brown people, Asian people, Indigenous people, Disabled people practice ballet every day all around the planet. We do it all the time. We love it. We know that it's not the rest of the world, and that it doesn't answer the needs of life in the world. We know that we're not house dancing when we're doing ballet. Ballet has a particularity.

Clare: I would also add that ballet takes up space in our civic imaginations. I think that having a ballet company marks smaller cities as being a certain kind of city. There's something about ballet, because of its relationship to whiteness, that connects it to a civic aspiration. It's also connected to a certain pedagogy around gender that has gotten held up as different from every other dance form, and dance departments have taken ballet out of their audition practices even though they have it in their curriculum because of the particularities of its history. So, I guess I'm chewing on your first question again of what it would look like to have a world where ballet could be in the mix without being this outsized presence in a negative way.

Tommy: I hear what you're saying in terms of our willingness to move in relationship to the biopolitical or structures of power. Ballet offers us a way to physically engage with exclusionary tactics and strategies, and that's one of the things it does well. So, this is a structural, systemic, civic, and biopolitical problem. I want to suggest that if it weren't ballet, it could be some other form. So, we have exclusionary sorts of practices built into how we understand race and class and gender and religion and sexuality. Ballet practice hits all the high notes in the West that those of us who are trying to understand other ways to be on the planet are chipping away at.

So, we write these books because we know that there's something wrong, ethically, and morally about participating in exclusion to understand creative expression. But I think if we zoom out to that level, maybe there's a way to think about, "Why Ballet?" Ballet ends up standing in for something else. There's no physiological reason that ballet takes up the space that it takes in the West.

Clare: The first thing we watch in my Dance in America course is the solo Kyle Abraham made, *Ces noms que nous portons*, for Taylor Stanley, who uses they/them pronouns. It has such a queer melancholy and queer strength, all woven into three minutes. It was filmed at Lincoln Center in front of the fountains in June 2020, in the immediate aftermath of George Floyd's murder by Minneapolis police officers and the Movement for Black Lives protests that followed. It was also Pride month. The lighting design is a rainbow background, and Stanley moves in the open space. There's something about the way that it brings attention to what's there and what's not there that I think is useful for questions we're asking about ballet. I'm curious about these kinds of ghostly specters and ways that pieces might point to histories that have been excluded. Not only is ballet a system, like whiteness, built on exclusionary tactics, it's also good at hiding them to some degree, the hiding of labor and rules—that's part of classical ballet.

Tommy: I just wonder if our anti-racist and proto-feminist, queer-affirming kind of critique could move ballet from the pedestal where its practices seem so incredibly irreplaceable. The pressure we put on it to keep acting as this agent of whiteness so that then we can exercise our practices of critiquing it. At the same time, I don't really know that older people, at this point, care about ballet the way that older people did 30 years ago.

So again, I want to zoom out from continuing a conversation that's already shifted. I think the scales of ballet companies are different now than 30 years ago, and the ways that companies act in civic life are quite different. So, these questions have different outcomes: what does a Black woman or a brown girl do when their director is terrible? Well, nowadays, we replace the director. The directors are part of the problem that we need to call out and say no to. And that's happening. We just need to do it more.

Iyun: Agreed. The broader dance industry already has leadership and organizational practices and somatic-based solutions that need to be adopted in ballet. How can these teaching, artistic, and leadership interventions propel the field in a different direction?

Tommy: That's such a great question, and it's also asked and answered. We have so many amazing somatic ways to think about healthiness in moving, accessibility of dance forms or dance practices for wheelchair users, for Deaf artists, for artists who are blind. We need to keep sharing information out so that more people have access to it, so a blind Black dancer in the US South has access to a contemporary dance class and feels they can learn something about expressive qualities of motion or an idea of a body among other people. That's what's amazing about dance. So, we have these resources: the question is how to share them? That's what a publication like this one does.

We must be vigilant because "ballet" keeps snapping back. The white ballerina on her toes in a diaphanous dress—for some people, that's still what ballet's supposed to look like. So maybe part of our task as critical thinkers in these arenas is to keep offering evidence of these multitudes of ways that we are inside of ballet and outside of ballet but pushing ballet towards the places it needs to be for us now.

Clare: I wonder a lot about why the pull to the normative remains so strong and violent. I taught a beginning ballet class while a graduate student at the University of Texas. I remember teaching some movement—I think it was arabesque—and a student raised their hand and said, "Clare, my body is in the way." And I was like, "Well wait, hang on a minute. Your body's not in the way. Your body is not the problem. The problem is either how I have introduced this, or we need a somatic way into this, rather than a line way." Yeah, we're trying to achieve a line, but there are a million ways to get there. Too often we've located the problem in individual people's bodies and taught them that their body was "in the way."

Iyun: How can we create opportunities for more people to access ballet?

Clare: I also think ballet training often gets oriented as though most of the people in the room are going to become professional ballet dancers. Of course, that's not true. There's something about this notion of becoming a professional that has bled into a wide range of spaces, which brings me back to this question of virtuosity and vocabulary and execution. I wonder if we could take a cue from the way people talk about camp, the idea of sensibility or style. What might it be for people to have an experience of the sensibility of ballet or the style of ballet? When I think about how ballet still lives in my body, I think about how I learned to use the full expanse of all my cells and my width and height. I'm curious about how that sensation is less predicated on a particular way you're supposed to execute the step.

Tommy: One of the things that whiteness seems to do so well is predict its eternalness, its reproduction towards an eternity. There's always going to be more white people who are always going to take more of the space and have more of the resources. In a similar way, as Clare just offered, some teachers think that the only reason to be in the ballet class is for its professional continuation. You come to take the class when you're four years old so that you could be a star in New York City Ballet, or at least in the corps of some company. That's the outcome.

But what we know as Black people is this basic thing: tomorrow's not promised. We dance for now and for today we dance towards the ancestors, towards the idea of a tomorrow, but certainly for the now. So, if we're taking ballet class and working in ballet for now, that's enough, and that enough-ness means that we can explore joy in class. We can explore an erotic sort of swivel of the hips or shaping of the foot. We can wonder at turning our skirt a different direction. And it's all for the now to help us imagine a togetherness, not an outcome that's product-based or in line with capital or even towards a career.

Although some Black people do have careers in ballet, generally, if we could turn our dance teaching towards the relationship between those of us who are in the room and the people who love us and whom we love, then maybe we could move towards a kind of shared activity and destiny and excellence in communication.

Clare: All you're saying makes me think about how reshaping ballet is also a way to create a different experience for ballet audiences. Ballet has a possibility that a lot of other dance forms for the stage don't and that is that more people in this country who see dance in a theater see ballet. It's ballet—and Ailey—where people see dance onstage mostly, so the stories told matter.

Tommy: The stories that we tell matter and who tells the stories matters. People who offer us evidence that they can find a way in and through, like Misty Copeland, means we feel the kind of achievement. It's a little bit of a Horatio Alger: you know Misty Copeland had to go through all kinds of challenges to be able to be on that stage.

And even the whitest of white people who never think about race understand that something different is happening because they see that person in that role on that stage. That's one way to think about the power of ballet to keep practicing exclusionary tactics and strategies: when will we see a black-Black woman, who we haven't seen yet on the stage of ABT, a black-Black woman, with no disrespect at all to my sisters who are like me, florescent beige? When black-Black women are engaged in ballet and doing those incredibly iconic "white" roles, something else happens.

There are some interesting Black femmes choreographing for New York City Ballet and Solange's writing music for New York City Ballet. We start to shift the narrative and the scenario and something else starts to happen. We as humans in the capitalist marketplace are drawn to this something else-ness. We go because we hear that there's a queer of color in a leading role, and we save up our money to be at a seat in the space to see what's going to happen. I do think that it matters that these companies change who's in which roles, who gets to do what, and that we shift the ways that we imagine something so incredibly exclusionary as ballet has been for the past 150 years or so. We want to see the next thing it's going to be.

Clare: Who is on stage matters. When I saw Misty Copeland dance *Swan Lake* in a matinee, the aisles were full of little Black girls who had worn their tutus. I can still see one kid. She didn't sit down the whole time. Those kids having that experience was great. It was joyful.

And I'm so glad City Ballet has commissioned Sidra Bell, but how are we in 2023 with Bell still the only Black woman who's choreographed for that company? The door's hopefully been cracked open now. But it's not enough.

Chris Rudd's *Lifted*, which just premiered with the first all-Black cast at ABT, excites me though. I don't think it's an accident that that happened after he made this super queer homoerotic duet, *Touche*, the first piece he made for ABT. There's something about the kind of web that unfolds through casting and stories. I'm fascinated by these webs: three men of color—Rudd, Calvin Royal III, and João Menegussi—make *Touché*. It's celebrated as part of ABT's online COVID programming, and then Rudd is invited to make *Lifted*. Fireworks shoot in a lot of different directions.

The Break

Dr. Brenda Dixon Gottschild (Professor Emerita, Temple University): I think the chapter, "Stripping the Emperor: The Africanist Presence in American Concert Dance," is a core conceptual way of theorizing what I have been doing: I've been "Stripping the Monarchy," and we find that the monarchy has always been naked in a sense. In the 20th century, we can look at Katherine Dunham, and she and Balanchine really partnered in doing the choreography for *Cabin in the Sky*. If you look at how Balanchine and Kirstein used to go "slumming" in Black New York, as cited in Jennifer Homans's book, *Mr. B.* [6] With these examples, and there are many, we see in Balanchine's "Americanization of Ballet," a distinctive Black accent. Everything about the modernization of the arts and culture of the 20th century in Europe and the Americas was intertextually linked to the Black presence. If you really think about W. E. B. Du Bois and the concept of "double consciousness," you could say that the 20th century was really shaped by a hidden consciousness of the Black presence. As I see it, white people had double consciousness too. It's at the heart of White Europeans and Americans who are unable to reconcile, acknowledge, and celebrate just how Black Euro-American culture is: from barbeque to ballet, so to speak! My all-time hero and friend Robert Farris Thompson once said, "You don't know how American you are if you don't know how Black you are!"

Ballet is shaped by a double consciousness of what it is today and how it might evolve: in 2016 I said in an interview that it had been "taboo" to say Africanist presence and Balanchine in the same breath.[7] I took a lot of heat for that... There was a time when dance conferences were not interested in me, and I wasn't interested in them.

Iyun: I had no idea you faced those challenges. Do you think there has been a trend of acknowledging Black and Brown dance artists, particularly in ballet, recently?

Brenda: In the mainstream ballet companies, by which I mean the white ballet companies, it's still difficult to find the Black ballerina. You will find a man of color—diasporic men of color—and you will find choreographers of color. But I think it is as important for there to be ballerinas. Balanchine had Debra Austin, who was in his company and then became a principal with what was then called Pennsylvania Ballet, and Aesha Ash worked with New York City Ballet, but they are still not in the books. So, when we think about my books and if revisionist histories create a more progressive future, my response is: dance is a measure of culture and a barometer of society. We're only a microcosm of the whole. I do feel that dance and the arts could be leaders in moving us to the next level of human endeavor. We hold the keys to this opening into a brave new world. But if we don't, it's because we are a part of the world as it is.

Iyun: Do you think this work, focused on dismantling racism in training, can affect choreographic, and professional practices in ballet?

Brenda: It depends on a lot of "if's" that could create an opening toward equity. If people acknowledged that every kind of concert dance is indebted to Africanist aesthetics, and there were African American dancers touring everywhere.

If one begins to teach, write, and lecture about the expansive routes of how we got to what we call ballet, and how it continues to be fed from underneath, that's a path. When Forsythe was at USC teaching in the Glorya Kaufman School of Dance, there were faculty like d. Sabela Grimes and E. Moncell Durden, and Forsythe was watching their classes, and picking up movements or what have you. It just gets so complicated. Francesca Harper was a member of his company in Frankfurt for 10 years, where again, in America, she couldn't have gotten a job. Francesca really celebrated the fact that he used Africanist tropes to choreograph, like "Oh, this makes us legit now… if he's using it, it's legit?" There's a tension between wanting to be true to oneself and one's culture, and the need to undo the whole "white supremacist capitalist patriarchy," as bell hooks says.[8] In order to make the world we deserve and that includes all of us, we need to let go of certain things.

For *The Black Dancing Body*, it was so interesting to talk to Jeffrey Gribler when he was retiring. I asked, "What do you wish that you could have done better?" And he said, "My feet." This is such an obsessive preoccupation with ballet dancers, more than anybody else, with the line, the feet, the turnout. If we want to look at the larger picture, ballet is like the satanic, demonic master for all human bodies. Everybody suffers, at different levels. It's like ballet itself is grappling with these things just as W. E. B. Du Bois described double consciousness: that "peculiar" sensation, this sense of always looking at oneself through the eyes of others, of measuring your soul by the person who looks at you with contempt, yet knowing in a sensorial, embodied, deep way that ballet needs us.

Educators

The Break: Tai Jimenez

Tai: I was a principal dancer with Dance Theatre of Harlem (DTH) and consider it my artistic home. I think that I did my best dancing here. There was a lot about the context of diversity that is at the heart of DTH that allowed me to flourish. I was also a principal dancer with Boston Ballet and danced on Broadway.

When I started teaching, I was called the alternative ballet teacher because I looked at it from a perspective of healing: wanting people to feel validated and seen, not only for their dancing, but as people. So, I would have the kids circle up and do breathing exercises and guided relaxation. These were all elements that found their way into my practice because even though I had managed to survive the ballet world, I hadn't focused on my healing. So, I started to focus on healing, including racial healing, and brought it to the ballet realm. When COVID-19 hit, I took a step away from dance and concentrated on yoga. It was a process of discovery. Even though I had experienced a profound physical practice in ballet, I discovered things in yoga about myself, physically, emotionally, and spiritually. Then Robert Garland called! I always knew in my heart that I was going to be drawn back to DTH.

Iyun: What are your immediate plans for the DTH School once you assume the directorship?

Tai: We're having three summer intensives: two virtual sessions, and an in-person component. I'm calling the second one a soft intensive and integrating yoga into the curriculum. So, I'm teaming up with Paunika Jones, my yoga-ballet friend, already doing work integrating yoga and ballet. We'll start with yoga in the morning, do a ballet class, and then do pointe work. That's it! It's a great opportunity to stay in shape but it also makes room for the healing practices that can be integrated into ballet.

An idea I'm also promoting is non-competition. In the ballet world, we're always looking at ourselves externally. Learning that we can free ourselves of that is huge. We should work to meet ourselves at our point of limitation with compassion.

We're also working to reestablish our presence in the Harlem community. A lot of our students commute to get here, so we want to bring back open classes to draw people from the community. We want to bring back our big summer street fair, which hasn't been held for several years.

Iyun: Do you have plans to connect with dancers in the Caribbean and the other parts of the Americas?

Tai: Now that DTH is much smaller, the dancers must be versatile. The company that you and I danced in was bigger, so someone could be a great contemporary mover, and not a classicist because the company could absorb them. We can't do that anymore. So, one country that's on our radar is Brazil. Mr. Mitchell had established relationships there that Robert is interested in reconnecting. Brazil produces many great ballet dancers. One thing we're finding in the States is that contemporary dance has become very popular, and it's seducing the ballet dancers into that world. I love contemporary ballet, but we also need dancers who are strong in classical ballet vocabulary.

For me, bringing Black and Brown people into the realm of classical ballet is crucial and what validates the art form in 2023. Ballet is an old art and I've often wondered, "Do we still need ballet?" or "Is it still valid as an artistic form?" For me, what makes ballet exciting and worth watching, is the fact that now everyone can participate in this once very exclusive art form. To have Black and Brown people in the classical ballet space is evidence of the healing. I still really love the art form, but if I go to the ballet and I don't see any BIPOC people on the stage, I'm not interested.

Let me say also, I have spent my time in white institutions and done what I could. Often what happens is that they hire Black and Brown people to check off their diversity box, and then you're left to sink or swim. And it's weird because suddenly the pressure is on you to do the Diversity, Inclusion, Equity work for them without support. At this point, I want to give my energy to supporting our institutions like DTH. I'm not spending my precious energy trying to work with institutions that are essentially using me to tick a box. There must be a cultural change. I'm more interested in cultivating a culture that is built around healing: building community and relationships, exercising creativity, and transparency and communication. I don't want to be a part of a place that's elitist and alienating. Canada's National Ballet School is a good example of an organization that is building community. This summer they are hosting an international conference, all expenses paid, and this year's theme is anti-Black racism. And I just think, kudos to National Ballet of Canada for hosting and getting people excited and inspired.

A Conversation among Educators (To explain the shift in tone: one respondent rewrote and redacted sentences that were shared during the December 2022 Zoom conversation, especially ideas about why ballet is included in the curriculum. The rewritten version is included is included here. - Kate Mattingly).

Iyun: I went to The Juilliard School from 1995–1999. During that time, Carolyn Adams was the only Black faculty, and in my senior year, Reginald Yates taught West African-based movement. We also performed fantastic repertoire, which included Jiří Kylián, José Limón, and Paul Taylor. To my recollection, we didn't dance any works by Black or Brown choreographers for main stage performances. And, outside of Lila York, we didn't work with many persons who identified as other than white men. So, I'm wondering, as you envision the future for The Juilliard School's Dance Division, can you speak about developments you'd like to make?

Alicia Graf Mack (The Juilliard School, Dean and Director of Dance): I was aware of these historic disparities when I came to Juilliard and was excited about joining President Damian Woetzel in championing the school's key pillars of equity, inclusion, diversity, and belonging. We began with creating and implementing a three-year plan to update the curriculum to reflect a multitude of perspectives, styles, and identities. We are still working to expand upon the legacy of our world-class teaching artists. That change is slower but steady. It is not enough to simply diversify the faculty and student body, but necessary to model the change that we want to see in the field, making a richer educational experience for all.

As an institution with the responsibility of preserving and celebrating the great works of the modern and contemporary dance canon, we recognized that in addition to the curriculum, we had to shift the narrative by bringing iconic choreographers of color to the forefront. In my first season, we presented Bill T. Jones' *D-Man in the Waters*, which was the first time Juilliard Dance presented a Black artist's work in over twenty years in a repertory performance. Then we staged Donald McKayle's *Rainbow 'Round My Shoulder*. In 2022 we performed Jawole Willa Jo Zollar's *Shelter*, the first time Juilliard Dance presented a Black female choreographer's work in a repertory concert. With a beautifully diverse student body trained in a multitude of modern and ballet-based techniques, West African dance, hip-hop and contemporary styles, we can perform works like Camille A. Brown's *City of Rain* with a sense of authenticity and shared movement experiences. This past New Dances: Edition 2022 performance, designed to commission new works, featured four Black choreographers—two female, two male.

Our student body is very diverse: currently, we have 86 dancers, and I think they feel supported because there are so many different types of students to lean on and be in community with. If we continue to work towards this idea, then having companies that are completely integrated with dancers of color, specifically ballet companies, won't be surprising. It won't be a thing.

Keesha Beckford (Joffrey Academy, Dance Lab Program Liaison): I am one of a few faculty of color at the Joffrey Academy. There are other faculty of color in the Community Engagement Division. I'm responsible for the Academy's Dance Lab Program, which is for students who want to assemble a weekly lineup of *a la carte* classes, as opposed to having a pre-professional schedule where they must come three to six times a week for several hours daily. We serve students who also want to participate in school events, are in academically rigorous programs, or who should be free of pre-professional ballet standards. My responsibilities include scheduling, faculty class assignments, and making sure parents and students are happy. I meet with parents if anything comes up, and I make sure teachers are aligned with our curriculum and are meeting students where they are. I work with the other division heads to ensure students are placed in the correct track. For instance, a Dance Lab student might show promise and benefit from moving into the Pre-Professional Division, or maybe a pre-pro student needs a less competitive atmosphere, and the Dance Lab Program would be would be a better fit.

Sometimes a parent would like their child in the Pre-Professional Division and asks me, "How can I make that happen?" I might have to explain under what conditions that could occur. Or I might have to explain how we think that this is the best place for your dancer and remind the parent that the Dance Lab Program is a viable pathway. Not everybody will be a professional ballet dancer. There are many routes to a professional dance career, and it's not always the pre-professional ballet track.

Alicia: Because of FERPA laws in higher education, I rarely speak with parents. However, I do have conversations with the students and those can be challenging. The dancers here are astute self-assessors, almost to a fault. Most of the time, I'm trying to encourage the dancer: "Yes, you can!" more so than "This might not be the path…" or a conversation of "You may think you want to go this way, but who knows? So, let's prepare ourselves for all the possibilities."

Endalyn T. Outlaw (University of North Carolina School of the Arts, Dean of Dance): Speaking with parents can be a challenge yet is essential because we have both a high school and undergraduate program. FERPA laws prohibits faculty and staff from speaking with college students' parents without their consent. We often speak with the parents of our high school students.

I have learned over time; my best asset is adaptability. If Plan A fails, Plan B need not be a concession, but a different way to find your path. All of your experiences are leading you toward that plan. When trying to deliver realistic messages there is the reminder: please don't compare yourself to others. Many of our students who were not touted or expected to be successful in the industry are the biggest change agents. They are the ones who are producing and coming up with new ways to present dance. So, my role is to encourage students to re-imagine what could happen because there are transferable skills in the arts, and dance in particular. Look at the broader picture of what dance can do for you and not just linear pathways.

Keesha: I think the task for ballet schools is to accept the idea that other dance genres aren't "less than" ballet. For me, a task is how to make that other pathway just as beautiful, viable and important, and never "less than" simply because it's different. It might be a different way of moving, conceiving the body, and even the world.

Endalyn: I am UNCSA's first Black Dean in any of the five arts schools [Dance, Music, Drama, Design & Production, Filmmaking], and the institution has been around for well over 60 years. This is an indicator that cultural shifts are happening. But with that, what does that look like in terms of infrastructure, or for someone new coming into a deanship with a legacy of elitism? Not only in terms of race, but also ballet aesthetics. Those factors bring close scrutiny. The challenge then becomes doing what I was hired to do, like diversifying our faculty, staff, and students. There's the questioning of credibility and standards. Can our program be diverse and maintain a high level of excellence? Absolutely! However, this is something that is challenged, and I think more so than with other deans.

Alicia: In 1951, Martha Hill founded Juilliard Dance, creating the model for conservatory style training, concentrating equally on ballet and modern dance techniques. Her role as a female, ground-breaking leader, set a path for someone like me to continue the legacy. I believe I was brought into this position because of my own personal experiences in the field and the values that I bring to my work. I feel very supported in my position.

Keesha: When I think about it, our faculty is female dominated, but the director level is mostly male. I don't feel people are ignoring me, my boss actively wants to make changes. Of course, change is slow—you can't change everything overnight. I have taken on the mantle of helping with student retention and trying to find out what families of color would like and need. People are often accustomed to being in a predominantly white institution, and might not know what an alternative could look like. Sometimes parents come to meetings and will say things are okay. Still, you can tell that there's something they would like to express, but are not really sure how. I am invested in getting people to speak openly and honestly.

Endalyn: Similarly, I have support, encouragement, and the ear of upper administration and many of the stakeholders within our institution. To manage the expectations of fulfilling the key pillars of our strategic plan—equity, diversity, inclusion and belonging—requires recognizing all of the stakeholders are *not* going to be in the same place at the same time. And so, in my role it becomes essential to establish that I'm not only here to diversify racially because I'm a woman of color.

My desire is to create a space that feels equitable and inclusive. While there may be assumptions that I am only looking to uplift Black students, that is not the case. While race matters, it has to do with the student's identity within the cultural community. There is an opportunity to demonstrate what ballet could be: a space where dancers can work at a high level and experience joy alongside dancers who may not look like them but are accepted and valued. I'm seeking to develop artists well-versed in classical vocabulary who also know how to translate the discipline, and codified form onto different bodies.

Alicia: I believe there are college dance programs designed for every dancer's unique interests and it is okay to define an institution by achieving desired learning outcomes. We look for dancers with a strong ballet base who demonstrate the ability and curiosity to know their body as an instrument for infinite movement possibilities. Juilliard Dance addresses biases by recognizing that all body types can dance with articulation and clarity, and we take an inclusive, anti-racist approach when auditioning students for the program. We have tailored the curriculum such that a student graduating from Juilliard Dance will have the tools to go in the direction of their dreams whether that be working in ballet, modern, contemporary, commercial dance, Broadway or in all of the above and in any other direction.

We talk a lot about why ballet is so prevalent at Juilliard, and I sort of steal William Forsythe's mantra that ballet is one of the most brilliant technologies to enhance a dancer's understanding of musicality, dynamics and range. It teaches precision, poetry in linear ideas and specificity. If a student is rigorously training in other techniques in tandem, the dancer can connect the dots and become a brilliant hybrid of many movement ideas while generating their own authentic way of engaging with the art form. I am not saying that this is the right approach for every college-aged dancer or institution, but this is the charge that we have set forth at Juilliard.

Yes, ballet has been fraught with issues. But personally, ballet gave me my life. It was a vehicle of sublime expression and my first love. Despite barriers and roadblocks with my height and race, ballet has always been a source of identity, feeling like home in my own body and spirit. I wore my brown ballet shoes and tights as a form of radical expression. There is a multiplicity inherent in being a Black ballerina that I love. I brought this confidence and knowledge to every facet of my dance career, even with companies outside of the ballet world. I think about my career at Ailey, and this idea that Mr. Ailey loved dancers with very refined technical ballet language, who could also access circular patterns and use a sense of grounding and floor work.

Iyun: Keesha and Endalyn, what are your leadership goals?

Keesha: I would like to see the Dance Lab Program develop a model where children get good ballet training, and solid modern technique—where they will become be those dynamic code-switching movers who can transition between being a strong ballet dancer, and getting into the floor, showing a fluid and articulated spine, and being grounded in African-based movement. They should be able use all that training in different ways when they are leaders and innovators in the front of the studio.

Endalyn: Centering a strategic plan on diversity, inclusion and belonging is a priority. For students to be successful and move to the next level, and the next iteration of how we want the industry to look—what does that include? It includes multi-talented dancers who, as Keesha said, can do many things well. Multiple disciplines inform and enhance each other. I also think that collaborative and interdisciplinary work are crucial. For instance, there are still industry events that use Zoom for auditions and initial introductions to dancers and artists. Artists who understand camera usage and how to present themselves in that medium are advantaged as are artists who are makers and muses. When you understand composition, you understand being a director and an entrepreneur. It might be scary to a conservatory to think in this way because it sounds like a liberal arts education. But I think we can have a conservatory education that doesn't protect the things we need to get rid of. We need to uphold the traditions that are at the base of our excellence, but we don't need to limit what excellence can be. This means being more open to collaborative and interdisciplinary work, and to developing students who understand history and the current industry.

Also, the well-being of faculty, staff, students, and anyone who makes up these institutions is important. When you add the arts on top of that, you have another layer of well-being that needs to be addressed. The competitive nature of the form and feeling like you don't belong is demanding physically and mentally. UNCSA has made a concerted effort to bring in facilitators, everything from work with intimacy to Title IX and health and nutrition awareness. Some of the things we face particularly in dance, our nutritional needs, anorexia, and bulimia, are not new issues but appear to be manifesting in students at younger ages. Social media platforms bear some responsibility because they give us a depiction of happiness, perfection and one dimension of reality. We need to have conversations to leverage its impact.

Keesha: We have a different situation because we are an academy and parents have an expectation for what should happen when they are paying for classes. That said, creating an environment of trust in the classroom and ensuring there are check-ins is vital. It's important to have levity and time to connect as people so that you're noticing even slight changes in the student. A student's body language can indicate that someone is not doing well or needs a break. Having moments in class when we are talking and relating as people is something we're encouraging. We also have a group of therapists that the students have access to—physical therapists are on site regularly and we have connections with psychological therapists.

Dr. Kate Mattingly: I'd like to ask Keesha and Endalyn what specifically in your ballet training equipped you to be such brilliant, thoughtful, phenomenal leaders?

Keesha: For me, as a dancer, I learned the difference between imitating and understanding. Are you sensing, or cramming your body into a preconceived idea? When I was training in the 1980s, my best friend had the body that did everything. I did not. So, now it is important to me that every student, especially a little Black girl, has the tools to understand technique. Do they understand what their body does, what it needs to do, how this concept is going to work differently for them? How it should and shouldn't feel? Less about what it looks like and more concern about themself. Being okay with the fact that I'm not going to look like them, and it doesn't matter if I do. I'm never going to look like that, so how do I work on myself? That's what I strive for with my students.

Endalyn: In ballet, when you're young, everything is guiding you towards a homogenous outcome: Imitate the teacher, emulate the student who is getting the most attention, or who has the stereotypical look. Along my path, I realized that there was just no way I was going to look like anybody else. The epiphany of my individuality being my strength was a turning point in my life. My focused shifted to how to navigate any avenue as my best self. What I bring into the room? I share that with students: You're going to get out of it what you put in. That doesn't mean it's going to be a sea of "Yeses." There will be many "Nos." But sometimes those "Nos" give you an opportunity to create your "Yes," and move away from that "No" with new knowledge.

Keesha: One of our struggles is a teacher shortage, and the question for me is, is this a viable profession? Can a person make a living as a studio teacher? It's a financial struggle. Those who are talented and brilliant, especially people of color who want and need to climb the social ladder—is this really what they're going to do? I don't know, particularly now that many are getting MFAs and choosing the more stable academic route. Back when I was dancing, fewer people were doing that. So, there's another huge piece to it: Can we afford the people of color who are abundantly qualified to do the work?

Endalyn: This is my first faculty search at UNCSA. Applications for the contemporary position has a slightly more diverse pool than the pool of ballet applicants. What does that indicate? It could be any number of things; previously, the deans for the School of Dance have been from ABT or NYCB. The ballet program held a kind of stature. It could be that a shift is happening. It could just be that there are few willing to teach for what we can offer financially in a location that is not considered an arts hub, which is also challenging. When I needed to fill the Ballet positions for an interim year I brought in two African American instructors, Akua Noni Parker and Keith Thomas, not because of the color of their skin, but because of their diverse body of work and potential to enhance the students' learning experience. Yet even with impressive and sustained credentials they were not readily welcomed, and their pedagogical practices challenged. So maybe there is a history to overcome for people of color to believe there is a place for them at UNCSA.

Keesha: We have full-time teachers of color in the Community Engagement program, like Linda Swayze and Michael Smith, who are Black, but in the Joffrey Academy, I am the only Black teacher right now. CE teachers work in the public schools and in the communities. They might teach at the Garfield Conservatory or other programs in the Greater Chicago area. The public school program is a conduit to the Bridge Program that brings a select group of students to study at the Joffrey Academy. Bridge students are provided with dancewear and training. Right now, I'm working with Linda to ensure that our Black and Brown Bridge families are comfortable transitioning into a predominantly white academy.

Endalyn: Absolutely. The ballet field mirrors the world, so one learns to adapt. You understand that you cannot relate to everyone in the same way. We have natural affinities but learn how to align ourselves in the moment. It helps to understand the differences: we've lived them, and we respect them. One thing that I would like to say, I'm grateful for this opportunity being in this space with Keesha and Alicia. It speaks to a desire I have in this position for us to create affiliations for our students. If we can put them in a place that will connect them to a company that will give them employment opportunities. That is our responsibility as nurturers.

Notes

1 "Sesame Street: Dance Theatre of Harlem," *YouTube*, https://www.youtube.com/watch?v=xKdDDUHDBL8
2 Archival footage available here: https://www.facebook.com/watch/?v=1768606056507044

3 Haley Hilton, "Paul Taylors Devon Louis," *Dance Teacher*, April 22, 2022, https://dance-teacher.com/paul-taylors-devon-louis-on-what-made-all-the-difference-in-his-training/
4 "Alisha Rena Peek," *Ailey II*, https://www.alvinailey.org/school/ailey-school/alisha-rena-peek
5 "Jazz Khai Bynum," *Ballet West*, https://balletwest.org/dancers/jazz-bynum.
6 Jennifer Homans, *Mr. B: George Balanchine's 20th Century* (New York: Random House, 2022).
7 Lynn Matluck Brooks, "Arrows at Racism in Dance and Beyond," *thINKingDANCE*, June 25, 2016, http://thinkingdance.net/articles/2016/06/25/Arrows-at-Racism-in-Dance-and-Beyond-Brenda-Dixon-Gottschild-.
8 bell hooks, "Cultural Criticism & Transformation," *Media Education Foundation* (1997), 7. https://www.mediaed.org/transcripts/Bell-Hooks-Transcript.pdf.

INDEX

abalone 49, 57–58
ableism 1, 23, 35
abonnés 199
Abraham, Kyle 208–209, 225
access 8, 30, 35, 37–38, 45, 47–48, 53, 55, 59, 60, 94, 104, 110n33, 112, 117, 146, 171, 180, 190–191, 221, 226–227, 238–239; accessibility 24, 26, 29, 226
accountability 7, 24, 30, 200–204, 212
Adams, Carolyn 234
Adams, Precious 180
Addison, Katlyn 180
Africanist aesthetics 98, 99n6, 231
Africanist impact 188
Ailey, Alvin 34, 119, 171, 176, 207, 221, 224
Ailey School, The 2, 164, 174, 176–177
Akinleye, Adesola 65, 101
Akinola, Modupe 84
al-Andalus 29, 137, 139, 143, 147
Alexander, Dorothy 186
Alexandre, Jane M. 116
algorithm 6, 10
Alhambra 140, 141, 148
alignment 36, 55, 79, 97, 147, 154–156

Alleyne, John 213
allyship 100, 200–202
Alonso, Alicia 173
Alonzo King LINES Ballet 66, 177, 214
Alterowitz, Gretchen 65
Alvin Ailey American Dance Theater (AAADT) 34, 119, 171–172, 176
American Ballet Theatre (ABT) 7, 9, 10, 12, 26, 41, 42, 126, 171, 189, 208, 210–211
American Ballet Theatre Studio Company 210
American Negro Ballet 6, 172
Anderson, Lauren 7, 171
anti-Blackness 23–25
antiracism 1, 23, 24, 30, 38, 66, 67, 101, 104, 107
arabesque 106, 108, 216, 227
Arbery, Ahmaud 67
Ash, Aesha 7, 27, 115, 180, 230
Atlanta Ballet 186, 210
Austin, Debra 7, 9, 230

Baker, Josephine 122
Balanchine, George 7, 50, 52, 56, 67, 78, 113, 114, 116, 124, 178, 188–189, 221, 229–230

Ballet Hispanico 2, 26, 27, 171, 173, 177, 221
Ballet Russe de Monte Carlo 76, 173
Ballet Tech 26, 37
Ballet West 2, 180, 221
Ballethnic Dance Company 206
Baltimore School of the Arts 174
Bambara, Toni Cade 105
Baptista, Mercedes 175
Barnes, Darius 178
Bass, Maudelle 9
Batson, Glenna 97
Battle, Hinton 32, 125, 178
Beatty, Talley 8
Bell, Sidra 163–170, 208–209, 229
Benjamin, Ruha 6
Bias 4, 11–15, 23, 25, 28, 67, 107, 168, 173, 175; racial bias 11–13, 15; unconscious bias 25, 28, 67
Blackface 10–11, 29
Blackness 2, 29, 57, 102, 110n35, 176, 195, 220
Blu Wakpa, Tria 51, 58, 61
Blunden-Diggs, Debbie 222
Boal, Peter 223
board of directors 43–44
Boodoo, Nardia 178, 207
Booker, Zane 12
Boston Ballet 43, 135, 180, 210, 232
Bourdieu, Pierre 185
Bradley, India 180
Brazil 173–175, 223, 233
Broadway 26, 34–36, 119, 177, 178, 188, 232, 238
Bronx Dance Theater 26
Brooks, Tyrone 207
Brown, Camille A. 234
Brown, Karen 7
Browne, Delores 76
Bukôngo culture/design 29, 137–140, 144–147
Butler, Judith 103
Bynum, Jazz Khai 221
Byrd, Donald 206–207, 213

Cabin in the Sky (choreography by George Balanchine and Katherine Dunham) 229

Campbell, Sylvester 32, 125, 178
Capitalism 24, 53–54
Capitol Ballet 32, 123, 125, 172, 207
Cardoso, Simone 174
Ces noms que nous portons (choreography by Kyle Abraham) 225
Chaleff, Rebecca 102
Chan, Phil 11, 116
Children's Television Workshop 221
Chisholm, Mary 33
Chouteau, Yvonne 50
Christensen, Harold 75
Clairmont, Keya 58
Coates, Ta-Nehisi 100, 103
Collage Dance Collective 177, 206, 212
Collins, Janet 173
Collins, Patricia Hill 1, 69
colonization 23, 138; uncolonization 100
Colorado Ballet 58
colorism 25, 173, 175, 176
Combahee River Collective 66
compassion 129–130, 232; compassionate truth 158
competition 10, 33–34, 53, 94–95, 123, 174, 191, 222, 232; non-competition 232
Complexions Contemporary Ballet 27, 171, 177, 207
Consuelo, Dona 175
Copeland, Misty 65, 117, 171, 195, 228
corrections 17, 112, 117, 125, 131, 133, 157–158
Coulthard, Glen Sean 52, 61
COVID-19 30, 68, 207, 232
Cox, Leonore 9
Crenshaw, Kimberlé 17n1, 66, 116
Creole Giselle 77, 176
Cristo, Cristiane 174
critical thinking 133–134
critical race theory 30
criticism/critics 25, 121, 168
Cuba/Cuban 39–40, 46, 48, 144, 172, 173, 223
cultural capital 5, 184–185, 188, 193

cultural competency 13, 24, 29, 121–122, 125–126

Dance Data Project 5, 24
Dancers Amplified 25, 30
Dance Theatre of Harlem (DTH) 2, 7, 9, 26–27, 33, 76, 77–78, 119, 123, 125, 164, 171, 174, 175–176, 188, 206, 207, 210–212, 218, 231
Danilova, Alexandra 40
de Baroncelli, Maria 76
decision-making 8, 24, 86, 97
DeFrantz, Thomas F. 5, 6, 54, 184–194, 224
Deloria, Philip 56, 61
De Mille, Agnes 8
Deo, Meera E. 107
DePrince, Michaela 117, 180
de Valois, Ninette 43
Diaz Cruz, Lydia 46
discipline (meaning strict commitment) 17, 81, 98, 121, 127, 147, 164, 178–179, 185, 194, 237
diversity 2, 12, 14, 15, 24–28, 51, 57, 58, 65, 84, 94, 97, 101, 104, 114, 117, 120, 153, 172, 177, 195–197, 201, 204, 208, 209, 222, 231, 233, 234, 237, 238
Doubrovska, Felia 40
Dove, Ulysses 166, 213
Duarte, Rejane 174
Du Bois, W.E.B. 230–231
Dunham, Katherine 229
Durden, E. Moncell 231
Dutch National Ballet 196
Duval, Sandra 94

Edwards, Ashton 65, 223
elitism 99, 199, 236
equity 7, 14, 25, 38, 51, 53, 94, 98, 114, 172, 195, 196, 203–204, 214, 216, 222, 231, 233, 234, 237
exclusionary practices/tactics 114, 173; exclusionary pedagogies 147exotic 78; exoticized 17, 114

feedback 5, 53, 85–89, 95, 96, 155–158
Felder, Kiara 65, 68
Fentroy, Chyrstyn 171
Fernandez, Royes 42, 46
Fichter, Nancy Smith 76, 78
Final Bow for Yellowface 11, 224
Fitz-Pegado, Lauri 119, 122–126
Florida State University 76
Flower, Lauren 65
Floyd, George 67
Fong, Sarah E.K. 9, 51–53
Ford Foundation 113, 124
Forsythe, William 2, 166, 231
Fortune-Green, Sandra 32–34, 119, 122–126
Freed of London 6
From Other Suns (choreography by Donald Byrd) 213

Gaines, Bahiyah Sayyed 178
Gaines, Kiyon/Kiyon Ross 178
Garland, Robert 6, 207, 221–223, 232
Garner, Amy Hall 208, 212
gay 2, 65
gender 8, 23, 24, 36, 37, 44, 64–66, 69, 83, 116, 191–192, 210, 215, 224, 225
Generosa, Angelica 171
Gibbon, Kathy 172
Gilreath, Nena 206
Gladstone, Richard 75
Goh, Choo San 5
Goldberg, K. Meira 149n11
Gomes, Bethania 174
Gottschild, Brenda Dixon 6, 12, 65, 173, 229
Graham, Martha 28, 52, 56, 139; Graham technique 28, 167
Grand Bal de la Douairière de Billebahaut 141
Grant, Kathleen S. 79
Graves, Lorraine 207
Gribler, Jeffrey 231
Grimes, d. Sabela 231
Guess Who's Coming to Dinner (choreography by Jennifer Archibald) 217
Gyrotonic system 79

hair 8, 15–17, 25–30, 47, 49, 53, 55, 106, 155, 176, 179–180, 216
Hamilton, Charles V. 4
Harper, Francesca 231
Haswell, Ebony 180
Haynes, Maxfield 65
Haywood, Claire 32, 35, 119
Hightower, Rosella 7, 33, 50, 55
Hippocratic Oath 158
Holder, Geoffrey 207, 221
homogeneity/visual uniformity 57, 71, 114; homogenous stages 28
homophobia 23, 101, 191; homophobic structures 224
Howard, Theresa Ruth 7, 65, 76, 83, 115, 117, 195–205, 207
Hughes, Zsilas Michael 223
Hunter, Charmaine 33, 207

improvisation 67, 68, 70, 89, 98, 132, 166, 168
individualism 52–55, 87–88
individuality 98, 129, 176, 179, 181, 216, 240
Inman, Tracy 177
interdependence 87
Indigenous worldviews/epistemologies 3, 51–52, 55, 60–61
International Association of Blacks in Dance 10, 195
Islamic culture/design 143–144

Jackson, Catrice 100
Jamaica 171–173, 223
James, Tobin 114
Jamison, Judith 222
Jefferson, Denise 176–177
Jimenez, Tai 222, 231–233
Joffrey Academy 235, 241
Johnson, Adanna J. 11
Johnson, Christina 207
Johnson, E. Patrick 64, 124
Johnson, Jermel 178
Johnson, Louis 7, 8, 32, 125
Johnson, Virginia 222
Jones, Ann 9
Jones, Bill T. 234

Jones, Doris 32, 35, 119–120, 122–126, 207
Jones, Paunika 180, 232
Jones Haywood Dance School (previously Jones Haywood School of Ballet) 32, 34–35, 123
Joseph, Marc Bamuthi 106
Juilliard School, The 2, 28, 171, 173, 211–212, 234

Kaufman, Sarah 9
Kendi, Ibram X. 66, 101
Kerr, Maurya 6, 66, 101–108
Key, Cortney Taylor 65, 68, 69
King, Alonzo 6, 29, 66, 83, 129, 136, 177, 207, 214–215
Kowal, Rebekah 56

La Bayadère 10
Lang, Pearl 176
Larkin, Moscelyne 51
LaViolette, Jenna Smith 51
Le, Vu 104
leadership 7, 12, 15, 24, 42, 43–44, 45, 58, 86–87, 112–117, 176, 196, 204, 208, 210, 222, 226, 238
learning environment 83, 133, 135, 174, 177
Lee, Brandye 34, 206–213
Lee, Keith 213
Lesbian 65
Liang, Edwaard 5
liberation 26, 67, 70, 101, 102, 169
Lifted (choreography by Chris Rudd) 229
Lighting 16–17, 134, 180, 226
Lopes Gomes, Chloé 12, 204
Long, Andrea 180
Louis XIV 142
Louis, Devon 221
Lucas, Waverly 206, 207
Lully, Jean-Baptiste 141, 147

Mahr, Martha 40
makeup 11–12, 15, 16, 179, 219
Malek, Audrey 65, 68
Maria Olenewa State School of Dance 174

Martin, John 8, 10, 55–56
Mason, Monica 43
Mata-Fragua, Leah 49, 57–58, 60
McIntosh, Peggy 103
McKayle, Donald 234
Menegussi, João 229
mentorship 35, 78
Miami City Ballet 39–48, 188
Microaggression 86
minoritized 12–13, 101; minority 29, 33, 43
misogyny 23, 101, 191, 192, 216
Mitchell, Arthur 7, 76, 78, 126, 171, 174, 176, 204
MoBBallet 195, 204
Moorish culture/design 143
Morrison, Toni 107
Mortimore, Zelda 75
Moultrie, Darrell Grand 208, 211
Mullikin, Alicia 103
Murphy, Ashley 180
music/musicality 9, 39, 41, 45, 70, 89, 95, 98, 112, 130–132, 139, 185, 186, 211, 218, 229, 236
Myers Brown, Joan 195, 222

National Ballet of Canada 233
"Negro Unit" of Ballet Theatre 9, 172
New York City Ballet (NYCB) 7, 27, 40, 41, 47, 56, 76, 114, 115, 124, 171, 188, 209, 228–230
Nigodoff, Alexander 39
Nijinska, Bronislava 41, 55
N'kisi Sarabanda cosmogram 138
North Carolina School of the Arts 236

Oga, Chisako 135
Okun, Tema 53, 82, 84–88
Osato, Sono 7, 173
Overton Walker, Aida 9

Pacific Northwest Ballet 2, 178, 188, 223
Parker, Akua Noni 180, 222
Pazcoguin, Georgina 11, 117
Peek, Alisha Rena 221
perfectionism 84–85, 94, 99

Perry, Ronald 207
Person, Melanie 177
Phifer, Cassandra 2
Philadelphia Ballet 178, 188
Pierce, Adriana 65
Pitts, Jamilah 105
pointe shoes/pointe work 26–28, 46, 49, 223, 232
primarily white institutions (PWI) 65, 104, 171, 224
privilege/privileged 13, 23, 87, 101, 103, 104, 107, 199–200, 202, 210
Pyle, Katy 65

quare 64–71
queer 64–71, 103, 223–229
queerness 2, 67

Rabel, Daniel 142, 143, 147
racialization 11–13; racialized pedagogies 191
racism 1, 3, 4, 6–8, 13, 14, 24, 25, 28, 35, 66, 85, 94, 98–105, 191–192, 197–200, 216, 230, 233; systemic racism 103, 196, 199
Rankine, Claudia 103
Reed, Dwayne 101
Reframing the Narrative (2022) 206, 208, 213
repetition 130, 131, 163, 185
resiliency 119, 124–126
Ringgold, Faith 196
Rivera, Chita 32, 125
Robinson, Renee 32
Romero, Cara 49, 50, 57–58
Rosella Hightower École de Danse 33
Rose, Nicholas 208
Royal III, Calvin 229
Rudd, Christopher 144, 208

Sabogal, Jessica 106
San Francisco Ballet School 2, 75, 135
Sarabande 137–138, 141–144, 146
School of American Ballet (SAB) 7, 27, 40–41, 46, 47, 113, 124–125, 177, 188

Schorer, Suki 113–115
Schreier, Claudia 6, 208, 210, 214, 215–216
self-reform 215, 218
Serrano, Lupe 46
settler colonialism 51–54, 59–60
sexism 1, 23, 24, 38
sexuality 64–66, 69, 225
Shabaka designs 147
Shayer, Gabe Stone 12
Shook, Karel 76
Silva, Ingrid 174
skin tone 10, 27–28, 86, 180; unearned skin advantage 101
Smith, Lowell 207
Smith, Michael 241
Smith, Therrell 124
Snipe Jr., Michael 178
social justice 107
social media 133, 181, 203, 207, 239
Soto, Jock 114
South African Suite (choreography by Arthur Mitchell, Augustus Van Heerden, and Laveen Naidu) 176
sovereignty 51, 58, 60
Spain 137, 140, 142–144, 146
Spivey, Jermaine 178
Stanger, Arabella 52
Stanley, Taylor 171, 225
stereotypes 12, 56, 120, 179
Swan Lake 16, 39, 56, 180, 229
Swayze, Linda 241

Tallahassee Civic Ballet 76
TallBear, Kim 53, 61
Tallchief, Maria 7, 49, 54–57, 115
Tallchief, Marjorie 50
Taylor, Breonna 67
Taylor, Sonya Renee 107
Thomas, Keith 241
Thomas, Kevin 206–207
Thompson, Robert Farris 145, 230
Tiger, Crickett 49, 50, 57–58
tights 26–28, 46, 57, 86, 112, 117, 155–156, 216, 221, 238

tokenism 24–25, 65
Toll, Shannon 56
Tran Myhre, Kyle "Guante" 106
transgender 210
transphobia 23
transparency 24, 202–204, 233
trauma 3, 11
trust 86, 93–95, 99, 107, 201–203, 239
Tulsa Race Massacre 219
Tumkovsky, Antonina 40
Ture, Kwame (Stokely Carmichael), 4
turnout 26, 36, 96, 154, 156, 157, 176, 231
Tyrus, Judy 207

University of Oklahoma 50–51

Van Heerden, Augustus 176, 207
Vollmar, Jocelyn 75

Wahzhazhe: An Osage Ballet (choreography by Jenna Smith LaViolette) 51
Washington School of Ballet 2, 126
Weisberger, Barbara 43
white supremacy 1, 3, 6, 7, 9, 35, 36, 53, 65, 82, 85, 100–107, 192, 197, 200
whiteness 3, 16, 27–29, 38, 53–55, 57, 82, 101–107, 120, 172–173, 180–181, 186, 197, 208, 224–227
Wilbur, Sarah 66
Wilkerson, Isabel 24, 213
Wilkerson, Lenai Alexis 178
Wilkinson, Raven 173
Williams, Stanley 40
Williams, Virginia 43
Wilson, Billy 125, 207
Wynn, Kevin 167

Yates, Reginald 234
Yogananda, Paramahansa 216

Zeller, Jessica 135
Zollar, Jawole Willa Jo 234

Made in the USA
Middletown, DE
02 April 2025